# GOD OF ALL

SRI RAMAKRISHNA

# GOD OF ALL

## Sri Ramakrishna's Approach to
## Religious Plurality

*by*

## CLAUDE ALAN STARK

## CLAUDE STARK, INC.
### CAPE COD, MASSACHUSETTS 02670

Library of Congress Catalog Card Number: 74-76001

International Standard Book Number: 0-89007-000-8

FIRST PRINTING

Printed in the United States of America

*To my spiritual father*
*SWAMI AKHILANANDA*
*and my spiritual mother*
*MAMA NDONA SANTU*
*from whom I learned of the living God*

(Matthew 16:16)

# *Note and Acknowledgment*

The author has in his possession a letter dated February 2, 1937 from Swami Akhandananda, then President of the Ramakrishna Order, addressed to Mrs. Anna M. Worcester (called Annapurna), explaining the attitude in which the artist approached the drawing of Sri Ramakrishna which faces the title-page of this book. A partial text of the letter follows:

". . . Herein I try to express some of the thoughts that crossed my mind since you left this place.

"Even this time, I think, I have not been able to entertain you properly, and to my satisfaction. In hurry, and in my joy, I forgot so many things I wanted;—the most important—being of course—to lead you through the hall and the rooms—where on the walls—there are some beautiful pictures,—specially the one of Sri Ramakrishna in oil colours, the work of an artist devotee—who, before he took up the brushes—with folded hands in front of a photo of the Master, prayed, 'I have shaped many an image [for he was a clay-modelist too]. I have painted many a figure, but never such a one of a great man with such ecstatic eyes. If Thou helpest me, then alone I may venture to attempt!' It was only at my constant inspiration and in my presence that he undertook the great task, and it came out as a wonderful likeness to the Master. But the artist was not satisfied; he admitted his failure to express the divine inwardness of the eyes of the Master in ecstatic state of absorption in meditation. I only wished you had seen it.

Again with love and blessings,

*Akhandananda*"

Appreciation is expressed to authors and publishers whose works have been quoted from or cited in this book. All such materials are indicated in the footnotes and bibliography.

Sri Ramakrishna's message was unique in being expressed in action. . . . Religion is not just a matter for study; it is something that has to be experienced and to be lived, and this is the field in which Sri Ramakrishna manifested his uniqueness. . . . His religious activity and experience were, in fact, comprehensive to a degree that had perhaps never before been attained by any other religious genius, in India or elsewhere.[1]

—ARNOLD TOYNBEE

---

[1] Foreword to *Sri Ramakrishna and His Unique Message* by Swami Ghanananda (3d ed.; London: Ramakrishna Vedanta Centre, 1970), p. vii.

# Contents

# *Foreword*

## *On Meeting the Neighbor / Stranger*

### by LEROY S. ROUNER

Sri Ramakrishna, a nineteenth-century Indian saint and mystic, experienced God directly and immediately in the context of Hinduism, Buddhism, Christianity, and Islam. Claude Alan Stark's recounting of this spiritual adventure is surely among the most carefully detailed and fully annotated of the current commentaries on Sri Ramakrishna's life and work. This labor of love is remarkable because it comes from an evangelical Christian whose conversion to Christianity was largely influenced by Swami Akhilananda of the Ramakrishna Mission in Boston, one of Sri Ramakrishna's recent disciples.

Dr. Stark is concerned with the dilemma of religious plurality. On the one hand are the great proselytizing religions—Christianity, Islam and Buddhism—claiming universality and seeking to convert all others to the one true faith. On the other hand are the non-proselytizing religions, including Confucianism, modern Judaism, and Hinduism, which preserve the integrity of their tradition by vigorously excluding others.

Dr. Stark is not happy with either an imperialistic struggle for souls among religious super-powers, or the exclusivism of the isolationist religions. Nor is he willing to settle for some lowest common denominator spirituality which avoids the hard issues of conflicting commitments in belief and practice. Perhaps most notably, he even rejects the more sophisticated and intellectually popular affirmation of a highest common denominator in the experience of the mystics of different religious traditions. As he reads them, the great mystics report widely divergent experiences of God.

He knows instinctively that there is no dialogue among religions as such; there is dialogue only among men and women of differing faiths and traditions. His own relationship with Swami Akhilananda was an experience of such a dialogue, and it resulted in a Hindu inspiring a secular Jew with his own devotion to Jesus Christ. The spirit of generosity, warmth, openness, and "Christian love," and the practical wisdom which Dr. Stark found in his *guru* have led him back to Sri Ramakrishna himself in the search for a method and model of dialogue among men and women of divergent religious beliefs and practices. Regarding mystical experience as an empirical and therefore scientific approach to religious knowledge, Stark proposes Ramakrishna's experience of practicing the presence of God in various religious contexts as a means of promoting the unity of mankind and overcoming both imperialism and exclusivism in inter-religious relationships.

Sri Ramakrishna, of course, was a spiritual virtuoso in a God-intoxicated culture, and we are secular citizens in a technological age. Dr. Stark's suggestion, however, is not that we should all become full-time religious experimenters, but that we should take Ramakrishna's method seriously. Sri Ramakrishna was the supreme example of a religious phenomenologist, and phenomenology is the methodology of love. It is the practical application of the New Testament injunction to lose one's life, for the sake of the neighbor and in Christ's name, if one would truly find it. This means that neither the attack of religious imperialism, nor the defense of religious exclusivism can be a valid Christian attitude toward inter-religious relationships. The method of love in relation to the neighbor who is a religious stranger is to lay aside one's own perspective, even one's own convictions and beliefs, and to take on the life and world and beliefs of the neighbor/stranger. In this context it is possible to discover the continually unfolding truth to which Christ promised the Holy Spirit would lead us. And only in this context is it possible to know the full meaning of the age-old

Christian affirmation that God has not left himself without witnesses in any age or human community.

Returning to one's own context of faith and culture and practice, two things will have changed. One will have a deeper knowledge of one's own tradition. As in geography, so in theology: one can never say that he knows his own country well until he has visited another. And because part of oneself will then belong to the belief-world of the neighbor/stranger, that world can never again be entirely alien.

Specialists in the history and philosophy of religions will search in vain for a philosophical or theological structure in this book which might predict the outcome of dialogue among the world's great religions, as in the work of Kraemer, Van Leeuwen, Toynbee, Radhakrishnan, Hocking, Northrop and others. Non-specialists will wonder why Sri Ramakrishna undertook his lifelong experiment, and must be content with Dr. Stark's confession that he does not really know. But the frustration of these unanswered questions, important as they are, need not stand in the way of Dr. Stark's primary purpose, which is spiritual, practical, and humane.

He has met a great soul, and is a better man for it. He would have us meet him and know him. In the pages that follow he has told Sri Ramakrishna's story with great scholarly care and spiritual empathy. It is his hope that his fellow Christians may find the authentic Spirit of the one true God at work in their inner dialogue with this Hindu neighbor/stranger. In the midst of this meeting and knowing, that Spirit may lead us into some as yet undiscovered new truth.

I join him in that hope.

LEROY S. ROUNER

# *Preface*

The objective of this work is to introduce Sri Ramakrishna's approach to the scholarship community; first to the Christian world since I am a Christian, and then to the broad fellowship of world religions. Sri Ramakrishna's life and teachings have received no more than token attention thus far in academic circles. It is submitted that his approach to the dilemma of religious plurality is a significant one in religious history and merits further study. This volume is offered as a start in such a direction.

My thanks to the friends and colleagues who have encouraged me in this effort, and my gratitude to the contributors who have added their reflections from the standpoint of their own disciplines and religious heritages.

CLAUDE ALAN STARK

# Introduction

## STATEMENT OF THE PROBLEM

The dilemma of religions is their plurality. Contemporary cultural and religious encounters in a mercurial world boldly point up this dilemma.

Further, the dilemma is heightened by the respective claims to universality of the world's great proselytizing religions, the Christian Faith, Islam, and Buddhism. (Modern exponents of Hinduism and Vedanta have been regarded by some thinkers to fall into this same category.[1]) Since the missionary enterprise is based squarely on this claim, the presentation by a proselytizing religion of its own position as universally applicable to the spiritual salvation of all men forms an integral part of its religious confession.

The dilemma is also magnified when the non-proselytizing religions are considered. While modern Judaism, Confucianism, Hinduism, and the Parsee tradition do not seek converts, nor do most

---

[1] J. Robert Nelson, "Signs of Mankind's Solidarity," in *No Man Is Alien: Essays on the Unity of Mankind,* ed. by J. Robert Nelson (Leiden: E. J. Brill, 1971), p. 4; Stephen Neill, *The Story of the Christian Church in India and Pakistan* (Grand Rapids, Mich.: Wm. B. Eerdmans, 1970), p. 127; cf. Swami Akhilananda, *Hindu View of Christ* (Boston: Branden Press, 1972 [c. 1949]), chap. xii, esp. pp. 275-279.

1

so-called primitive religions, their resistance to the principle of religious harmony rests on the assertion of a religio-cultural exclusivism which, rather than promoting universal salvation on a predetermined conditional basis, actually bars entry to others. Salvation here is simply a coefficient of probability: the accident of birth.

We are faced, then, with a total dilemma of religious plurality, the one group of religious traditions each seeking to include all men, the second group seeking to exclude all others. It is evident that this dilemma can neither be resolved by a dogmatic assertion of harmony, nor by a superficial dismissal of the profound differences among religions, nor by theological speculation alone, nor by ecclesiastical decree, nor by reference to scriptural authority. Neither can the dilemma itself be ignored by the serious student of religion, for to do so would be to yield to the spiritual indifference and apathy of which secularists of all traditions are today heirs.

The dilemma is also not resolved merely by advancing the postulate that all religions are valid paths to the one God. Scriptural or ecclesiastical authority cannot adequately demonstrate this postulate, even if that were generally their intent:[2] their authenticity would be challenged by adherents of other religious traditions.

The question is set forth in this book whether the approach of Sri Ramakrishna, an approach based on the experience of God, offers a workable hypothesis toward solving this central dilemma. The problem of this investigation is to present Sri Ramakrishna's approach as fully as possible, using the extensive documentation of his life and teachings as well as those of his principal successors, and then to show how his approach may adequately fulfill the conditions of such a hypothesis.

## DEFINITIONS

It is recognized here that the word "God" defies precise definition in any language. While terms denoting the ultimate Reality such as "God," "Allah," "Brahman," "Tao," "Dharma," "Nzambi" vary considerably from one tradition to another in their conceptual orientation, in all cases the great scriptures and prophets of these traditions point to something beyond the term and the concept which

---

[2] E.g., Rig Veda I.164.46$^C$; "Declaration on the Relationship of the Church to Non-Christian Religions," *The Documents of Vatican II,* ed. by Walter M. Abbott (London: Geoffrey Chapman, 1967), pp. 660-668.

cannot be delimited in human language, nor fully captured by human thought.

Thus while conceptions of God represent man's attempt to know him, and God's attempt to reveal himself, the very conceptions themselves are ultimately inadequate to reveal God's nature. This does not negate the sanctity nor the utility of scripture or prophetic oracle, but it does establish their limitation. That is, it can be affirmed without fear of contradiction that the knowledge of God, while based on scripture, is beyond scripture; to know him as he is, one must go beyond "him" and "is," or beyond concepts, language, and thought-forms.

Here is where the term "mysticism" enters in. Throughout this study Rufus Jones' definition of mysticism will be used. According to Jones, mysticism is "the type of religion which puts the emphasis on immediate relation with God, on direct and intimate consciousness of the Divine Presence. It is religion in its most acute, intense, and living stage."[3] That is, mysticism is the *direct and immediate* experience of God. As William James states, "God's knowledge cannot be discursive, but must be . . . immediate."[4]

Another important term requiring clarification is "the scientific method." This method of science, also used in scholarship, has normally been applied to data from the objective world, in which "experience" is limited to evidence gathered through the five senses and through instrumentation to refine and to identify the elements of objective reality. The single most important assumption in this study is that elements of subjective reality can be introduced as primary evidence in the scientific method of scholarship, and on an equal footing with elements of objective reality. The following statements are offered in support of this assumption:

'I am going to make an appeal here that we must find a way to make subjective empiricism as valid as objective empiricism.'[5]

---

[3] Rufus M. Jones, *Studies in Mystical Religion* (London: Macmillan, 1925), p. xiv. Cf. William James, *The Varieties of Religious Experience,* The Modern Library (New York: Random House, 1902), chap. xx, "Conclusions," pp. 416-417. Cf. Rudolf Otto's statement on the subject in *Mysticism East and West,* trans. by Bertha L. Bracey and Richenda C. Payne (New York: Macmillan, 1960), p. 13. Note Evelyn Underhill's discussions in *Mysticism* (4th ed.; London: J. M. Dent, 1912).

[4] *Varieties of Religious Experience,* p. 397.

[5] Captain Edgar D. Mitchell, astronaut who performed the first ESP experiment in outer space, quoted by Bill D. Schul in "Science & Psi: Transcultural Trends,"

Experience of nonordinary reality is no less real for being unverifiable in the realm of ordinary experience. Internal reality, in all of its varied forms, is a different order of reality that is self-validating.[6]

In the year 1600 . . . the Copernican revolution led to consequences as diverse as a tremendous acceleration in physical science and a decline in the political power of the Church. . . . A group of questions relating to the position of the Earth in the universe, and the nature and significance of the heavenly bodies passed out of the realm of the theological and philosophical and into the realm of empirical inquiry. . . .

A later similar event occurred with the work of the geologists, paleontologists, and biologists of the nineteenth century culminating in the controversial evolutionary hypotheses. Questions relating to the origin of the earth and of man were relabeled 'empirical' instead of 'theological.' Again the consequences reverberated throughout the worlds of research, education and politics.

I believe there is good reason to suspect that we are in the midst of another such saltation today. Much evidence suggests that *a group of questions relating to the commonality of and interpretation of man's subjective experience, especially of the 'transcendental,' and hence to the bases of human values, are shifting from the realm of the 'philosophical' to the 'empirical.' If so, the consequences may be even more far-reaching than those which emerged from the Copernican, Darwinian, and Freudian revolutions.*

The science of man's subjective experience is in its infancy. Even so, some of its foreshadowings are evident. With the classification of these questions into the realm of empirical inquiry, we can anticipate an acceleration of research in this area. As a consequence there is new hope of consensus on issues which have been at the root of conflict for centuries (just as earlier there came about consensus on the place of the Earth in the universe, and on the origin of man). The new science will incorporate the most penetrating insights of psychology, the humanities, and religion.[7]

Other technical terms will be defined in the body or notes of the book.

report of a symposium at the American Psychiatric Association Convention, *Psychic Magazine,* September, 1972, p. 42.

[6] Andrew Weil, *The Natural Mind: A New Way of Looking at the Higher Consciousness* (Boston: Houghton Mifflin, 1972), as excerpted in *Psychology Today,* October, 1972, pp. 51-96 (p. 56).

[7] Willis Harman, "The New Copernican Revolution," *The Journal of Transpersonal Psychology,* I (Fall, 1969), 21-23.

## LIMITATIONS

While the study is documented by reference to secondary sources, no attempt has been made here to cover the following basic categories of religious studies: sociology of religion, psychology of religion, history of religions or phenomenology of religions, biographical portrait of Sri Ramakrishna, theology, revelation, comparative mysticism, scriptural exegesis, or a review of the history of other approaches to encountering the dilemma of religious plurality.

Nor is a defense of Hinduism in and of itself or vis-à-vis other religions intended here. Such a defense would negate the value of the hypothesis. Hinduism is presented as a relevant background to Sri Ramakrishna's spiritual life.

## PREVIOUS RESEARCH

There has not been to date any comprehensive study on the specific area of Sri Ramakrishna's approach to the dilemma of religious plurality using the methodology here employed.

The most authoritative and exhaustive biography of Sri Ramakrishna, upon which all subsequent biographies are based, was written by his contemporary and intimate disciple, a monastic of high spiritual attainment, Swami Saradananda.[8] *The Gospel of Sri Ramakrishna,*[9] a compilation of sayings and conversations of Sri Ramakrishna, addressed largely to his householder disciples, is a thousand-page record of his teachings and personal religious experiences covering the last four years of his life. These two books, along with statements made by his direct disciples which are scattered throughout other works, represent the core of primary evidence.

## METHODOLOGY

This book represents an attempt to delineate one possible approach to the dilemma of religious plurality. The approach is based on the value of direct and immediate knowledge of God.

---

[8] *Sri Ramakrishna, The Great Master,* trans. by Swami Jagadananda (2d ed; Mylapore, Madras: Sri Ramakrishna Math, 1952). Saradananda saw God in all; see p. 108, note 7 *infra.*

[9] Trans. with an Introduction by Swami Nikhilananda (New York: Ramakrishna-Vivekananda Center, 1942).

The study will set forth a relevant catalogue of Sri Ramakrishna's spiritual experiences as its major elements. These elements of experience are here regarded as primary evidence.

The presentation is essentially divided into two main sections: Chapters I through IX set forth the basic "facts" of Sri Ramakrishna's lifelong experimentation in religion, his experiences of God, while Chapters X-XII present his teaching career and the account of his disciples and successors.

It must be stressed that Sri Ramakrishna did not overlook or negate the important differences among religious traditions, even within Hinduism. His experiments in the field of religion led him to declare not that all religions are the same, but that, if followed, they lead to the same One God. Sri Ramakrishna therefore cannot be legitimately challenged as a *syncretist* or an *eclectic*,[10] for he neither sought to establish a new religion, taking elements from each, nor attempted a syncretic *mélange* of diverse religious traditions. He was a true *hermeneutician* in his practice of religious discipline—upholding the value and sanctity of each tradition that he tried—both within and outside Hinduism. Thus his testimony of God-consciousness which occurred a century ago remains fully in step with contemporary methods of religious study.

Anyone even casually familiar with the life and teachings of Sri Ramakrishna will note that the significance of his life extends far beyond the material presented here. In this respect the treatment has been one-dimensional: to show his contribution toward advancing the unity of mankind through his experiences of God in the spirit of thoroughgoing integrity.

Some thoughtful persons, especially those who are unfamiliar with the general body of mystical testimony in both East and West, may challenge as dubious the facts of Sri Ramakrishna's religious experiences which are applied here as data.

In response to such a challenge, the following points should be noted. First, Sri Ramakrishna's spiritual experiences were verified in a systematic and conscientious manner by responsible and qualified disciples, all of whom (except one) had been trained in Western-style universities. The testimony of such men as Swami

---

[10] See Alan Richardson, *A Dictionary of Christian Theology* (Philadelphia: Westminster Press, 1969), p. 331.

6

Vivekananda—who was offered the Chair of Eastern philosophy at Harvard University in 1896[11]—and the Swamis Brahmananda, Saradananda, Premananda, Shivananda and others fully corroborates Sri Ramakrishna's experiences. In fact, Swami Saradananda stated, " 'Nothing beyond my spiritual experience has been recorded in the book, *Sri Ramakrishna Lila-prasanga.'* "[12]

Secondly, a number of leading contemporary Western scholars have unambiguously given their stamp of authenticity from the perspective of their own understanding and their special fields of discipline to Sri Ramakrishna's spiritual experimentation: in the historical field, Arnold Toynbee; in the physical sciences, Robert Oppenheimer, Erwin Schrödinger, Sir Arthur Eddington, Harlow Shapley, James Houston Shrader, and Dana L. Farnsworth; in the social sciences, Pitirim Sorokin, Robert Ulich, O. Hobart Mowrer, Paul E. Johnson, and Gordon W. Allport; and among Christian religious leaders, Rudolf Otto, Joachim Wach, Edwin Booth, Walter H. Clark, George Williams, James Luther Adams, Henry Cadbury, Harold DeWolf, Huston Smith, Geoffrey Parrinder, Edgar S. Brightman, S. Paul Schilling, John Lavely, Peter Bertocci, and Walter G. Muelder. Thus it can be asserted that from the point of view of Western academic scholarship a strong case can be made for the admissability of Sri Ramakrishna's spiritual experiences as historical fact in the implementation of the method used here.

The most radical demonstration, however, of the validity of his experiences from the religious viewpoint is that not only did they have a transforming and integrating effect on his own life but he was able subsequently to transform the lives of others. This is documented in Chapters X and XI.

Sri Ramakrishna himself would not discourage the questioning spirit of skeptics and sincere seekers after truth. He would welcome anyone's challenge of the authenticity of his experiences of God and answer such questioners with his own challenge that, by turning their attention to this pursuit, they verify the truths of their own scripture with the direct and immediate experience of God.

---

[11] *The Life of Swami Vivekananda* by His Eastern and Western Disciples (4th ed.; Mayavati, Almora, Himalayas: Advaita Ashrama, 1949), p. 396.

[12] Quoted by Swami Nirvedananda in his Introduction to Saradananda's *Sri Ramakrishna, The Great Master,* "The Book and Its Author," p. xxiv.

**CHAPTER I**

# *Prologue: Does God Exist?*

## SRI RAMAKRISHNA'S FORMATIVE PERIOD

*His Scientific Attitude*

Sri Ramakrishna's life was a series of experiments with different methods of realizing God. His approach to religious experience can be compared to the attitude of the man of science who investigates the functionings of objective reality. In fact, Sri Ramakrishna tested the value of religion itself by seeking to verify the very existence of God. Reflecting this viewpoint, Swami Akhilananda states:

> How can we know that God exists unless we experience Him? We may hear or read about Him or learn theology and philosophy on His existence, but all this will bring no direct and immediate knowledge of Him. Individuals may struggle to be religious but they cannot attain that without direct and immediate experience of Reality. So true religion is thoroughly scientific as it is based on experience of God.
>
> Some people criticize religion, claiming that it has nothing to do with the scientific methods of observation and experiment and logic. This viewpoint is not based on fact. In the light of what Sri Ramakrishna tells us, religion is based on observation and experiment. Unless one has im-

8

mediate and direct knowledge of God . . . one has not attained the goal of religion.[1]

The necessary condition for verification in the scientific method is a passion for truth.[2] This passion permeated the life of Sri Ramakrishna: "Truthfulness," he declared, "is the austerity of this age. . . . Through truth one can realize God."[3] The spirit of truth

[1] Swami Akhilananda, *Modern Problems and Religion* (Boston: Branden Press, 1964), chap. i: "Science and Religion," p. 21. See also Swami Ranganathananda, *Vedanta and Science* (Calcutta: The Ramakrishna Mission Institute of Culture, 1966) and *Swami Vivekananda's Synthesis of Science and Religion* (Calcutta: The Ramakrishna Mission Institute of Culture, 1967); Swami Pavitrananda, *Modern Man in Search of Religion* (Mayavati, Almora, Himalayas: Advaita Ashrama, 1947), chap. ii: "Reverence for Science," pp. 30-54; Gerald Heard, "Vedanta as the Scientific Approach to Religion," in *Vedanta for the Western World,* ed. by Christopher Isherwood, Compass Books (New York: Viking Press, 1960), pp. 51-55. Cf. these views with those of William Ernest Hocking and Henry Nelson Weiman: "The empirical philosophy of religion insists that religious belief should be shaped . . . to apprehend the greatest good human life can ever attain. I believe Professor Hocking and I are united in the claim that religious belief should not be about the unknowable but should be about what is empirically and rationally knowable." H. N. Weiman, "Empiricism," in *Philosophy, Religion, and the Coming World Civilization: Essays in Honor of William Ernest Hocking,* ed. by Leroy S. Rouner (The Hague: Martinus Nijhoff, 1966), p. 197. Finally, cf. the foregoing with the following statement by William James: "Our testing of religion by practical common sense and the empirical method, leave it in possession of its towering place in history." *Varieties,* p. 368.

[2] See William James, "Pragmatism's Conception of Truth," *Essays in Pragmatism* (New York: Hafner, 1952), pp. 159-176, esp. pp. 160-162. "True ideas are those we can assimilate, validate, corroborate and verify" (p. 160). In this connection note especially James's discussion of verification which follows. Also see James, "The Pragmatism Account of Truth and Its Misunderstanding," *The Meaning of Truth* (Ann Arbor: University of Michigan Press, 1970), pp. 180-215. Cf. the following statement by Akhilananda: "In the scientific world we find a tendency not to accept anything unless the facts are actually proven to us. . . . Sri Ramakrishna was a man of that type. He was, in fact, a product of this modern age. He would not accept even God-consciousness until he had himself verified it, until he had realized the fact. He would not accept anything whether given him by a Hindu, Christian or Mohammedan teacher. He tested it first as you and I test the different facts of science by our own experiments." *Sri Ramakrishna and Modern Psychology* (Providence: The Vedanta Society, 1937), pp. 15-16. "This outlook shows that Sri Ramakrishna was the pragmatist of all modern pragmatists" (*ibid.,* p. 7). Cf. Swami Vivekananda, *Practical Vedanta* (Mayavati, Almora, Himalayas: Advaita Ashrama, 1946).

[3] *Sayings of Sri Ramakrishna* (7th rev. ed.; Madras: Sri Ramakrishna Math, 1949), p. 168.

shone as the starting-point, the means, and the end of his religious activities. Speaking of his own attitude, he said:

> One is sure to realise God, if only one has great devotion to truth. On the contrary, if one has no regard for truth, everything of his will be destroyed gradually. After attaining to this state (of God-realisation), I told Mother, taking flowers in my hand, 'O Mother, here take back Thy knowledge and Thy ignorance, Thy purity and Thy impurity, Thy good and also Thy bad, Thy virtue and Thy sin; give me only pure Bhakti, Mother.' But when I said all these to Mother, I could not say, 'Take back Thy truth and untruth.' All I could return back to Mother, but not truth.[4]

This statement gives us an important clue to Sri Ramakrishna's mental constitution. Like a scientist, he would not renounce truth under any circumstances. This attitude was evidently a family characteristic, for his father had already gained a reputation for strict truthfulness prior to Sri Ramakrishna's birth. In this connection, Swami Abhedananda, one of Sri Ramakrishna's immediate disciples, writes the following:

> His father, Khudiram Chattopadhyaya was very orthodox, prayerful and lived up to the high ideals of a spiritual life. He never spoke an untruth. He was honoured and revered as a 'Vak-siddha Purusha'—that is, whatever he uttered invariably came true.[5]

In fact, so steadfast was Khudiram's devotion to truth that he incurred extreme poverty by refusing to perjure himself in court when requested to do so by the landlord who ruled his village. Knowing full well the dangerous consequences of arousing the landlord's vindictiveness, he nevertheless refused to bear false witness and "had to sacrifice all of his landholdings in consequence. He was ruined."[6]

### Early Years

It was in this condition of abject poverty that Sri Ramakrishna was born on February 17, 1836. He was born to noble parents. "His mother was equally pious and full of devotion. She was like the

[4] *Ibid.,* p. 317.

[5] Swami Abhedananda, *Sri Ramakrishna* (Calcutta: Ramakrishna Vedanta Math, 1940), p. 6.

[6] Christopher Isherwood, *Ramakrishna and His Disciples* (London: Methuen, 1965), p. 11.

embodiment of simplicity and kindness. Her mind was free from earthly desires, pride and egotism."[7]

Sri Ramakrishna was raised in the small village of Kamarpukur.[8] Although eighty-six miles from Calcutta, it was completely untouched by Western influence. Gadadhar (as he was then called) was a product of the timeless village life of India, in which the roots of spiritual culture are deepest, nourished from the heroic Vedic tradition of the remote past, and from the rich variety of spiritual ideals supplied by the Puranic, Tantric and other traditions.[9] The

[7] Abhedananda, *Sri Ramakrishna*, p. 6.

[8] See Isherwood, pp. 3-6, for an excellent exposition of Bengali villages of this type, and of Kamarpukur in particular. Note especially the author's following comments: "The Bengal village does not present, like the English village, an outward appearance of order. It will contain a number of temples and small shrines, but these are not meeting-places as Christian churches are, because Hinduism is primarily a household religion and its rites of daily worship are mostly practised in each individual home. . . . On the whole, life in such a village was happy. Poverty is a relative evil; and in this case it was widely shared, and prevented from becoming extreme by the helpfulness of your neighbors. As a community, Kamarpukur met one of the most important demands of the modern social psychologist; no one could feel rejected there. Everybody had his or her place in the caste-structure. The family recognized total responsibility for all its members, even the most distant. The old were honoured. Women were treated with respect. Children were indulged and petted by all. As we study the personality of Ramakrishna, we see in him the sublimation of the village child he once was; innocently secure in his love for his mother and his certainty of being loved. You cannot imagine a less frustrated childhood than his, or one less likely to produce conflicts and neuroses in later years. It will be important to bear this in mind when we consider the psychological states which Ramakrishna afterwards passed through" (pp. 5-6).

[9] For a comprehensive sweep of the Vedic tradition, see "Vedic Civilization," Part III of *The Cultural Heritage of India*, Vol. I: *The Early Phases* (2d ed.; Calcutta: The Ramakrishna Mission Institute of Culture, 1958), pp. 163-389. An interesting viewpoint is expressed by Govind Chandra Pande of the University of Allahabad in his *Studies in the Origins of Buddhism*, Ancient History Research Series No. 1 (Allahabad: University of Allahabad, Department of Ancient History, Culture and Archaeology, 1957), chap. viii, "Review of the Vedic Background," pp. 251-309. For the philosophical aspect of that period, note "The Vedanta," Part II of *Cultural Heritage*, Vol. III: *The Philosophies*, ed. by Haridas Bhattacharyya (2d ed.; Calcutta: Ramakrishna Mission Institute of Culture, 1953), pp. 187-387; also Sarvepalli Radhakrishnan and Charles A. Moore, eds., *A Source Book in Indian Philosophy* (Princeton, N. J.: Princeton University Press, 1957); and for a more popularized version, Heinrich Zimmer, *Philosophies of India* (Princeton, N. J.: Princeton University Press, 1967). For a contemporary interpretation of the Vedanta which will be used extensively here, see *The Complete Works of Swami Vivekananda* (Mayavati,

real culture of India, the repository of its more than four milennia of religious unfoldment, is to be found in its village life.

Thus Sri Ramakrishna's formative period was influenced to an important extent by the deeply religious atmosphere which surrounded him, both in his family and in the larger village society. This environmental effect produced an intensification of his innate desire to know the truth, to pursue the religious quest to its ultimate conclusion. Other aspects of his boyhood personality are presented by Isherwood as follows:

> He was vigorous and healthy, never suffering from sickness of any kind. From his earliest years, he had a strongly defined character. He was lively, affectionate, ready to be friends with everybody. But, at the same time, he had a curious streak of obstinacy in him. Although his memory was unusually retentive, he absolutely refused to remember any of the rules of arithmetic. And whatever he was forbidden to do—flatly and without explanation—he would do immediately; and never lie or try to hide the fact that he had done it. . . . He was strangely fearless, even of

Almora, Himalayas: Advaita Ashrama, 1948-1955), I-VIII. For the Puranic tradition, see "The Puranas," Part III of *Cultural Heritage,* Vol. II: *Itihasas, Puranas, Dharma and Other Sastras* (Calcutta: Ramakrishna Mission Institute of Culture, 1962), pp. 223-298; also helpful here are Milton Singer and Daniel H. H. Ingalls, eds., *Krishna: Myths, Rites and Attitudes* (Honolulu: East-West Center Press, 1966); Bharatan Kumarappa, *The Hindu Conception of the Deity* (London: Luzac, 1934), chap. iii, "Conception of the Deity in Pancaratra and Puranic Literature," pp. 86-126; J. Gonda, *Change and Continuity in Indian Religion* (The Hague: Mouton & Co., 1965), chap. v, "The Isvara Idea," pp. 131-163; Swami Ramakrishnananda, *God and Divine Incarnations* (Madras: Sri Ramakrishna Math, 1947) and his *Sri Krishna, Pastoral and Kingmaker* (Madras: Sri Ramakrishna Math, 1960); A. C. Bhaktivedanta Swami, *Teachings of Lord Chaitanya* (New York: International Society for Krishna Consciousness, 1968); M. Winternitz, *A History of Indian Literature,* Vol. III, Part I: *Classical Sanskrit Literature,* trans. by Subhadra Jha (Delhi: Motilal Banarsidass, 1963). On the Tantric tradition, see the works of Sir John Woodroffe, especially *Sakti and Sakta* (Madras: Ganesh & Co., 1965), *The Serpent Power* (Madras: Ganesh & Co., 1964) and *Introduction to Tantra Sastra* (Madras: Ganesh & Co., 1969); see also M. P. Pandit, *Lights on the Tantra* (Madras: Ganesh & Co., 1968) and *Gems from the Tantras* (Madras: Ganesh & Co., 1969); cf. Swami Pratyagatmananda, "Philosophy of the Tantras," in *The Philosophies,* ed. by Bhattacharyya, Part II, pp. 437-448. An overview of the three traditions up to and including the present is offered by the recent substantial volume, *India's Contribution to World Thought and Culture,* ed. by Lokesh Chandra, Devendra Swarup, Swarajya Prakash Gupta and Sitaram Goel (Madras: Vivekananda Rock Memorial Committee, 1970).

those things which children are apt to fear most; the dark and the super-natural. He would go deliberately to places that were popularly sup-posed to be haunted by ghosts and ghouls. . . . But Gadadhar showed curiosity rather than awe. . . . People were naturally drawn to him—not only his own school-fellows but grown-up men and women. Among boys of his age, he was always the centre of the group, the inventor of new games. . . . If Gadadhar was not at all a lonely child, he was certainly not dependent on the company of others. He would roam off happily alone and lose himself in the sense of Nature around him. It was thus that, at the age of six or seven, he had his first intense spiritual experience.[10]

### First Superconscious Experience

This spiritual experience, Sri Ramakrishna's first "taste" of God,[11] is described in the following way by Swami Akhilananda:

[10] Isherwood, pp. 27-28. Cf. Swami Gnaneswarananda, *Ramakrishna, The Man and the Power* (Chicago: The Vedanta Society, 1936), pp. 7-18.

[11] Cf. *dhawq* ("taste") in the Sufi Islamic tradition. See al-Ghazali, *Ihya' 'Ulum Al-Din* ("The Revival of the Religious Sciences"), trans. by L. Zolondek (Leiden, Netherlands: E. J. Brill, 1963). In this his major work, al-Ghazali proposes three possible conditions in which man may be related to God: 1) *iman* or faith, 2) *'ilm*, science or knowledge giving reasons for faith, and 3) *dhawq*, "taste" or direct experience. See W. Montgomery Watt, *Muslim Intellectual: A Study of Al-Ghazali* (Edinburgh: Edinburgh University Press, 1963), pp. 164-165. *Dhawq* or direct experience is the quintessence of spiritual knowledge, and is achieved through the "science of the heart": "Al-Ghazali's conception of the heart is intimately linked to his conception of man. . . . To al-Ghazali the heart does not signify the 'cone shaped flesh in the left side of the chest'; it is rather a 'transcendental spiritual subtlety which is connected to the physical heart'; this subtlety is the essence of man, which comprehends, learns, and knows; and it is this which speaks, opposes, censures, and holds to account.' Moreover, this spiritual essence of man is similar to the essence of God, for God created man in His own image. Because of this relationship between man and God, every man, not only the prophets, can . . . reach the realization of the knowledge of God." L. Zolondek, Introduction to Book XX of al-Ghazali's *Ihya'*, p. 2. Al-Ghazali himself attained *dhawq*, and contributed immensely to Islamic religious history by thus infusing orthodox Islamic tradition with the spirit of mysticism, striking a balanced harmony between the two. It can be noted here that the Sufi Islamic term *dhawq* is fully comparable to the term *samadhi* in the Hindu tradition. *Samadhi* will be used extensively here to denote superconscious experience, but it should not therefore be surmised that other religious traditions lack a precise vocabulary of mystical experience. The constant emphasis of this thesis is that mysticism, or the direct and immediate experience of God, is a universal phenomenon—occurring wherever man is man—and is in no way confined to boundaries set up by religious traditions, nationalities, languages, and so forth. Al-Ghazali's *dhawq* is offered as an illustration.

... he was going to visit a temple. On the way, a beautiful scene: a deep speck of cloud with a number of cranes flying in front of it, made him realize God-consciousness. Beauty, the *Sundara* aspect of the Divine, transported him and gave him divine joy. That was the first experience of this hero in the spiritual realm.[12]

## Subsequent Superconscious Experiences

There are at least two other distinct recorded occasions mentioned by his biographers[13] when Sri Ramakrishna, in his early boyhood, lost external consciousness and became merged in *samadhi*.[14] In each instance the boy became completely absorbed in an aspect of God with form—one or another familiar to him as part of his rural religious heritage.[15]

[12] Akhilananda, *Sri Ramakrishna and Modern Psychology*, p. 9.

[13] Swami Saradananda, *Sri Ramakrishna, The Great Master*, pp. 56-57. Cf. Isherwood, pp. 30-31, 34-35; *The Life of Sri Ramakrishna* (Mayavati, Almora, Himalayas: Advaita Ashrama, 1948), pp. 24-25, 27-29.

[14] "First is the conscious plane, in which all work is always accompanied with the feeling of egoism. Next comes the unconscious plane, where all work is unaccompanied with the feeling of egoism. That part of mind-work which is unaccompanied with the feeling of egoism is unconscious work, and that part which is accompanied with the feeling of egoism is conscious work. In the lower animals, this unconscious work is called instinct. In higher animals, and in the highest of all animals, man, what is called conscious work prevails. But it does not end here. There is a still higher plane upon which the mind can work. It can go beyond consciousness. Just as unconscious work is beneath consciousness, so there is another work which is above consciousness, and which also is not accompanied with the feeling of egoism. The feeling of egoism is only on the middle plane. When the mind is above or below that line there is no feeling of 'I', and yet the mind works. When the mind goes beyond this line of self-consciousness it is called *Samadhi,* or superconsciousness." Swami Vivekananda, *Raja-Yoga,* a translation with commentary of Patanjali's *Yoga Aphorisms* (rev. ed.; New York: Ramakrishna-Vivekananda Center, 1955), p. 76. Vivekananda further states: *"Samadhi* is the property of every human being. . . . Each one of the steps to attain *Samadhi* has been reasoned out, properly adjusted, scientifically organised, and, when faithfully practised, will surely lead us to the desired end." *Raja-Yoga or Conquering the Internal Nature* (8th ed.; Mayavati, Almora, Himalayas: Advaita Ashrama, 1947), p. 102. For further elaboration of *samadhi,* see Akhilananda, *Hindu Psychology: Its Meaning for the West,* with an Introduction by Gordon W. Allport and a Foreword by Edgar Sheffield Brightman (New York: Harper & Row, 1946), chap. x, "The Superconscious State," p. 150 ff. I cite both these authors as authentic sources on this point, because both were thoroughly scientific in their approach. In addition, each was intimately acquainted with *samadhi* through personal experience and frequent observation of others in this state.

[15] In these cases the goddess Visalakshi and the god Shiva, respectively.

From now onwards, Gadadhar was in this kind of ecstasy from time to time. He would forget himself and his surroundings when meditating or listening to songs, music, etc. in praise of gods and goddesses. Then his mind would remain indrawn for a time—short or long—during which it would not be susceptible to any external stimulus. On occasions, when his absorption became very deep, he would appear like a lifeless statue.

When that state was over, he would say, if asked, that he had experienced a marvellous joy in having a divine vision when meditating on some god or goddess or listening to songs glorifying them. All this caused much alarm to Chandra [his mother] and other members of the family for a long time. But that fear passed away when they found that the boy's health was not affected in any way, and that he was efficient in all kinds of work and was always happy. Gadadhar was now so often in this condition, that he gradually got accustomed to it and could almost control it as he wished. . . . This made him very happy and he was never afraid of experiencing that state.[16]

## SRI RAMAKRISHNA'S SEARCH AFTER TRUTH

*Naturalness of His Religious Attitude*

One must marvel at this documentation of the religious experiences of a boy barely completing his first decade of life. It clearly demonstrates his intense yearning after ultimate Truth from a very early age. While the average man and woman can manage to acquire devotion to God and the accompanying habitual practices of prayer and meditation[17] only after years of struggle and constant

[16] Saradananda, pp. 58-59.

[17] What is meant here by the word "meditation" is comparable to the technical Sanskrit word *dhyana.* "In order to reach the super-conscious state *(samadhi)* in a scientific manner it is necessary to pass through the various steps. . . . When the mind has been trained to remain fixed on a certain internal or external location, there comes to it the power of flowing in an unbroken current, as it were, towards that point. This state is called *Dhyana."* Vivekananda, *Raja-Yoga,* Mayavati edition, p. 98. Swami Akhilananda writes: "The practice of concentration is, no doubt, the kernel of religious evolution. Without the practice of concentration and meditation, no man can ever expect to reach the highest state of spiritual evolution. When we study the lives of the great Christian, Jewish, Hindu, Buddhist, and Mohammedan mystics, we fully realize that they reached the highest spiritual consciousness through development of the power of concentration." Akhilananda, *Hindu Psychology,* pp. 102-103. He further explains: "When concentration is very deep and the mind does not waver but remains focused on the object of thought, that is meditation *(dhyana).* According to Hindu psychologists, meditation is not merely a nice thought, a poetic flight, or loose fancies of even pleasant experiences; it is the depth

15

effort, these attributes became natural to Gadadhar long before his "formal" search for God was under way at age seventeen.

Gadadhar's father died in 1843. This event profoundly stimulated the boy's desire to verify the existence of God. His father's death accented the transitoriness of life for him. In this changeable world he sought that which is permanent. He delighted to pass long hours in the company of itinerant monks *(sadhus),* serving them, joining in their religious discussions, in prayer, and imitating their ways in his play.[18]

### His Goal of Education

Young Gadadhar found the objective of schooling to be opposite to his own goal of verifying God, for it emphasized the changeable aspect of life and not the search for permanence *(sat)*[19] to which he was dedicated. What is usually of paramount importance to the average person in both East and West is the development of competence for earning money and gaining a good reputation and position in the world. This is the foundation upon which the modern educational system is based.[20] Generally speaking, ethical training,

---

of concentration in which the mind flows continuously to an object without any cessation as 'oil poured from one vessel to another.' It is not a succession of many thoughts of the same object. The mind must not waver whatsoever. So a man is really meditating when his mind is freed from all other thoughts and is wholly focused on the object of his concentration" *(ibid.,* p. 113). Cf. Swami Siddheswarananda, *Meditation according to Yoga-Vedanta,* with a Foreword by S. Radhakrishnan (2d ed.; Puranattukara, Trichur: Sri Ramakrishna Ashrama, 1969); *Meditation,* by Monks of the Ramakrishna Order (London: Ramakrishna Vedanta Centre, 1972).

[18] *Life of Sri Ramakrishna,* pp. 21-24.

[19] For the Hindu, *Brahman* is beyond description; it transcends the categories of name and form *(nama-rupa),* of time, space and causation *(desa-kala-nimitti),* and therefore of language. The expression *Sat-Chit-Ananda,* representing the divine qualities of Existence or Truth, Knowledge or Consciousness, and Bliss or Love is regarded by the Hindu as the nearest that human language can come to describing the Indescribable. These three qualities are interrelated and inseparable, similar to our Christian Trinity. Here the term *sat* or truth has a very specific meaning: i.e., truth is that which remains the same at all times under all conditions. Expressed in another way, truth is that which cannot be denied. Therefore, Sri Ramakrishna's search for a *permanent* entity behind a changing universe was in fact a search for truth *(sat),* a search for Brahman. See Vivekananda, *Works,* II, 193-194. Cf. works of Raymond Panikkar.

[20] Akhilananda, *Modern Problems,* chap. iv, "Philosophy of Life and Education," pp. 59-74.

the development of a theocentric system of values, and the intensification of man's innate desire to know God are little stressed, if at
all, in post-Renaissance Western education, which has become the
model for the whole world.[21] This was true even for Sri Ramakrishna's rural school, although it had not been influenced by Western ways. What is *practical* in our type of education is the potential
for worldly wisdom, in contrast to spiritual insight. The pragmatic
concept of truth is measured by its utility,[22] and utility in this case is
measured ultimately in "dollars and cents." Thus truth is restricted
to the changeable universe, and pragmatism is reduced finally to
materialism.

But this is not the only alternative, and for Sri Ramakrishna as a
young boy it was definitely not so. For him that which was most
immediately useful was the knowledge of God. Utility lay in a longing for a changeless truth—that which cannot be negated—the
quest for permanence in God. Pragmatism here has a completely
different foundation.[23] Like the materialistic view, it also rests on an
experiential or empirical foundation,[24] but not that of sense data:
"If God exists, can I experience Him now, directly and immediately?" This burning question alone motivated Sri Ramakrishna, so
that nothing but the ultimate answer could satisfy him. God was his

[21] *Ibid.,* chaps. v and vi, "Personality Development in Education," pp. 75-87, and
"Emotional Integration in Education," pp. 88-99. Cf. Pitirim A. Sorokin, *Reconstruction of Humanity,* Bhavan's Book University (3d ed.; Bombay: Bharatiya Vidya
Bhavan, 1962), Part I, chap. iii, pp. 43-60. Professor Sorokin comments that "even
the intellectual elite of the past four centuries, distinguished for their genius, have
hardly been ethically superior to the rank and file" (p. 46). He further documents this
point in considerable detail in one of his last books, *Power and Morality: Who Shall
Guard the Guardians?* by Sorokin and Walter A. Lunden, Extending Horizons
Books (Boston: Porter Sargent, 1959).

[22] See William James, *Essays in Pragmatism* (New York: Hafner, 1952), "What
Pragmatism Means," pp. 141-158.

[23] "Now pragmatism, devoted though she be to facts, has no such materialistic
bias as ordinary empiricism labors under" *(ibid.,* p. 154). "She [pragmatism] has in
fact no prejudices whatever, no obstructive dogmas, no rigid canons of what shall
count as proof. She is completely genial. She will entertain any hypothesis, she will
consider any evidence. It follows that in the religious field she is at a great advantage.
. . . In short, she widens the field for God. Pragmatism is willing to take anything. . . .
She will count mystical experiences if they have practical consequences" *(ibid.,* p.
157).

[24] "The Vedantists['] . . . test of its [*samadhi's*] purity, like our test of religion's
value, is empirical: its fruits must be good for life." James, *Varieties,* p. 392.

17

only utility. Nothing else for him was practical.[25]

Thus at a very early age, this young Brahmin, for whose caste the development of formal learning should have been of paramount importance, recognized the two alternatives as presented before him: school, or learning the three R's, the object of which "was to earn a few more handfuls of rice and an extra bunch of bananas,"[26] and spiritual experience in the realization of God. In effect, this became the touchstone by which all his future decisions would be tested: that is, "will this particular course of action lead me Godward or away from God?" Although he continued to go to school for a time and learned to read and write in Bengali,

> he never developed a liking for book learning. When he saw the longing for worldly enjoyment and wealth of learned pandits, Battacharyas, etc., he became averse to acquiring knowledge like them. For, his keen insight made him first ascertain the motives underlying all actions and then judge their value by the standard of his father's good qualities, like detachment from the world, devotion to God, truthfulness, righteous conduct, etc. That comparison revealed to his surprise that the goal of most people was entirely different from that of his father. But he felt more sad than surprised to find that such people always suffered from delusion because they looked upon this transitory world as permanent. . . . As a

[25] Cf. the following statement by Sri Ramakrishna's foremost disciple, Swami Vivekananda, in a lecture delivered in London in 1896: "Vedanta preaches the ideal, and the ideal as we know, is always far ahead of the real, of the practical, as we may call it. There are two tendencies in human nature: one to reconcile the ideal with life and the other to elevate life to the ideal. . . . Now, if any man comes to preach to me a certain ideal, the first step towards which is to give up selfishness, to give up self-enjoyment, I think that that is impractical. But when a man brings an ideal which can be reconciled with my selfishness, I am glad and at once jump at it. That is the ideal for me. As the word *orthodox* has been manipulated into various forms, so has the word *practical.* 'My doxy is orthodoxy; your doxy is heterodoxy.' So with practicality. What I think is practical is to me the only practicality in the world. If I am a shopkeeper, I think shopkeeping the only practical pursuit in the world. If I am a thief, I think stealing is the best means of being practical; others are not practical. You see how we all use this word *practical* for things that *we* like and can do. Therefore I ask you to understand that Vedanta, though it is intensely practical, is always so in the sense of the ideal. . . . To many this is, no doubt, a terrible ideal, and most of us think that this ideal can never be reached; but Vedanta insists that it can be realized by everyone." *Jnana-Yoga* (rev. ed.; New York: Ramakrishna-Vivekananda Center, 1955), pp. 211-212.

[26] Gnaneswarananda, p. 10.

result of this discovery, there arose in his mind a desire to conduct his own life differently.[27]

This was an extremely bold posture for a young boy to take. In our culture it would have been equivalent to renouncing all the values that society holds dear. That is because our society is at heart thoroughly hedonistic instead of theocentric.[28] Had he pursued such a course in Europe or America, he would have become a misanthrope, an outcaste, unfit to lead a normal, productive life. Yet in his village society, especially among the poor and illiterate, there existed a profound religious culture completely accessible to him through oral tradition, through the living example of his family and elders, and through the media of religious drama, recitation, worship, and myth. In other words, Gadadhar did not need books to teach him about God. Such instruction was daily being carried on.

[27] Saradananda, p. 59.

[28] See Sorokin, *Reconstruction of Humanity,* Part III, chap. vi, "Two Basic Principles," pp. 91-98. Sorokin states in defining the central thesis of his sociological position: "Western medieval culture['s] . . . major principle, or the true-reality value, was God. All the important sectors of medieval culture articulated this fundamental principle-value as formulated in the Christian Credo. . . . Its dominant mores, ways of life, and mental outlook stressed union with God as the only supreme end, and a negative or indifferent attitude toward this sensory world, with all its wealth, pleasures, and values. . . . Such a unified system of culture based upon the principle of a supersensory and superrational God as the only true reality and value may be called *ideational.* A basically similar major premise respecting the superrational and supersensory reality of God though differently perceived in its properties, underlay also the integrated culture of Brahmanical India, the Buddhist and Taoist cultures, Greek culture from the eighth to the end of the sixth century B.C., and some other cultures. They have all been predominantly ideational. The decline of medieval culture consisted precisely in the disintegration of this ideational system. It began at the end of the twelfth century, when there emerged the germ of a new, and profoundly different major principle, namely, that *the true reality and value is sensory.* Only what we see, hear, smell, touch, and otherwise perceive through our sense organs is real and has value. Beyond such a sensory reality, either there is nothing, or, if there is something, we cannot sense it; therefore it is equivalent to the nonreal and the non existent. As such it may be neglected. . . . Beginning roughly with the sixteenth century, the new principle became dominant, and with it the new form of culture that was based upon it. In this way the modern form of our culture emerged, the sensory, . . ., secular, and 'this-worldly' culture. It may be called *sensate.* . . . It is precisely this principle that is articulated by our modern sensate culture in all its main compartments: in its arts and sciences, philosophy and pseudo-religion, ethics and law; in its social, economic, and political organization; in its dominant ways of life and mentality" (pp. 94-95).

## Contact with Sadhus and Village Art

Considering further influences on his learning process, special note should be taken of Sri Ramakrishna's remarkable memory, whereby he is said to have had total recall, even years later, of things he had heard but once.[29] This represented an important aspect of learning for him throughout his life, but especially in his boyhood, when he would spend hours sitting with the *sadhus* (wandering monks),[30] listening to their spiritual instruction, their recital of traditional religious stories and Vedic chants, and internalizing through an oral tradition characteristic of early Vedic times the groundwork of religious mythology and spiritual values he was to work out during the course of his life.

It may be surmised that the boy's close contact with *sadhus* representing different aspects of the Hindu tradition (and there are many) not only sharpened his appetite for the experience of God and increased his detachment toward worldly pursuits, but also permeated his consciousness with an appreciation for *different* modes of cultic worship. He expressed this appreciation in the many village art forms that were available to him:

> An amateur dramatic company was formed in the village, and Gadadhar was asked to join it and take the chief roles. As he did not have time for both school and study of the various dramatic presentations, he chose the thing that appealed to him, and was thus able to give up school with

[29] "One could see him drinking in every word of the village Kathak—story teller—as he narrated and sang the stories of the enlightened ones from ancient texts. Nothing escaped the retentive memory of the little boy who could reproduce a whole religious opera with its music by hearing it only once. From these sources he gathered enough food for years of contemplation, and also cultivated an effective means for artistic expression." Gnaneswarananda, p. 12.

[30] The Indian institution of *Sannyasa,* dating back to pre-Buddhistic times, has a twofold function from society's point of view. Traditionally the *sadhu* or monk preserves the spiritual ideal for society by completely identifying himself with the religious goal. He goes from door to door begging food, depending on the will of God for his sustenance. In exchange for the bowl of rice he might receive, he in turn imparts spiritual instruction, recites scripture, etc., as the need may arise. Thus this age-old institution of *Sannyasa* acts for India as a means of imparting religious instruction. See Vivekananda, *Karma-Yoga and Bhakti-Yoga* (rev. ed.; New York: Ramakrishna-Vivekananda Center, 1955), *Karma-Yoga,* chap. ii, "Each is Great in His Own Place," pp. 13-31. Cf. *The Way of a Pilgrim,* trans. by R. M. French (New York: The Seabury Press, 1965). See Vivekananda, *Works,* II, 462-463; see especially the footnote on page 463.

a clear conscience. . . . Gadadhar not only played the chief roles but took upon himself the task of training the other boys. Incidents from the lives of Sri Rama and Sri Krishna were dramatized. From the start, the project was a success. Gadadhar was in his element, and we are told of his frequent trances during the performances.

At this time Gadadhar showed marked talent in painting and clay modelling, though he had had no special training. His powerful concentration and intuitive idealism were great help. He would often surprise professional moulders by pointing out inaccuracies in the execution of some delicate part of an image, the eyes, for instance, and would direct them how to set them aright. In his ecstatic moods he saw various divine forms; and these visions, coupled with his artistic faculty, developed his critical faculty and enabled him to produce figures of great beauty.[31]

These activities developed his devotional response to various forms of God in a way which is completely unfamiliar to Western theological understanding today. They are an integral part of the Indian cultural setting of village life which has given rise to great religious leaders and movements, based as it is on what Professor Sorokin calls the "ideational" as opposed to the "sensate" value system. Such art forms within a culture preserve and transmit living religious ideals, thereby providing an education *par excellence* for the refinement of spiritual perception. This was eminently true in the case of Sri Ramakrishna.

As a healthy boy reared on the lap of benign nature, loving humanity and being loved by all, constantly feeding his intellect with the ancient lore of his race, through artistic medium, and also learning to give exquisite expression to what he spontaneously absorbed, Gadai received an education which made him the man he was destined to be. If later in life men with university degrees and world-wide reputation for scholarship sat at his feet like undeveloped children and marveled at the wisdom, culture, refinement and spiritual glory of the illiterate Ramakrishna, it might be taken for a dramatic representation in his life of the highest ideal of education.[32]

At age seventeen Sri Ramakrishna joined his older brother in Calcutta where the latter hoped to remedy his delinquency as a student, but Sri Ramakrishna's discriminative faculty[33] again reasoned

[31] *Life of Sri Ramakrishna,* pp. 40-41.

[32] Gnaneswarananda, p. 14.

[33] More precisely, the faculty of discrimination of the "real from the unreal," or

strongly against worldly learning. His was the eternal quest to go beyond the senses, beyond the finite, to a union with the Infinite. Toward this end he became a temple priest at a temple dedicated to the worship of Kali, the Mother Goddess,[34] in a place four miles from Calcutta—Dakshineswar. It was here that he spent the remainder of his life.

---

*viveka,* is considered by Hindu teachers to be an important tool for attaining super-conscious experience *(samadhi).* The particular path which stresses this is called *jnana marga,* or the way of knowledge. For a complete elaboration of this method, see Vivekananda, *Jnana-Yoga* (rev. ed.; New York: Ramakrishna-Vivekananda Center, 1955). Cf. *Shankara's Crest-Jewel of Discrimination (Viveka-Chudamani),* trans. with an introduction to Shankara's philosophy by Swami Prabhavananda and Christopher Isherwood (Hollywood, Calif.: Vedanta Press, 1947); or for a more literal translation, *Vivekachudamani of Shri Shankaracharya,* trans. by Swami Madhavananda (7th ed.; Calcutta: Advaita Ashrama, 1966); *The Quintessence of Vedanta (The Sarva-vedanta-siddhanta-sarasangraha) of Acharya Sankara,* ed. by V. A. Thyagarajan, trans. by Swami Tattwananda with an Introduction by Swami Agamananda (Kalady, Kerala: Sri Ramakrishna Advaita Ashrama, 1960); and especially the *Brahma-Sutra-Bhasya of Sri Sankaracarya,* trans. by Swami Gambhirananda (Calcutta: Advaita Ashrama, 1965). Also useful here is *The Bhagavad-Gita with the Commentary of Sri Sankaracharya,* trans. by A. Mahadeva Sastri (Madras: V. Ramaswamy Sastrulu & Sons, 1961). It can be noted here that with respect to methodology and type of spiritual experiences, the *jnana marga* of Hinduism is very similar to early Buddhistic practices. This will be developed later in chapter IV.

[34] See Swami Kirtidananda, *The Glory of the Divine Mother* (Calcutta: The Ramakrishna Mission Institute of Culture, 1969); Sister Nivedita, *Kali the Mother* (Mayavati, Almora, Himalayas: Advaita Ashrama, 1950); Arthur Avalon, *Hymns to Kali* (Madras: Ganesh & Co., 1965) and his *Kama-Kala-Vilasa* (Madras: Ganesh & Co., 1961) as well as his *Hymns to the Goddess* (Madras: Ganesh & Co., 1964); Sir John Woodroffe, *The Garland of Letters* (Madras: Ganesh & Co., 1969); and especially *The Devi-Mahatmyam or Sri Durga-Saptasati,* trans. by Swami Jagadisvarananda (Mylapore, Madras: Sri Ramakrishna Math, 1955). Note poems to Divine Mother written by Swami Vivekananda, *In Search of God and Other Poems* (2d ed.; Calcutta: Advaita Ashrama, 1968), especially "Kali the Mother," p. 15.

# CHAPTER II

# *First Experience of God*

## KALI, THE DIVINE MOTHER

*Kali an Aspect of God*

Sri Ramakrishna's family deity was Raghuvir, an aspect of Ramachandra.[1] Although he and his family were extremely devoted to this deity, the sources on his life indicate the ease with which he transferred his worship to a totally different aspect of God—a phenomenon seldom seen in Western religious history except in cases of total conversion, but one completely acceptable and commonplace in the Hindu tradition. For a Hindu, God is formless, nameless, attributeless, yet can take innumerable forms, names, and attributes so that his devotees can worship him according to their own particular taste and temperament. This is the Hindu position. It justifies the many gods and goddesses of the Hindu pantheon, for all these are but different aspects of the same All-Loving Being.

Sri Ramakrishna first verified the existence of God with his experience of Kali, an aspect of Divine Mother.[2] This experience oc-

[1] See Ramakrishnananda, *God and Divine Incarnations,* "The Parasurama Avatara," pp. 141-149; C. Rajagopalachari, *Ramayana,* Bhavan's Book University No. 44 (Bombay: Bharatiya Vidya Bhavan, 1965).

[2] While God the Divine Mother as well as Father of all is recognized chiefly in

curred as a result of his intense yearning for her vision, a yearning
so intense that he could no longer satisfactorily perform his regular
duties of temple priest, which consisted chiefly in serving the image
of Divine Mother. He regarded this image as the embodiment of
truth, consciousness, and bliss. It was the all-pervading Brahman
that had become for him solid and concrete to accept his worship,
like ice congealing in an endless ocean.[3]

Hinduism among the world religions, this tendency can be traced in other religious
traditions, if not so prominently. Dr. James M. Judd presents a good case for this
based on scriptural interpretation and historical data in both the Jewish and Christian traditions in his recent article, "The Universality of Mother God," *Vedanta for
East and West* (London), No. 122 (November-December, 1971), pp. 9-15. In Mahayana Buddhism the *Srimalasinhanada Sutra* (untranslated) focuses on the *tathagata-
garbha,* or Buddha's womb, providing rich maternal symbolism. We also note the
goddess Tara in late Mahayana scriptures, in addition to the abundance of mother
ideology prevalent in tantric Buddhism, beginning with the early *Guhyasamaja tantra* right through to the later *Kalacakrayana* and *Sahajayana* tantras (see Lal Mani
Joshi, *Studies in the Buddhistic Culture of India* [Delhi: Motilal Banarsidass, 1967],
chap. x, "Origin and Growth of Esoteric Buddhism," pp. 302-348). Emphasis on worshipping God as Mother in African Christianity is more common than generally
recognized (note matrilineal social units). Quoting Isaiah 49:15, a Lutheran African
minister's Holy Communion service in Zululand included the following remarks:
"Consider the greatness of a woman's love of her child. . . . The child lives from the
mother and receives strength from her day by day. The child eats from the mother,
drinks her blood, and yet, the mother never tires of the child. . . . God has borne us
through Jesus Christ. *Jesus is our Mother.* He was constrained by his love for us."
(Italics mine.) Quoted by Bengt Sundkler in *The Christian Ministry in Africa* (London: SCM Press, 1960), p. 123. Cf. the life and teachings of Mama Ndona Beatrice
and the Antonian Movement which she founded; see Sigbert Axelson, *Culture Confrontation in the Lower Congo* (Falköping, Sweden: Gummessons, 1970), pp. 136-
146; and Georges Balandier, *Daily Life in the Kingdom of the Kongo, From the
Sixteenth to the Eighteenth Century* (New York: World Publishing Co., 1968), p. 13;
pp. 257-263. Also see R. Batsikama ba Mampuya ma Ndwala, *Ndona Beatrice:
serait-elle temoin-du Christ et de la foi du vieux Congo?* (Kinshasa: Éditions du
Mwanza, 1969), an appeal to Pope Paul VI for the canonization of Mama Ndona
Beatrice.

[3] "God with form and God without form are not two different Beings. He Who is
with form is also without form. To a devotee God manifests Himself in various
forms. Just think of a shoreless ocean—an infinite expanse of water—no land visible
in any direction; only here and there are visible blocks of ice formed by intense cold.
Similarly, under the cooling influence, so to say, of the deep devotion of his worshipper, the Infinite reduces Himself into the Finite and appears before him as a Being
with form. Again, as on the appearance of the sun, the ice melts away into the
formless." *Words of the Master,* comp. by Swami Brahmananda (10th ed.; Calcutta:
Udbodhan Office, 1945), p. 9.

*His Experience of Kali*

He pined for a direct and immediate realization of the spiritual form of Divine Mother, saying, "Mother, if Thou exist, reveal Thyself to me."[4] Later in his life he made the sincere longing for the vision of God one of the central points of his teachings: "As the drowning man pants hard for breath, so must one's heart yearn for the Lord before one can find Him."[5] The following statement in Sri Ramakrishna's own words describes his first experience of Kali, which formed the foundation for all his subsequent ventures in the spiritual life:

> 'I was then suffering from excruciating pain because I had not been blessed with a vision of the Mother. I felt as if my heart were being squeezed like a wet towel. I was overpowered by a great restlessness, and a fear that it might not be my lot to realize Her in this life. I could not bear the separation any longer: life did not seem worth living. Suddenly my eyes fell on the sword that was kept in the Mother's temple. Determined to put an end to my life, I jumped up like a madman and seized it, when suddenly the blessed Mother revealed herself to me, and I fell unconscious on the floor. What happened after that externally, or how that day or the next passed, I do not know, but within me there was a steady flow of undiluted bliss altogether new, and I felt the presence of the Divine Mother.[6]

*Basis of Authenticity of His Experience*

If this experience verifies the existence of God, answering the cardinal question of life, on what basis can it be conclusively authenticated? What factors differentiate this type of experience from hallucination, from autosuggestion, from insanity? Swami Akhilanan-

---

[4] Swami Ghanananda, *Sri Ramakrishna and His Unique Message* (3d ed.; London: The Ramakrishna Vedanta Centre, 1970), p. 27.

[5] *Sayings of Sri Ramakrishna,* p. 191. Cf. "Some men shed streams of tears because sons are not born to them, others eat away their hearts in sorrow because they cannot get riches. But alas! how many are there who sorrow and weep for not having seen the Lord! Very few indeed! Verily, he who seeks the Lord, who weeps for Him, attains Him" (*ibid.,* p. 190). Cf. James, *Varieties,* pp. 353-354: James aptly compares St. Augustine with Sri Ramakrishna in regard to their longing for God. See *The Confessions of St. Augustine,* trans. by John K. Ryan, Image Books (New York: Doubleday, 1960); Peter Brown, *Augustine of Hippo* (Berkeley: University of California Press, 1969); Etienne Gilson, *The Christian Philosophy of St. Augustine,* trans. by L. E. M. Lynch (New York: Random House, 1967).

[6] *Life of Sri Ramakrishna,* p. 71.

da presents a critical evaluation of these objections which apply to mystical experiences of saints of all religious traditions:[7]

> God-vision is not abnormal nor is it created by an insane mentality. . . . [It is] supernormal. In abnormal cases we find that a man's mind is disintegrated; his emotions have no harmony; his intellect and emotions do not co-ordinate; and his actions are incongruous and inconsistent. . . . On the contrary, one who has experienced superconscious realization attains complete integration of mind; his emotions are fully controlled; his intellect, emotions and will are co-ordinated. . . .

> It is also often said that these experiences may not be actual pathological conditions; yet they may be projections of one's thoughts, products of creative imagination, or instances of self-hypnosis and autosuggestion. . . . If such were the case, the effects would not be elevating, as already described. Autosuggestion can bring a person to a state of oblivion and stupor where he lives in a dream world. On the contrary, *superconscious experience gives definite new knowledge and transforms the personality* [italics mine], which could not be accomplished by self-hypnosis and creative imagination. However powerful imagination or suggestion may be, it cannot give more than the mind contains nor can it change the personality by integrating the emotions. . . .

> Another objection has been made that these so-called superconscious experiences are epileptic fits. . . . Our answer is that in an epileptic fit or swoon a man loses his consciousness, and after the fit his whole nervous system and mind are affected and made weaker. It can be said definitely that he does not gain anything in the seizure and he acquires no new knowledge. The effect is often the same from narcotics. On the other hand, a man enters into the superconscious state as an ordinary person and comes out of it a better man. His entire personality is transformed; . . . he is master of himself; . . . and he gains knowledge which he never previously had. . . .

> The superconscious experiences not only change the intellectual side of the mind by giving it a new fund of knowledge of the reality behind

[7] "It is meaningless to say that these are Oriental ideas alone. They are common ideas of all deeply spiritual persons who have superconscious realization. This shows that criticism against superconscious experiences is not based on facts and is, consequently, unscientific." Akhilananda, *Hindu Psychology,* p. 156. Cf. the following statement by Rudolf Otto: "Mysticism is *the same* in all ages and in all places, that timeless and independent of history it has always been identical. East and West and other differences vanish here." *Mysticism East and West,* p. 13.

the phenomenal world, but they also change the quality of the emotional life of a person. *A mind that has had superconscious experience needs no inference or logic to understand the existence of God. It immediately experiences and senses that Reality and has dynamic conviction of the existence of God and soul* [italics mine]. The intellect is fully illumined, and . . . there is great refinement and exaltation of the contents of the emotion[s]. . . . His happiness knows no bounds, for he has reached the culmination of consciousness—the mine of bliss. His whole inner life is extremely peaceful, so much so that everyone can feel the radiance of peace and bliss.[8]

[8] Akhilananda, *Hindu Psychology,* pp. 153-160. Cf. the following statement by Swami Vivekananda: "What makes the difference? From one state a man comes out the very same man that he went in, and from another state the man comes out enlightened, a sage, a prophet, a saint, his whole character changed, his life changed, illumined. These are the two effects. Now the effects being different, the causes must be different." *Raja-Yoga,* Mayavati edition, p. 90. Cf. also the statement by St. Teresa of Avila in her autobiography concerning the validity of her spiritual experiences: "If a vision were a mere product of one's own mind . . . the soul would remain confused, not sustained and strengthened, but tired and disgusted. But in the real vision, it is impossible to exaggerate the riches of the soul and the health and comfort of the body which remain after the experience." Translated by Edgar S. Brightman from *La Vida de La Santa Madre Terasa de Jesus,* Cop. 28, parts of 10 and 11, in D. Vedinti de Fuenti, *Abras de Santa Terasa de Jesus* (1881), I, 165-166, as cited by Akhilananda, *Hindu Psychology,* pp. 157-158; see *The Life of St. Teresa of Jesus,* trans. by David Lewis (London: Thomas Baker, 1924). For further clarification of the validity of the experience of God in the superconscious state *(samadhi)* such as the one Sri Ramakrishna had, see James, *Varieties,* pp. 391-392, where Professor James, citing Swami Vivekananda as an authority, discusses the test of authentic superconscious experience. See also Sorokin, *The Ways of Power and Love* (Chicago: Henry Regnery Co., 1967), chap. vi, "The Superconscious in Man's Mental Structure, Creativity, and Cognition," pp. 98-100. Here Sorokin attempts to "lay down the very minimum of evidence for the reality of the supra-conscious and . . . describe some of its properties" (p. 98). See also pp. 96-97 and 109-112. For additional discussion of the authenticity of superconscious experience from a rational point of view, although not as thoroughgoing and completely reliable as the foregoing, see Richard Maurice Bucke, *Cosmic Consciousness* (New York: E. P. Dutton & Co., 1967). Note especially the section, "Ramakrishna Paramahamsa," pp. 311-314. Bucke's sources (in 1901) on the life of Sri Ramakrishna were Max Müller (who had met Swami Vivekananda and Swami Abhedananda) and Protap Chandra Mazoomdar, a questionable source: see Mazoomdar's article, *Ramakrishna Paramahamsa* (Calcutta: Udbodhan Office, 1928), originally published in the *Theistic Quarterly Review* (October, 1897). For an articulate, comprehensive, and conclusive summary of the scientific basis of *samadhi,* see Akhilananda, "Extra-Sensory and Superconscious Experiences," in *The Philosophies,* ed. by Haridas Bhattacharyya, pp. 520-

27

And it was so in the case of Sri Ramakrishna. According to his description of that first experience of God, his was a "steady flow of bliss," which he had never before experienced, one "altogether new." He also said that in that vision of the Mother of the Universe he saw "an infinite shoreless sea of light; a sea that was consciousness."[9] He had thus gained access to new knowledge through a different category of perception which transformed his total mind. According to the foregoing criteria for authenticity, his was a valid instance of superconscious experience or *samadhi*. This was the beginning of a spiritual life dedicated to vast experiments in the field of God-consciousness. "Of the few mystics who ever reach samadhi, the majority do so toward the end of their lives or at the moment of death. Ramakrishna, as we shall see, entered samadhi not once but several times a day, over a period of many years!"[10]

*Further Experience of Divine Mother*

Although Sri Ramakrishna was "conscious of the Divine Mother as the inner core of . . . [his] being," during that first experience, calling aloud, "Mother! Mother!" when he regained consciousness,[11] he later saw Her vividly during periods of normal conscious-

531, esp. the section titled "Modern Criticism of Superconsciousness," p. 527 ff. It is noted that here and elsewhere (*Hindu Psychology,* pp. 166-169) Akhilananda clarifies further the technical conception of the superconscious state by insisting that it must not be confused with the "deep unconscious" as set forth by Dr. Jung (see Carl G. Jung, *Integration of the Personality,* trans. by Stanley Dell [London: Kegan Paul, 1939], p. 15). Rudolf Otto's statement bears directly on this point: "I shall speak, then of . . . a definitely 'numinous' state of mind. . . . This mental state is perfectly *sui generis* and irreducible to any other; and therefore, like every absolutely primary and elementary datum, while it admits of being discussed, it cannot be strictly defined. . . . It can only be evoked, awakened in the mind." *The Idea of the Holy* (2d ed.; London: Oxford University Press, 1950), p. 7.

[9] Isherwood, p. 65.

[10] *Ibid.,* p. 63. See *Srimad-Bhagavad-Gita,* trans. by Swami Swarupananda (8th ed.; Mayavati, Almora, Himalayas: Advaita Ashrama, 1948), chap. viii, sloka 10, p. 185, as follows: "He who meditates on Him thus, at the time of death, full of devotion, with the mind unmoving, and also by the power of Yoga, fixing the whole Prana betwixt the eye-brows, he goes to the Supreme. . . . (Power of Yoga—which comes by the constant practice of samadhi. *Prana:* the vital current)." Cf. chap. vii, sl. 30: "Those who know me . . . continue to know Me even at the time of death, steadfast in mind." *Ibid.,* p. 178. Cf. *Sukhavativyuha* Literary Corpus, esp. *Amitayur-dhyana* sutra, in early Mahayana Buddhism.

[11] Ghanananda, p. 47.

ness as well as in *samadhi*. As Saradananda relates, "When that vision came to an end, there arose in the heart of the Master an eager, incessant cry of lamentation for a constant immediate vision of the divine Mother's form, consisting of consciousness only." Because of that "unbearable anguish" he would lose external consciousness again and again, and see "that form of the Mother consisting of consciousness . . .,—the form that smiled, spoke and consoled and taught . . . [him] in endless ways!"[12]

The Master's worship, meditation, etc., underwent novel changes. It is difficult to explain to others that wonderful state of complete absorption in Her. . . . Whenever one saw him, one thought he had merged his little will and the little ego in Her will, Who was the source of all wills, and did everything as if he was completely an instrument in Her hand, praying in his heart of hearts, 'Mother, my only refuge, kindly make me, Thy boy, say and do what I should.' . . . Although in the world, he was not of it. . . . The universal Mother's form, consisting of pure consciousness and bliss, was now known to him as the only reality. . . .

. . . Now he saw, even at times other than those of worship and meditation, the full figure of the effulgent Mother, smiling and speaking, guiding him, accompanying him and saying, 'Do this, don't do that.'

. . . when he offered cooked food etc., to the Mother, . . . [she] sat down to take the offerings in Her very person, illumining the temple with the effulgence of Her holy person. . . .

Previously, . . . he saw that there appeared a wonderful living presence in the stone image before him. Now he did not see that image at all when he entered the temple; but saw instead, standing there the living Mother Herself, all consciousness. . . . The Master said, 'I put the palm of my hand near Her nostrils and felt that Mother was actually breathing. I observed very closely, but I could never see the shadow of the Mother's divine person on the temple wall in the light of the lamp at night. I heard from my room that Mother, merry like a little girl, was going upstairs, her anklets making jingling sounds. I came up to test it and found that She, with Her hair dishevelled, was actually standing on the verandah of the first floor of the temple and was now viewing Calcutta, now the Ganga.'[13]

[12] Saradananda, pp. 143-144.

[13] *Ibid.,* pp. 146-147. There are many illustrations in the religious history of both East and West of mystics who have seen the ultimate Reality in corporeal, concrete form with their naked eyes subsequent to their first experience of God. Foremost among these in our own Christian tradition is Saint Anthony of Padua, twenty-ninth Doctor of the Church, who talked and played with the Bambino in his daily life and

## HIS SPIRITUAL PRACTICES (SADHANA)

### *Kali as Guru*

As in the case of Saint Anthony and the Bambino, the constant presence[14] of Divine Mother became a natural function of Sri Ramakrishna's life now. He could see her whenever he wished. He moved in intimate communication and rapport with her as a child does with his own mother, importuning her for his daily needs and wants, referring to her all the decisions of his life, no matter how small, and seeking her guidance with regard to his spiritual path.[15] The Divine Mother herself had become, in a sense, his first spiritual teacher or *guru*.[16]

---

even scolded him at times, in the attitude of a loving father. See P. Bernardino Barban, *Saint Anthony of Padua,* trans. by Alexander Piasentin (New York: Society of St. Paul, 1933); Sophronius Clasen, *St. Anthony,* trans. by Ignatius Brady (Chicago: Franciscan Herald Press, 1961). In the Hindu tradition, cf. Mira Bai, who had similar experiences with the Lord Krishna. See Lajwanti Madan, Ph.D., "Mira Bai," in *Women Saints of East and West,* with a Foreword by Vijaya Lakshmi Pandit and an Introduction by Kenneth Walker (London: The Ramakrishna Vedanta Centre, 1955), pp. 51-57. In the modern age, cf. Aghormani Devi, known as Gopal's Mother: see Swami Ghanananda, "Some Holy Women Figuring in the Life of Sri Ramakrishna," *Women Saints,* pp. 125-127; also Saradananda, Part IV, chaps. vi and vii, pp. 639-668. The three instances cited above—Saint Anthony, Mira Bai, and "Gopal-Ma"—are all examples of the Absolute taking the personal form of God in response to the worshipper's devotion in the same way as the Absolute took the form of Divine Mother for Sri Ramakrishna.

[14] Cf. Brother Lawrence, *The Practice of the Presence of God* (London: A. R. Mowbray, 1965). Although Brother Lawrence's experience of God differed from that of Sri Ramakrishna's now under discussion, it is noteworthy that he advocated the presence of God as a spiritual practice which, in and of itself, could lead to God-realization. This technique represented both the means and the end. See Akhilananda, *Hindu Psychology,* p. 156, for a discussion of the mental training required for superconscious experience in which Brother Lawrence is quoted.

[15] For Sri Ramakrishna's feelings and attitude toward Divine Mother in his own words, see *The Gospel of Ramakrishna,* revised by Swami Abhedananda from M.'s original English text (New York: Vedanta Society, 1947), *passim.*

[16] For a clear and comprehensive exposition of the Hindu concept of *guru* or spiritual teacher, see Akhilananda, *Spiritual Practices* (Boston: Branden Press, 1972), chap. ii, "Requirements of a Spiritual Teacher," pp. 25-36. Cf. the remarkably erudite and scholarly treatment, cutting across multiple cultures, of the etymological, historical and scriptural roots of the *guru* tradition in Gonda, *Change and Continuity,* chap. viii, "The Guru," pp. 229-283. Quoting Gandhi, he establishes the Hindu viewpoint: " 'I believe in the Hindu theory of guru and his importance in

## The Necessity of Sadhana

In seeking this first experience of God, however, Sri Ramakrishna did not have recourse to a spiritual guide. It was, as has been pointed out, his intense longing to see God in the form of Divine Mother which attracted the grace of God,[17] giving him the vision and experiences he had. He did, nevertheless, perform spiritual practices *(sadhanas)* in a systematic manner as preparation for these experiences. According to his own statement, "(Sadhanas) are absolutely necessary for Self-knowledge, but if there is perfect faith then a little practice is enough."[18]

---

spiritual realisation. I think there is a great deal of truth in the doctrine that true knowledge is impossible without a guru. Only a perfect *jnani* (one who having spiritual knowledge knows the path to Release) deserves to be enthroned as guru.' Most of those who want to reach God must follow such a guide, who is no mere man, but 'a channel through which Gods [*sic*] communicates Himself to the adept.' Hence the conviction that the guru alone can guide his disciples on the path of spiritual progress to full knowledge of the Highest which leads to ultimate emancipation" (p. 282). Cf. the teachings of Sri Krishna to Arjuna on the battlefield as set forth in the *Bhagavad-Gita,* where God Himself assumes the position of the guru. In this connection cf. the following comment by Sri Ramakrishna as quoted by Swami Tyagisananda in his explanatory note to sloka 38 of the *Narada Bhakti Sutras* (Mylapore, Madras: Sri Ramakrishna Math, 1955), pp. 180-181: " 'God alone is the guide and Guru of the Universe. He who can himself approach God with sincerity, earnest prayer, and deep longing, needs no Guru. But such deep yearning of the soul is very rare; hence the necessity for a Guru. When going to a strange country, one must abide by the directions of the guide who knows the way.' " For Sri Ramakrishna's teachings on the *guru,* a good summary is found in *Words of the Master,* ·pp. 24-28. Cf. also the teachings of Swami Brahmananda, considered the spiritual son of Sri Ramakrishna: "Disciple: 'Is it possible to realize God without a *guru?*' Maharaj [Swami Brahmananda]: 'It is, but it is not so easy without a *guru.* The *guru* is one who shows the path to God through a *mantram* (holy name). He gives the secret of spiritual practices. He watches over his disciple and protects him. A *guru* must be a knower of Brahman.' " *The Eternal Companion: Brahmananda, Records of His Teaching,* with a biography by Swami Prabhavananda (Hollywood, Calif.: The Vedanta Press, 1947), p. 200. Cf. Shankara's *Vivekachudamani,* slokas 33, 37 and 38.

[17] According to Sri Ramakrishna's concept of grace, "In this age of Kali three days' ardent yearning to see God is enough for a man to obtain Divine grace." *Sayings of Sri Ramakrishna,* p. 193. Cf. Vivekananda, *Works,* I, 11.

[18] *Sayings of Sri Ramakrishna,* p. 184. "Even Sri Krishna went through tremendous spiritual practises relating to the worship of the Radha-yantra" *(ibid.,* p. 183). Cf. Swami Akhilananda, *Hindu View of Christ,* chap. iv, "Christ and Spiritual Practices," pp. 100-127. Note especially the following: "Spiritual practices are the means of the cultivation of divine love. They are not mysterious as some critics seem

## The Nature of His Sadhana

Sri Ramakrishna's own spiritual disciplines were characterized by a remarkable vigor, intensity, and one-pointedness. He renounced all for the sake of God. His allegiance to truth took the form of a literalness[19] whereby he immediately gave up whatever he reasoned would not bring him a step closer to God-realization.

> Sri Ramakrishna . . . conquered all attachment to wealth and women not by running away from them, but by living in their midst and yet rising above them. Sri Ramakrishna conquered all attachment to wealth by practicing a unique 'Sadhana.' He would take some dust of earth in one hand and gold or silver coin in the other and repeat: 'Taka mati; mati

to think. They are not incantations or processes of propitiation of certain deities. They are not allurement of God so that He will shower us with His blessings. Neither are they processes of self-hypnosis. They are mainly a method of cultivation of the thought of God, a method of manifestation of divine love. . . . Jesus Himself practiced the path of love and repeatedly told His disciples to do the same through systematic methods of manifestation of love. . . . Jesus made it apparent that people who are watchful and vigilant in their spiritual attitudes and practices can realize God. On the other hand, those who are lazy and careless in their spiritual life miss the mark and do not become aware of God. 'Watch therefore, for ye know neither the day nor the hour wherein the Son of man cometh.' (Matt. 25:13.)" *(Ibid.,* pp. 107-108.) See also chap. iii, *ibid.* For a presentation of *sadhana* according to the Hindu tradition, see Ananda, *Spiritual Practice* (Mayavati, Almora, Himalayas: Advaita Ashrama, 1930); Akhilananda, *Spiritual Practices.* Especially to the point is *The Spiritual Teachings of Swami Brahmananda* (2d ed.; Mylapore, Madras: Sri Ramakrishna Math, 1933) and Swami Shivananda, *For Seekers of God,* trans. by Swami Vividishananda (Mayavati, Almora, Himalayas: Advaita Ashrama, 1947); both these works represent the distillation of exalted spiritual experiences of two fully illumined souls, as told mainly to monastic disciples to guide them in their spiritual practices. Vivekananda's *Raja-Yoga* treats the technical aspects of *sadhana* for the Western reader in a most authoritative fashion, reflecting his own high spiritual realizations. In the Christian tradition, cf. *The Spiritual Exercises of St. Ignatius,* trans. by Anthony Mottola, Image Books (Garden City, N. Y.: Doubleday, 1964), St. Teresa, *Way of Perfection* (London: Thomas Baker, 1935), and especially Thomas à Kempis, *The Following of Christ* (New York: D. & J. Sadlier, 1885). It should be pointed out that Swami Vivekananda carried only two books in his wanderings the length and breadth of India: *The Bhagavad-Gita* and the *Following [Imitation] of Christ.*

[19] "Literalness was characteristic of Sri Ramakrishna. He was never content with a merely mental renunciation; the thought must be accompanied by a deed. . . . For example, in order to humble his caste-pride, he cleaned out a privy with his own hands." Isherwood, p. 59. Sri Ramakrishna was of Brahmin caste, and that would have been the duty of an Untouchable, or outcaste.

taka'—'Gold is dust, dust is gold,' and after realizing the sameness of both, he would throw them into the Ganges. Since then, nothing of the world appeared valuable to him. . . . From this time he could not bear the touch of any coin. . . . Thus he renounced wealth because an attachment to it is an obstacle in the path of God-consciousness. . . . Sri Ramakrishna conquered all lust and attachment to woman by realizing that every woman, young or old, is the earthly representative of the Divine Mother. He worshipped all women by seeing the Divine Mother in them. He did not run away from his wife but worshipped her and called her the embodiment of the Divine Mother. Even when he was taken by Mathur Babu to the house of a public woman, Sri Ramakrishna said: 'My Divine Mother appears before me in the form of an unchaste woman.'[20]

It is evident that sincerity was the keynote of Sri Ramakrishna's spiritual practice. Such sincerity required of him that his thoughts, words and actions be completely consistent. Upon testing the value of a particular course of action, or of an insight derived from the scriptures, he would commit himself wholly to it and follow it to its final conclusion. He realized early in his *sadhanà* that the spirit of dispassion toward worldly enjoyments[21] is an important factor in the process of self-purification leading to God-consciousness. As Swami Brahmananda later declared, "It is hard indeed to kindle any thought of God within the human heart without the fire of renunciation. . . . We saw a true and living representation of discrimination and renunciation in Sri Ramakrishna. . . . We read of discrimination and renunciation in the scriptures, but we saw them personified in him."[22]

[20] Abhedananda, *Sri Ramakrishna,* pp. 22-24.

[21] "Sri Ramakrishna used to say: 'He who has given up sense enjoyments for God's sake has already covered three parts of the journey.' Is it easy to renounce bodily cravings? Only if one has God's grace . . . can he have the strength to renounce the world in this life." *Eternal Companion,* p. 150.

[22] *Ibid.,* p. 185. Cf. *Vivekachudamani of Shri Shankaracharya;* the following slokas are especially pertinent to this discussion in that they define discrimination and renunciation: "17. The man who discriminates between the Real and the unreal, whose mind is turned away from the unreal, who possesses calmness and the allied virtues, and who is longing for Liberation, is alone considered qualified to inquire after Brahman." "20. A firm conviction of the mind to the effect that Brahman is real and the universe unreal, is designated as discrimination (Viveka) between the Real and the unreal." "21. Vairagya or renunciation is the desire to give up all transitory enjoyments (ranging) from those of an (animate) body to those of Brahmahood (having already known their defects) from observation, instruction and so forth"

*Meditation the Key to Sadhana*

While disciplines such as the above are important, meditation is the very heart of *sadhana*.[23] Sri Ramakrishna used to meditate at a quiet spot in a grove of five trees known as the Panchavati. As K. S. Ramaswami Sastri states, "His life was then one of continuous meditation and devotion."[24] Swami Ghanananda writes:

> The manner in which he prepared himself for the meditation was remarkable: he would strip himself of all clothing and divest himself even of the sacred thread till he had finished his meditation. He considered these to be marks of shame and family ties, and believed that one should give up the eightfold fetters of hatred, shame, pedigree, culture, fear, fame, caste and egotism, when calling on God. He was passing through a part of the purificatory stage in mystic life.[25]

*The Hindu concept of meditation is based on the understanding that God is within man.*[26] " 'He who does not find God within himself will never find God outside of himself. But he who sees Him in the temple of his own soul sees Him also in the temple of the universe.' "[27] Meditational techniques are intended to unify the mind, make it one-pointed and single in the thought of a particular aspect of God or *ishta*,[28] thereby intensifying the devotion toward God

---

(pp. 8-9). See also slokas 19, 22, 45, 56, and 78. Shankara is regarded as the principal exponent of spiritual practices emphasizing *viveka* and *vairagya* to attain *samadhi.* Cf. Vivekananda, *Works,* I, 410-411, 99, 209; II, 99, 173; IV, 4-5; V, 102-189; VI, 331, 340. Swami Vivekananda's definitions of *viveka* and *vairagya* in a modern framework are particularly useful. The development of these two spiritual qualities as effective means of knowing God is not exclusive to Hinduism. Cf. Shankara and Meister Eckhart in this respect, as Rudolf Otto does in *Mysticism East and West,* "Conformity," Part A, pp. 19-156.

[23] See Akhilananda, *Hindu Psychology,* chap. vi, "Meditation," pp. 102-125.

[24] Sastri, *Sri Ramakrishna Paramahamsa* (Mylapore, Madras: Sri Ramakrishna Math, 1928), pp. 7-8.

[25] Ghanananda, p. 46.

[26] Cf. Luke 17:21.

[27] A saying of Sri Ramakrishna, as quoted in Sastri, p. 16. Cf. the statement "Ana 'l-Haqq" of the Sufi tradition attributed to al-Hallaj; see Reynold A. Nicholson, *The Mystics of Islam* (London: Kegan Paul, 1966), pp. 150-155. Cf. Akhilananda, *Modern Problems,* p. 132, which compares the Christian, Hindu, Sufi and Buddhist traditions on this point.

[28] *Ishta* or "Chosen Ideal" is defined as "the aspect of the Godhead selected by a spiritual aspirant, or by his *guru* for him. Through meditation on his Chosen Ideal, the aspirant gradually attains concentration of mind, love of God, and ultimately,

*(bhakti).*[29] Sri Ramakrishna's *sadhana* in preparation for his first experience of God was based on the cultivation of divine love, *parabhakti.*[30] His intimate relationship with Divine Mother, both be-

---

illumination." *Narada's Way of Divine Love: The Bhakti Sutras,* trans. with commentary by Swami Prabhavananda (Hollywood, Calif.: Vedanta Press, 1971), p. 166. See the chapter, "The Chosen Ideal" in *Bhakti-Yoga* by Vivekananda, *Karma-Yoga and Bhakti-Yoga* (rev. ed.), pp. 158-161.

[29] Shankaracharya defines *bhakti* from the *Advaita* standpoint as the "seeking after one's real nature." *Vivekachudamani,* sloka 31, p. 11; cf. sloka 32. Sandilya states, "It is extreme attachment to Ishvara, the Lord" *(ibid.).* If the Supreme Lord is the essence of one's real nature, or the Self of the self *(Atman),* as most Hindus maintain (cf. note 27, p. 34 *supra*), then these two statements are not contradictory, but merely define *bhakti* from two different angles of vision. Cf. *Vedartha-Sangraha of Sri Ramanujacharya,* trans. by S. S. Raghavachar, with a Foreword by Swami Adidevananda (Mysore: Sri Ramakrishna Ashrama, 1968). Note the discussion of Sri Ramanuja's interpretation of the text, *"Tat Tvam Asi"* (Chandogya Upanishad, VI, 8, 7), from the *Vishishtadvaita* perspective in the Foreword, p. v. Cf. Madhva's *Dvaita* position on this text and on his definition of *bhakti* as explicated by H. N. Raghavendrachar, "Madhva's Brahma-Mimamsa," in *The Philosophies,* ed. by Bhattacharyya, Part II, pp. 313-332. Cf. Vivekananda, *Jnana-Yoga:* "Dualism and all the systems that preceded it are accepted by Advaita, not in a patronizing way, but with the conviction that they are true" (rev. ed., p. 275).

[30] See *Narada Bhakti Sutras,* trans. by Swami Tyagisananda. Narada defines *parabhakti* as "nothing less than the immortal bliss . . . which comes unsolicited by the grace of God and by self-sacrifice (sloka 3). Realizing that, man becomes . . . completely immersed in the Bliss of the Atman, the truest and highest self" (sl. 6). "Bhakti (described . . . as Paraprema or Supreme Love) is not of the nature of lust, because it is a form of renunciation" (sl. 7). "Now this renunciation . . . is only a consecration of all activities, sacred as well as secular" (sl. 8). "The characteristics of Bhakti are described variously on account of differences in view-points" (sl. 15). "But Narada is of the opinion that the essential characteristics of Bhakti are the consecration of all activities, by complete self-surrender, to Him, and extreme anguish if He were to be forgotten" (sl. 19). "Such indeed was the Bhakti of the Gopis of Vraja" (sl. 21). The latter were considered to have manifested the highest type of *parabhakti* or *prema* (see Ramakrishnananda, *Sri Krishna, Pastoral and Kingmaker,* and Singer and Ingalls, *Krishna: Myths, Rites and Attitudes).* In this connection, note the following statement by Vivekananda, as quoted by Swami Prabhavananda in his translation of the *Srimad Bhagavatam, The Wisdom of God* (Hollywood, Calif.: Vedanta Press, 1943): " 'Who can conceive the throes of the love of the gopis—the shepherd girls—the very ideal of love, love that wants nothing, love that even does not care for heaven, love that does not care for anything in this world or in the world to come?' " (p. 200). Also see Swami Abhedananda, *Human Affection and Divine Love* (Calcutta: Ramakrishna Vedanta Math, 1952). One may understand from the foregoing definition of *parabhakti* that although this technical term has been discussed in the context of Hindu *sadhana,* the concept expressed has universal application for the

fore and after the initial experience, reflected a ripening of this particular mood *(bhava)*[31] which he had chosen for his relationship with God. He states,

> Brahman and Sakti are identical, like fire and its power to burn. [It is] Brahman alone [who] is addressed as the Mother. This is because a mother is an object of great love. One is able to realize God just through love.... Listen to a song:
> As is a man's meditation, so is his feeling of love;
> As is a man's feeling of love, so is his gain;
> And faith is the root of all.[32]

---

love of God in all religious traditions (see Vivekananda, *Karma-Yoga and Bhakti-Yoga* (rev. ed.), *Bhakti-Yoga,* pp. 117-210). "'As oil poured from one vessel to another falls in an unbroken line, so, when the mind in an unbroken stream thinks of the Lord, we have what is called *para-bhakti,* or supreme love'" (*ibid.,* p. 189).

[31] Quoting Sri Ramakrishna, Saradananda writes, "He is realizeable by means of spiritual moods (Bhava) alone.... One should cultivate a particular mood and then call on Him. It is through a mood that love sprouts. . . . Do you know what a spiritual mood is? Establishing a relationship with God and keeping it bright before our eyes at all times—at the times of eating, drinking, sitting, sleeping, etc. . . . For example, 'I am His servant,' 'I am His child,' 'I am a part of Him'—this is what is called the 'ripe I,' the 'I' of knowledge.... The 'I's of spiritual ignorance (Avidya) . . . should be renounced. . . . A person who has renounced everything for God's sake and made Him his own, exerts pressure of love on Him and says, 'I have renounced everything for you, say whether you will now show yourself to me or not'" (p. 381).

[32] *The Gospel of Sri Ramakrishna,* trans. by Swami Nikhilananda (New York: Ramakrishna-Vivekananda Center, 1942), p. 108. "Sri Ramakrishna Paramahamsa has stressed again and again that for the Kaliyuga the Path of Devotion as described by Narada is, indeed, the best and the easiest. This is but an echo of the experience and verdict of innumerable saints and holy men who have preceded him." Tyagisananda, Preface to *Narada Bhakti Sutras,* p. v. Cf. *Narada Sutra,* trans. with commentary by E. T. Sturdy (a Western disciple of Swami Vivekananda) (2d ed.; London: John M. Watkins, 1904). In Sri Ramakrishna's own words, "It is difficult in this materialistic age (Kali-yuga) to get through all the works, all the duties laid upon us by the Sacred Books. Verily in this age, earthly life depends entirely upon material food. Works and duties, there is scarcely time enough for them. It will be all over with the patient suffering from the burning fever of this world if he is allowed to go through the slow process of treatment practised by the old-fashioned Hindu physicians. People are short-lived and the malaria carries one off in a few days. The specific for the present day is Dr. D. Gupta's patent fever mixture, which produces a miraculous effect at once. Yes, in this age the one means of realizing God is Bhakti or sincere devotion and love for Him, and earnest prayer." *The Gospel of Ramakrishna,* Abhedananda revision, pp. 172-173.

# CHAPTER III

# Verification of God in Hinduism

## EXPERIMENTATION WITH OTHER
## FORMS OF HINDUISM

*His Desire to Verify Diverse Paths*

Subsequent to this first experience, an irrepressible urge arose in the mind of Sri Ramakrishna to experience God in different ways. It is a mystery of his personality why this occurred, since he had already become established in the uninterrupted vision of God in the form of Divine Mother. He had achieved the goal of his intense spiritual practices; he had reached the *summum bonum* of religious life which satisfies the great majority of saintly personalities. But it was his peculiar nature, as has been shown, to test or verify values of the spiritual world. If Divine Mother was true, what of the other aspects of God? Were they equally real?

The same principle applied to diverse methods of spiritual practice: were they also valid? It must be remembered that direct experience was the only criterion that Sri Ramakrishna used to verify the existence of God in any of his forms. In his terms of understanding religious inquiry, an aspect of the ultimate Reality exists only *if,* and *when,* it can be experienced or perceived directly. It followed that any spiritual practice would be validated as methodology if it led to the experience of God when sincerely and systematically pursued.[1] Thus in verifying by experience different forms of God in his own tradition, Sri Ramakrishna concurrently sought to validate the particular path *(sadhana)* associated with that aspect of God.

### His Scientific Approach

He did not, however, calculate in his mind, "Now I will follow this or that path in order to prove to the world that a basic harmony exists among diverse *sadhanas*." Rather, his desire to enjoy God in his different forms was fully spontaneous,[2] arising as it did in the heart of a true *bhakta* or lover of God. Sri Ramakrishna's attitude can be adequately compared to the search for knowledge of a "pure scientist"—one not necessarily concerned with the degree of efficiency his discoveries will produce in the mundane world—but one who continues his quest for truth after each new discovery. Such were the cases of men like Eddington,[3] Schrödinger,[4] Stromberg,[5]

[1] See Akhilananda, *Modern Problems,* pp. 22-24; *Hindu Psychology,* Chap. xi, "Methods of Superconscious Experience," pp. 171-189; "Extra-Sensory and Superconscious Experiences," p. 530; *Hindu View of Christ,* chap. iii, "Christ, a Yogi," pp. 72-99; *Mental Health and Hindu Psychology* (New York: Harper & Row, 1951), chap. xvi, "Power through Religious Practices," pp. 205-220; *Spiritual Practices, passim.*

[2] "It never seemed to me that he had practised the different religions with any definite motive of preaching the harmony of religions. Day and night he remained overwhelmed with the ecstatic thought of God. He enjoyed the sport of the Divine by practising spiritual disciplines, following the paths of the Vaishnavas, Christians, Mussalmans and the rest. But it seems to me, my child, that the special feature of the Master's life is his renunciation. Has any one ever seen such a natural renunciation? Renunciation was his ornament." *Thus Spake the Holy Mother,* comp. by Swami Suddhasatwananda (Mylapore, Madras: Sri Ramakrishna Math, 1953), p. 21.

[3] A. S. Eddington, *Philosophy of Physical Science* (New York: Macmillan, 1929). Swami Akhilananda writes of Eddington: "A great scientist of this country related to us a conversation he had with Einstein, who told him: 'I do not have a glimpse of the Absolute, but Eddington has it.' We had met Eddington in India during 1937 when he accompanied a Calcutta scientist to our monastery. From his facial expression then, we had the distinct impression that he was on the borderline of spiritual realization. Our friend, the American scientist, asked, 'Swami, can we scientists have a glimpse of the Absolute?' The answer was, 'Yes, positively. Your minds are being trained in scientific study and research. To know the Absolute, you merely have to change the object of your concentration.' " *Spiritual Practices,* p. 18.

[4] Erwin Schrödinger, *What is Life?* (New York: Macmillan, 1947); note especially the final chapter. Note also *Science and Humanism* (London: Cambridge University Press, 1952).

Shapley[6] and Einstein, whose relentless search after knowledge in the objective world can be compared with that of Sri Ramakrishna in the realm of God-consciousness. As Akhilananda states, "The life of Sri Ramakrishna demonstrates that there should be no quarrel between religion and science. . . . His desire to know the truth was the starting point of his experimentation with religion, just as the scientist starts experimenting when he has the desire to know the truth."[7] For Sri Ramakrishna, the laboratory was the vast open field of religious traditions; the instrument of experimentation was his own mind. And "the secret of his success in these diverse Sadhanas . . . was— in one word—sincerity, a complete correspondence between thought and action—and entire absence of duplicity."[8]

## HIS DASYA SADHANA

*Experience of Rama*

Nowhere was this "correspondence between thought and action" more evident than in his first attempt at experiencing an aspect of God other than Divine Mother. His sincerity and concentration were such that not only were his habits of life and mental structure completely transformed during that period when he practiced the *dasya sadhana,*[9] but his physical characteristics were changed as well. According to a reliable biographer,

---

[5] Gustaf Stromberg, *The Soul of the Universe* (Philadelphia: David McKay, 1940).

[6] Harlow Shapley, *Of Stars and Men* (Boston: Beacon Press, 1959).

[7] Akhilananda, *Modern Problems,* p. 26.

[8] *Life of Sri Ramakrishna,* p. 83.

[9] The *dasya sadhana* is that spiritual practice in which the devotee assumes the attitude of a servant towards God as Master. Such an attitude predominates in the Judeo-Christian tradition as well as in Islam. See George E. Mendenhall, *Law and Covenant in Israel and the Ancient Near East* (Pittsburgh, Pa.: The Presbyterian Board of Colportage, 1955). Mendenhall's posture on the Mosaic Covenant (based on previous work by Victor Korosec), which has been widely adopted up to now (see G. Ernest Wright, *The Old Testament and Theology* [New York: Harper & Row, 1969], chap. iv, pp. 97-120), is that at Sinai the ancient Israelites became the servants of Yahweh under a covenant modelled after the Hittite international suzerainty treaties of the mid-second millenium (see James B. Pritchard, *Ancient Near Eastern Texts* [Princeton, N. J.: Princeton University Press, 1950], pp. 120-127; pp. 188-196), a covenant whose treaty text was the Decalogue itself, the stipulations of which

It was shortly after his vision of Kali that his attention was directed to Rama, the king of Ayodhya, who is regarded as an incarnation of the Lord Himself. Convinced that the quickest way to realise Him would be to become thoroughly imbued with the spirit of His greatest devotee, Hanuman, he took upon himself the task of reproducing as faithfully as possible Hanuman's attitude towards Rama—that of the faithful servant

---

bound the covenant people to Yahweh in obedience, out of gratitude for His former redemptive acts and His promises of land and progeny. The essential relationship of man to God running through the religious life of ancient Israel was thus based on a legal form, spiritualized and used to represent the relationship of a perfect God with his often troublesome and imperfect people, whose activities more frequently bespoke breach of covenant than they did covenant-keeping (see Deuteronomy; G. Ernest Wright, *God Who Acts* [London: SCM Press, 1966]). Nonetheless, the ideal relationship for ancient Israel was the covenant relationship. Cf. G. van der Leeuw, *Religion in Essence and Manifestation,* trans. by J. E. Turner (2 vols.; Gloucester, Mass.: Peter Smith, 1967), "The Covenant," I, 252-260. It was reinterpreted, of course, by Jesus in the New Testament. Cf. Jeremiah 33:31-33; see I Corinthians 11:23-26. This relationship of humble servant to omnipotent Lord precisely fits the pattern of *dasya bhava* in Hinduism, only there the context for such a relationship is taken from the Hindu's world of spiritual ideals as compared with the Semitic legal form. Despite the obvious theological variance of *Vishishtadvaita* with Semitic anthropomorphism, this parallel on the point of *dasya* or servantship may be aptly illustrated by Sri Ramanuja's *Vishishtadvaita* and *bhakti* themes as treated in his earliest work, the *Vedartha-Sangraha.* The Lord's *Krpa* (redemptive grace) and the devotee's *prapatti* (self-surrender) are for him the essence of *bhakti* (love of God). Although the law of *karma* (causation) regulates the nature of experience for individual souls, no amount of good works can in themselves generate the conditions for God-realization. Only the grace *(Krpa)* of Ishvara can produce these conditions. *Bhakti* is the means of attracting this grace. But the essence of *bhakti* for Ramanuja, and its final beatification, unfolds with *prapatti,* in which the metaphysical statement of *Vishishtadvaita* (qualified non-dualism) becomes personal and concrete in the complete self-surrender of the *sesa* (servant) to the *Sesin* (Master). As the ontological basis for *prapatti* in the context of *bhakti* within the doctrine of *Vishishtadvaita,* Ramanuja states, "Further, the individual self, so constituted, is wholly subservient to the Lord, and is controlled by Him and has Him for its sole support" (sloka 103). But self-surrender co-exists with service, for out of the continuous remembrance of the Lord comes a spirit of service in utter dependence on the Supreme Lord and none else (cf. Hanuman). This idea is fully developed in the closing slokas of the *Vedartha-Sangraha,* where Ramanuja answers Manu's objection that "service is a dog's life. Therefore one should give it up" (Ma. IV, 6) and remain dependent solely on oneself. Ramanuja asserts that "service to one who is unworthy of service is a dog's life" while service to the Supreme *Sesin* is the ultimate service, through which dependence one attains freedom (sls. 244, 250). For Ramanuja, then, this "service in the form of *bhakti"* (sl. 251) is regarded as the highest knowledge, wherein the soul realizes its true relationship to Brahman. The Lord himself, through His infinite

towards the master. The following are his own words about the process and results of this form of practice: 'By constant meditation on the glorious character of Hanuman I totally forgot my own identity. My daily life and style of food came to resemble those of Hanuman. I did not feign them, they came naturally to me. I tied my cloth round the waist, letting a portion of it hang down in the form of a tail, and jumped from place to place instead of walking. I lived on fruits and roots only, and these I preferred to eat without peeling. I passed most of the time on trees, calling out in a solemn voice, "Raghuvir!" My eyes looked restless like those of a monkey, and most wonderful of all, my coccyx enlarged by about an inch. It gradually resumed its former size after that phase of the mind had passed on the completion of that course of discipline. In short, everything about me was more like a monkey than a human being.'[10]

### Experience of Sita

The *sadhana* of servantship *(dasya)* ended in a vision of Sita, Rama's eternal consort—a vision which Sri Ramakrishna had with his eyes open, in his normal state of mind rather than in *samadhi* as

---

grace, bestows this knowledge: "If a seeker meditates on the Supreme with a full consciousness of this relationship *(sesin* and *sesa)* as the principal entity and the subsidiary entity, and if the Supreme Brahman so meditated upon becomes an object of supreme love to the devotee, then He Himself effectuates the devotee's God-realization" (sl. 243). The devotion of Hanuman the monkey-god for Sri Rama is regarded as the model of such faithful service *(dasya bhava)* in the Hindu tradition (see *Life of Sri Ramakrishna,* p. 81). "When Rama and Lakshmana . . . [sought] everywhere for Sita, they came across a group of monkeys, and in the midst of them was Hanuman, the 'divine' monkey. Hanuman, the best of the monkeys, became the most faithful servant of Rama and helped him in rescuing Sita, . . . His devotion to Rama was so great that he is still worshipped by the Hindus as the ideal of a true servant of the Lord. You see, by the monkeys and demons were meant the aborigines of Southern India." Vivekananda, "The Ramayana," *Karma-Yoga and Bhakti-Yoga* (rev. ed.), p. 265. In the modern age Swami Ramakrishnananda, a direct disciple of Sri Ramakrishna, manifested this same type of service and devotion in his life; see *The Story of a Dedicated Life* (Madras: Sri Ramakrishna Math, 1948).

[10] *Life of Sri Ramakrishna,* p. 82. It may be observed that physical changes resulting from intense spiritual practices is not a phenomenon unique to Sri Ramakrishna or to Hinduism. Cf. the stigmata of St. Francis. See G. K. Chesterton, *St. Francis of Assisi* (New York: Doubleday, 1957); Johannes Jorgensen, *St. Francis of Assisi,* trans. by T. O'Conor Sloane, Image Books (Garden City, N. Y.: Doubleday, 1955). Also see *The Writings of St. Francis of Assisi,* trans. by Benen Fahy (Chicago: Franciscan Herald Press, 1963) for expressions of St. Francis' devotional attitude in his own words.

before. This experience occurred while he was sitting quietly amid the grove of five trees (Panchavati) where he usually meditated. As he described the experience,

'All of a sudden a luminous figure of exquisite grace appeared before me. The place was illumined with her lustre. I perceived not her alone but also the trees, the Ganges and everything. I observed that it was a human figure, being without such divine characteristics as three eyes and so on. But such a sublime countenance, expressive of love, sorrow, compassion and fortitude, is not commonly met with even in goddesses. Slowly she advanced from the north toward me, looking graciously on me all the while. I was amazed and was wondering who she might be, when a monkey with a cry suddenly jumped and sat by her. Then the idea flashed within me that this must be Sita, whose whole life had been centered in Rama and who had misery only as her lot! In an excess of emotion I was about to fall at her feet crying, "Mother," when she entered into my body, with the significant remark that the smile on her lips she bequeathed to me! I fell unconscious on the ground, overpowered with emotion.'[11]

## HIS TANTRIC SADHANA

### The Bhairavi Brahmani

This and other visions experienced by Sri Ramakrishna occurred without benefit of a *guru*. But he did accept the guidance of spiritual teachers on many occasions, especially when the *sadhana* required systematic training in precise methodology. His first spiritual preceptor was a woman, called the Bhairavi Brahmani. She was a highly developed spiritual personality who was fully qualified[12] to be Sri Ramakrishna's mentor. She was a person of con-

[11] *Life of Sri Ramakrishna*, p. 83. With regard to Sita's gift of her smile to Sri Ramakrishna in that experience, Isherwood writes: "Everyone who knew Ramakrishna agreed that he had a smile of unforgettable sweetness. Saradananda believed that his smile was literally the same as Sita's smile." *Ramakrishna and His Disciples*, p. 72.

[12] See *Hindu Psychology*, pp. 191-194, for Akhilananda's summary of the qualifications of a *guru*. See also Woodroffe, *Introduction to Tantra Sastra*, "Guru and Sisya," pp. 66-68, esp. the following: "There is in reality but one Guru. The ordinary human Guru is but the manifestation on the phenomenal plane of . . . the Supreme Guru. . . . He it is who enters into and speaks with the voice of the earthly Guru at the time of giving mantra [initiation]. . . . It is the Guru who initiates and helps, and

siderable spiritual attainment, having reached *samadhi*, and she was well versed in both technical and practical aspects of the *sadhanas* through which she guided Sri Ramakrishna, with a full command of the scriptures involved. It is significant that Sri Ramakrishna accepted a woman as his first *guru* because it indicates the importance he gave throughout his life to the role of womanhood in the spiritual world as well as in the temporal: "His mission was to establish the worship of the Divine Mother and thus to elevate the ideal of womanhood into Divine Motherhood."[13]

## Initiation into Tantric Sadhana

In this connection, Sri Ramakrishna was initiated[14] by the Bhairavi Brahmani in the esoteric *tantra sadhana,*[15] a spiritual practice

---

the relationship between him and the disciple *(sisya)* continues until the attainment of monistic siddhi" (p. 66). "When, however, siddhi is attained, both Guru and Sisya are above this dualism. With the attainment of pure monism, naturally this relation, as all others, disappears" (p. 68). "According to the Tantra, a woman with the necessary qualifications may be a guru and give initiation" (p. 67). Cf. *The Eternal Companion,* pp. 162-163. Swami Brahmananda states: "If a man truly longs for God, if he sincerely desires to practice spiritual disciplines, he is bound to find an illumined *guru.* . . . Sri Ramakrishna used to say: 'When a man finds an illumined *guru,* he is soon freed from the sense of ego, and he himself becomes illumined' " (p. 163).

[13] Abhedananda, Introduction to *The Gospel of Ramakrishna,* p. 19.

[14] See Akhilananda, *Spiritual Practices,* chap. iv, "Initiation," pp. 48-56. Note the comparison Akhilananda makes between Hindu initiation and Christian conversion, Jewish *bar mitzvah* or confirmation, similar Islamic practices, and Buddhist *diksha.* He also critically evaluates the point of view of modern religious psychology on the subject of conversion from the perspective of mystics of various traditions. Cf. Gonda, *Change and Continuity,* chap. x, "Diksha," pp. 315-462. Gonda traces the historico-religious roots of initiation from the Vedic period through the Vishnu Puranas, Shaivism, the Tantric *sadhanas* and Mahayana Buddhism down to modern Hindu practices. Cf. Woodroffe, *Introduction to Tantra Sastra,* "Initiation: Diksha," pp. 69-70.

[15] The most authoritative works in English on the Hindu Tantras to date are those of Sir John Woodroffe (pseudonym Arthur Avalon). Among these, the most detailed are *Shakti and Shakta* and *The Serpent Power.* For background information well founded in scholarship, see the following in *The Cultural Heritage of India,* Vol. IV: *The Religions,* ed. by Haridas Bhattacharyya (2d ed.; Calcutta: The Ramakrishna Mission Institute of Culture, 1956): P. C. Bagchi, "Evolution of the Tantras," pp. 211-226; Swami Pratyagatmananda, "Tantra as a Way of Realization," pp. 227-240; Atal Behari Ghosh, "The Spirit and Culture of the Tantras," pp. 241-251; R. K. Venkataraman, "Sakti Cult in South India," pp. 252-259; Chintaharan Chakravarti, "Sakti Worship and the Sakta Saints," pp. 408-420. Sri Ramakrishna's conversa-

which emphasizes the worship of God as Power *(Shakti),* embodied in the Female Principle of the Godhead, or Divine Mother. Here, the Male *(Shiva)* and Female *(Shakti)* Principles are in essence the same Reality viewed from two different perspectives. As Sri Ramakrishna explains,

tions are filled with reminiscences of his own spiritual experiences during his *tantra sadhana; see Gospel of Sri Ramakrishna,* trans. by Nikhilananda, *passim.* Sri Ramakrishna is regarded as the foremost exponent of the Shakti Principle in the Tantras in the modern age. Along with his disciple, Swami Vivekananda, Sri Ramakrishna influenced Sri Aurobindo *(The Life Divine* [New York: The Greystone Press, 1949]) and others. Akhilananda writes in this connection, "Many know of Mahatma Gandhi, but they do not know that Tilak and Aurobindo Ghose inspired Gandhi in the political field. Both of these men were in turn inspired by the teachings of Sri Ramakrishna and Swami Vivekananda." *Modern Problems,* p. 126. Swami Vivekananda's observations on the *tantra sadhana* or Shakti worship reveal a thoroughly original approach to this subject, as is evidenced by the following: "Saktas worship the Universal Energy as Mother, the sweetest name they know; for the mother is the highest ideal of womanhood in India. When God is worshipped as 'Mother,' as Love, the Hindus call it the 'right-handed' way, and it leads to spirituality but never to material prosperity. When God is worshipped on His terrible side, that is, in the 'left-handed' way, it leads usually to great material prosperity, but rarely to spirituality; and eventually it leads to degeneration and the obliteration of the race who practise it. Mother is the first manifestation of power and is considered a higher idea than father. With the name of Mother comes the idea of Shakti, Divine Energy and omnipotence, just as the baby believes its mother to be all-powerful, able to do anything. The Divine Mother is the Kundalini sleeping in us; without worshipping Her we can never know ourselves. All-merciful, all-powerful, omnipresent are attributes of Divine Mother. She is the sum-total of the energy in the universe. Every manifestation of power in the universe is 'Mother.' She is life, She is Intelligence, She is Love. She is in the universe, yet separate from it. She is a person and can be seen and known (as Sri Ramakrishna saw and knew Her). Established in the idea of Mother we can do anything. She quickly answers prayer. She can show Herself to us in any form at any moment. Divine Mother can have form (Rupa) and name (Nama), or name without form, and as we worship Her in these various aspects we can rise to pure Being, having neither form nor name . . . . The sea calm is the Absolute; the same sea in waves is Divine Mother." Vivekananda, *Works,* VII, 24-25. "Without Shakti (Power) there is no regeneration for the world. Why is it that our country is the weakest and the most backward of all countries?—Because Shakti is held in dishonour there. . . . Without the grace of Shakti nothing is to be accomplished. What do I find in America and Europe?—the worship of Shakti, the worship of Power. Yet they worship Her ignorantly through sense-gratification. Imagine, then, what a lot of good they will achieve who will worship Her with all purity, in a Sattvika spirit, looking upon Her as their mother!" *Ibid.,* pp. 416-417. "The Dharma of the Westerners is worship of Shakti, the Creative Power regarded as the Female Principle. It is with them somewhat like the Vamachari's worship of woman. As the

There is no distinction between Impersonal God *(Brahman)* on the one hand and Personal God *(Shakti)* on the other. When the Supreme Being is thought of as inactive, He is styled God the Absolute *(Suddha Brahman);* and when He is thought of as active—creating, sustaining and destroying—He is styled *Shakti* or the Personal God.[16]

Although Sri Ramakrishna had experienced the form of Divine Mother as Kali, the goddess in the temple at Dakshineswar, he now sought to realize her in yet a different aspect by following the intricate disciplines of the *tantras* under the guidance of his new *guru.*[17] Before proceeding on this path, Sri Ramakrishna asked permission of Divine Mother to do so, which she granted.

---

Tantrika says: 'On the left side the women . . . on the right, the cup full of wine; in short, warm meat with ingredients . . . the Tantrika religion is very mysterious, inscrutable even to the Yogis.' It is this worship of Shakti that is openly and universally practised [in the West]. . . . Our Shakti-worship is only in the holy places, and at certain times only is it performed; but theirs is in every place and always, for days, weeks, months, and years. Foremost is the woman's state, foremost is her dress, her seat, her food, her wants, and her comforts; the first honours in all respects are accorded to her. Not to speak of the noble-born, not to speak of the young and the fair, it is the worship of any and every woman, be she an acquaintance or a stranger. This Shakti-worship the Moors, the mixed Arab race, Mohammedan in religion, first introduced into Europe when they conquered Spain and ruled her for eight centuries. It was the Moors who first sowed in Europe the seeds of Western Civilisation and Shakti-worship. In course of time, the Moors forgot this Shakti-worship and fell from their position of strength, culture, and glory, to live scattered and unrecognised in an unnoticed corner of Africa, and their power and civilisation passed over to Europe. The Mother, leaving the Moors, smiled Her loving blessings on the Christians and illumined their homes." Vivekananda, *The East and the West* (Mayavati, Almora, Himalayas: Advaita Ashrama, 1963), pp. 65-67. "At the present time God should be worshipped as 'Mother,' the Infinite Energy. This will lead to purity, and tremendous energy will come here in America." *Works,* VII, 92.

[16] *Words of the Master,* p. 6. Sri Ramakrishna would not agree, nor would the main body of Hinduism, nor, for that matter, would an important segment of medieval Christianity agree with the following statement by van der Leeuw: "The relation to the father, again, can be spiritualized and moralized; that to the mother never completely so. . . . When he may no longer be the fructifier, the father may be the creator; the mother can only bear offspring. The father acts with power: the mother is merely potent. The father leads his people to their goal: the mother's child-bearing renews the cycle of life. The mother creates life: the father history." *Religion in Essence and Manifestation,* chap. x, "The Form of the Mother," I, 100. Sri Ramakrishna and Hinduism would in part concur, however, with his next statement: "She is Form and Power: he Form and Will" *(ibid.).*

[17] The Bhairavi Brahmani was the first Hindu scholar to attest to the authenticity of Sri Ramakrishna's spiritual experiences according to the standards set forth by

## His Practice of the Sixty-four Tantras

Thus at age twenty-five, Sri Ramakrishna was led to practice the sixty-four *tantras* during the period of 1861-1863.[18] He performed the *tantric sadhanas* in complete chastity without the assistance or companionship of a female sex-partner, showing the true spirit of these practices to be symbolic of the union of the soul and God rather than sexually-oriented on the level of the pleasure principle.[19]

---

Hindu scriptures, thus removing any doubts of their validity. Her conclusions were fully confirmed by other reputable scholars who met Sri Ramakrishna during that period of his life: Vaishnava Charan, Pundit Gauri Kanta Tarkabhushan of Indesh, Pundit Padmalochan Tarkalankar, Pundit Narayan Sastri of Rajputana, Pundit Jaynarayan, Krishnakisore, and others. See Saradananda, pp. 185-193, 499-525; cf. *Life of Sri Ramakrishna,* pp. 114-120, 146-165. Sri Ramakrishna found in the Bhairavi Brahmani a spiritual teacher who could shed light on the intense spiritual experiences he had undergone during the five-year period of his *sadhana* prior to their meeting. "Sri Ramakrishna . . . related to her every incident of his Sadhana—his wonderful visions, his total loss of outward consciousness in the meditation of God. . . . The Sanyasini listened to his recital full of joy and wonder . . . [and replied], 'Your state is what is called Mahabhava in the Shastras. . . . Sri Radha experienced that state and so did Gauranga. All these are recorded in the Bhakti texts. I have these books with me, and I shall show you that whoever has sincerely yearned for God has experienced this state, and everyone doing so must pass through it.' . . . The Brahmani had dived deep into the various Hindu scriptures, specially the Tantras and the Vaishnava literature. . . . The Master's questions as to his various experiences she would settle by quoting from authoritative texts wherein are recorded similar experiences of previous seekers after truth." *Ibid.,* pp. 115-118.

[18] His biographers are vague about the precise duration of this period, stating that it commenced at the end of 1861, lasted throughout 1862, and was completed in 1863. See Saradananda, p. 203, 207; cf. Isherwood, p. 102.

[19] Cf. Sorokin's "sensate" vs. "ideational" world views. See *Reconstruction of Humanity, passim; Ways of Power and Love,* pp. 83-84, 88, 154, 238-240; *Power and Morality, passim.* In his discussion of monasticism, self-denial and "self-isolation," he states the following: "Religious, moral, artistic, scientific and other potential creators retreat into solitude *voluntarily.* They carry with them the highest values of their culture. . . . The total body of evidence seems to indicate that the strong seekers of the superconscious did become in voluntary solitude more spiritual . . . more altruistic. . . . Hermits of the past, like St. Francis, St. Ignatius, and of recent time, Serafim of Sarov, . . . Sri Ramakrishna, Vivekananda . . . and a legion of others are the most effective instrumentalities of altruization of the human world (while their sensate denunciators have hardly exerted any such influence and in their own life have shown little if any unselfishness)." *Ways of Power and Love,* p. 233, 240. Here and elsewhere Sorokin answers the critics of celibacy who claim that monasticism is a denial of society, its values and its perpetuity. He asserts that those who choose celibacy in order to know God generate the greatest altruism, and thereby benefit

He maintained a filial relationship with the Bhairavi throughout this episode, as he did with all women during his lifetime, including his own wife.

Sri Ramakrishna's experiences along the path of the *tantras* are documented with a remarkable precision and detail by Saradananda,[20] especially considering the historically secretive nature of these practices and their instruction. These experiences and their documentation represent a valuable legacy for the scientific study of religion. According to Sri Ramakrishna,

> 'There was . . . no limit to my visions and experiences, all very extraordinary. The Brahmani made me undertake one by one, all the sadhanas prescribed in the main sixty-four Tantras, all difficult to accomplish, in trying to practise which most of the sadhakas go astray; but all of which I got through by Mother's grace.'[21]

### His Purity

On one occasion the Brahmani brought a beautiful young woman for him to worship as a representation of Divine Mother. When the worship was over, she commanded him to sit on the girl's lap and repeat the name of God. He became fearful lest he lose self-control, and prayed for strength. No sooner had he sat on her lap than he plunged into *samadhi.* On another occasion he was told by his teacher to witness a pair of lovers enjoying intercourse in order to test and fortify his equanimity. He said that he saw " 'nothing in it but the blissful sport of the divine." " His " 'mind, instead of descending even to the neighborhood of ordinary human feelings, soared higher and higher merging at last in a deep samadhi.' " Upon regaining external consciousness, his teacher told him, " ' "You have reached the desired end of a very difficult Tantric sadhana and become established in the divine mood. This is the ultimate sadhana

---

society. Cf. Akhilananda, *Modern Problems,* p. 122 ff.; Vivekananda, *Karma-Yoga,* "Each is Great in His Own Place," pp. 13-31. For the specific value of celibacy for God-realization, see Chapter IX of this study.

[20] Saradananda, Part II, chap. xi, "Tantric Sadhana," pp. 194-206.

[21] *Ibid.,* p. 198. Regarding the rapid rate of his progress, Sri Ramakrishna stated, "'It did not take me more than three days to succeed in any of the sadhanas. When I took up a particular sadhana and asked divine Mother importunately with a glowing eagerness of heart for the realization of its result, She benignly crowned me with success in three days only.'" *Ibid.,* p. 202.

of the (heroic) mode of worship." ' " Sri Ramakrishna stated that his " 'mental attitude toward all women, viz., that of a child towards its mother, remained intact during the long period of the Tantra sadhana.' "[22]

### Vision of Mahamaya

His biographers relate the following vision which occurred during this period:

> At this time, Ramakrishna felt a strong desire to experience Mother Kali's power to delude—her play of seeming creation, preservation and destruction, which is called Maya. He was granted a vision which would have terrified a lesser devotee. One day, he saw a woman of exquisite beauty come up from the Ganges and approach the Panchavati. As she came nearer, she seemed to become more and more obviously pregnant. Her womb swelled visibly, until she gave birth to a beautiful child, which she suckled with the greatest tenderness. But suddenly her expression changed. She became ferocious and terrible. She began to eat the child, grinding its flesh and bones between her teeth and swallowing them. Then she turned and went back into the Ganges.[23]

### Psychic Powers

He also developed extraordinary psychic powers as a result of practicing the *tantras*. He did not want to hold on to these powers, however, because he felt they would become obstacles to further

[22] *Ibid.,* p. 199. Saradananda repeatedly heard from Sri Ramakrishna that "he never in his life kept the company of a woman even in a dream" (p. 202). Note Saradananda's observations on the original intent of the *tantric* practices and the cause for their subsequent degeneration, pp. 201-202.

[23] Isherwood, p. 102. For a philosophical statement of the Advaitic understanding of *maya* or cosmic nescience, see the works of Shankaracharya: *Vivekachudamani; Brahma-Sutra-Bhasya; Upadeshasahasri* ("A Thousand Teachings"), trans. with notes by Swami Jagadananda (Mylapore, Madras: Sri Ramakrishna Math, 1961), etc. Sir John Woodroffe's *The World as Power* (Madras: Ganesh & Co., 1966) offers an excellent supplement to Shankara from the Tantric interpretation, also essentially Advaitic. Vivekananda's three chapters on *maya* in *Jnana-Yoga* (rev. ed.), pp. 24-74, further clarify this concept for the Western reader. He considered these London lectures on *maya* as among his greatest intellectual achievements, in that they simplified and made concrete this most abstruse of all Vedantic philosophical concepts. Cf. the *Vedantasara of Sadananda Yogindra Saraswati* of the later Shankarite school, trans. by Swami Nikhilananda (Calcutta: Advaita Ashrama, 1968) with its detailed exposition of "superimposition" in the concept of *maya*.

spiritual realization. As a student of human nature, he knew the dangers of vanity which arise when a man finds he can fathom or manipulate the laws of nature by the sole power of his own mind.[24] The aim of religion, especially in the mystical approach, is not directed at the objective world but at the "direct and immediate knowledge of God,"[25] the Creator and substratum of the changing phenomenal universe.

Examples of the occult powers that came unsolicited to Sri Ramakrishna at this time are an ability to know the meaning of the language of birds and animals, to become as small as an atom, to hear spontaneously the great sound of the universe (called *anahata dhvani,* a harmony of all sounds), and to radiate light from his body. He "acquired for a time a strange and celestial beauty," a golden complexion which was "vouched for by many witnesses."[26] He said of this:

'It was as if a golden light was shining forth from my body.' . . . 'People used to stare at me in wonder, so I always kept my body covered with a thick wrapper. Alas, I thought to myself, they're all charmed by this outward beauty of mine, but not one of them wants to see Him who dwells within! And I prayed to the Divine Mother earnestly, "Mother, here's your outward beauty—please take it back and give me inner

---

[24] *Sayings of Sri Ramakrishna,* pp. 129-131, especially the following: "Siddhis or psychic powers should be avoided like filth. Those come of themselves by virtue of Sadhanas or religious practices, and Samyama or control of the senses. But he who sets his mind on Siddhis remains stuck thereto, and cannot rise higher" (p. 130). "Krishna once said to Arjuna, 'If you desire to attain Me, know that it would never be possible so long as you possess even a single one of the eight psychic powers (Ashta Siddhis).' For occult powers increase man's egotism and thus make him forgetful of God" (p. 129). See Vivekananda, *Raja-Yoga,* for a catalogue of these powers and how they arise. In sloka 3:38 Patanjali himself states that occult powers are obstacles to the knowledge of God. See Akhilananda, *Hindu Psychology,* p. 148, 153. The foregoing refute statements of some Indologists with an incomplete grasp of Yoga, exemplified by the following: "Yoga has arisen from magical conceptions and practices, and it always remains a refined form of magic. Its ultimate goal . . . is magical—a miraculous state; . . . it consists in attaining . . . a supernatural, miraculous 'glory' with an abundance of power and knowledge." Otto, *Mysticism East and West,* p. 160. Regarding the origin of Sri Ramakrishna's own insight here, "Divine Mother showed him in a vision that these powers were worthless for a real devotee." Ghanananda, p. 62.

[25] Rufus Jones, p. xiv.

[26] Isherwood, pp. 101-102.

beauty instead!" And at last that light went in, and the body became pale again.' . . .

It was at this time, also, that Ramakrishna was made aware by a vision that many disciples would come to him in his later life and receive enlightenment from him.[27]

### Effects of His Tantric Sadhana

One of the most significant results of his *tantra sadhana* was, however, not the emergence of psychic phenomena, nor even the extent and multiplicity of his divine visions, but the permanently transforming influence they had on his personality: he became childlike, and completely without egotism. Regarding such supranormal religious experiences, Akhilananda states: *"The real criterion is the effect on the character of the person."*[28] In this connection, Saradananda writes,

> We have heard from the Master himself that from the time of his Tantric sadhana, the door of his Sushumna, the canal Centralis, was fully opened and his nature was permanently converted into that of a boy. From the latter part of that period, he could not, in spite of all his efforts, retain his wearing cloth, sacred thread, etc. on his person for any length of time. He did not feel where and when all these things slipped off. This condition was, it is needless to mention, caused by the absence of his body-consciousness, on account of his mind remaining always absorbed in the lotus feet of the divine Mother. We have it from the Master himself that, unlike the ordinary Paramahamsas (a class of naked sannyasins), he never practised going about or remaining naked —it naturally came to him with his gradual loss of body-consciousness. At the end of those sadhanas, his knowledge of non-duality with regard to all things, the Master said, increased. . . . The Master, [was] devoid of egoism.[29]

As an important aspect of this permanent transformation of Sri Ramakrishna's personality, the sex idea was completely eradicated from his mental structure. While Sri Ramakrishna's attitude toward women had always been very pure—he had regarded them as veritable representations of Divine Mother—it was during the *tantra sadhana* that he actually "saw . . . the divine Mother Herself

---

[27] *Ibid.,* pp. 102-103.

[28] *Hindu Psychology,* p. 148.

[29] Saradananda, p. 205.

dwelling in the female form."[30] Comparing his own regard for womanhood to that of Ganesh, the elephant god who is considered the ideal of continence in Hinduism, he related, " 'My attitude to women is also the same; that is why I had the vision of maternal form of the universal Cause, in my married wife and worshipped her and bowed down at her feet.' "[31]

## OTHER EXPERIMENTATIONS IN HINDUISM

Sri Ramakrishna's verification of God in Hinduism was by no means limited to the foregoing illustrations. The gamut of his experiences in his own religious tradition was enormous. Among such experiences, he verified the path of the ancient *rishis* of the Upanishads in the *santa bhava* by attaining the pinnacle of Advaita Vedanta, the state known as *nirvikalpa samadhi;* he pursued the *vatsalya bhava* and the difficult *madhura bhava* practices, which are the parent-child relationship and the paramour or "sweet" relationship respectively of the spiritual aspirant toward God; and he performed the worship of his own wife, Sri Sarada Devi, as the embodiment of Divine Mother (the worship of Shodasi). These *sadhanas* and their consequences are treated separately in subsequent chapters.[32]

---

[30] *Ibid.,* p. 204. Also see pp. 200-201.
[31] *Ibid.,* p. 201.
[32] See Chapters IV, VII, and IX herein.

# CHAPTER IV

# Verification of 'God' in Buddhism

## ANALYSIS OF BUDDHIST PERSPECTIVE

### Buddhism not Atheism

Buddhism is not, as many people think, an atheistic religion.[1] What it is is difficult to define: Buddhist scholarship according to Western standards is very recent; therefore no consensus of opinion exists. Historically speaking, Buddhism rests on an enormous aggregate of distinct scriptures which afford a rich variety of perspec-

[1] In emphasizing the Middle Way or *majjhimapatipada* the Buddha sought assiduously to avoid the extremes of both "Absolutism" or "Nihilism" with regard to the existence or non-existence of ultimate Reality. It is therefore indefensible to call him an atheist. While Buddhist scholars differ widely on many points, they appear to concur in regarding the Buddha and classical Buddhism as non-atheistic. As Conze states, "If Atheism is the denial of the existence of a God, it would be quite misleading to describe Buddhism as atheistic." Edward Conze, *Buddhism: Its Essence and Development,* Harper Torchbooks (New York: Harper & Row, 1959), p. 42. John Blofeld explains, ". . . many people, . . . are apt to equate Buddhism with atheism as ordinarily understood, although in fact they have no affinity. . . . Mystics of other religions who take the term 'God' to mean ultimate, divine reality . . . come very close to the Buddhist position. . . . As with what Christian mystics call the Godhead, Buddhists think of divine reality not as a *person* to be adored but a *state* to be attained. . . . Mahayana Buddhists have no one name for divine reality. . . . Various

tives, from a theistic *bhakti*-oriented Buddhology[2] in some Mahayana schools[3] to what has been called "ethical idealism"[4] in the

names are given to it in different contexts." *The Tantric Mysticism of Tibet* (New York: Dutton, 1970), pp. 51-52. It should be pointed out that in Mahayana Buddhism a theistic tendency developed in what is called the Buddhism of faith. In many Mahayana schools the Buddha himself, and the Dharma which was identified with him (e.g., *Dharmakaya*), was installed and worshipped as the Omniscient Being. Dr. Joshi states, "For the Buddhists *dharma* is the Ultimate Truth revealed by an Omniscient Being for the weal and welfare of living beings." "Truth: A Buddhist Perspective," *The Journal of Religious Studies,* IV (Spring, 1972), p. 65. Cf. Conze, p. 40. From the Hindu viewpoint, "Those who believe that Buddha was an atheist are very wrong. His silence about God or soul was that of a mystic. He was a Jnani." *The Story of a Dedicated Life,* p. 104.

[2] Regarding the complex development of *bhakti* in Buddhism, see *Saddharmapundarika* (Lotus Sutra) (ca. first century B.C.) as a Buddhist *bhakti* text, with its *ekayana* principle and appeal to lay society, the personification of Eternal Dharma, *stupa* worship where sutras, Dharma and Buddha are enshrined, sutra copying as a form of *bhakti,* and multiple *bodhisattvas.* Cf. the *bhakti* orientation of *Sukhavativyuha* scripture, with its notion of a "Pure Land" *(Sukhavati)* where the Amitabha or Amitayus Buddha resides; note also Maitreya and the Tusita heaven. Erotic motifs on a symbolic level in Buddhist scripture represent another development of *bhakti,* first appearing in the *Avatamsaka* corpus about 100 A.D. and continuing down to the Buddhist Tantric period in various texts (cf. *Guhyasamajatantra,* etc.). Note *Buddhist Texts Through the Ages,* ed. by Edward Conze *et al.,* Harper Torchbooks (New York: Harper & Row, 1964): "Faith," p. 52 ff., "The Buddhism of Faith," pp. 185-206, "The Tantras," pp. 221-268. Note the development of *bodhisattvas* from the *Mahavastu* of the Mahasanghika onward, emphasizing *bhakti* and salvation by *sraddha* (faith) in the Dharma, which the *bodhisattvas* embody. In this connection, see Geoffrey Parrinder, *Avatar and Incarnation* (London: Faber & Faber, 1970) pp. 131-180. Although Parrinder lacks precision in his comparisons and the method by which he sets forth his Buddhology and theory of Hindu *avatar,* his courageous attempt in this area succeeds in bringing out the salient points. Cf. Richard V. de Smet, review of *Avatar and Incarnation* by G. Parrinder, in *The Journal of Religious Studies,* III (Spring, 1971), 171-173. Note also Asanga's *trikaya* theory in the later Buddhology of the scholastic period (*trikaya* or threefold Buddhabody: *Dharmakaya, Sambhogakaya,* and *Nirmanakaya*); as *Dharmakaya* the Buddha and his Dharma are identical, and can be worshipped. This is the justification for *bhakti* in an essentially non-theistic religion. It also represents a *rapprochement* to Advaita Vedanta in the recognition that the *Dharmakaya* or eternal Buddha nature is immanent in all sentient beings. For a thoroughgoing scholarly treatment of the post-Gupta period in Buddhist scholasticism in India, see Joshi's monumental work, *Studies in the Buddhistic Culture of India.*

[3] See E. B. Cowell *et al.,* eds., *Buddhist Mahayana Texts* (New York: Dover Publications, 1969); D. T. Suzuki, *On Indian Mahayana Buddhism,* ed. by Edward Conze, Harper Torchbooks (New York: Harper & Row, 1968); Edward Conze, *Bud-*

early Pali Canon. Contrary to Christianity, Islam, Judaism and Hinduism, in which a single body of scripture is taken as "orthodoxy," *all* the Buddhist scriptures are valid references for spiritual development.

## The Content of Buddha's Enlightenment (Nirvana)

The reference point for this chapter will be the essential nature of the Buddha's enlightenment: *Nirvana,*[5] and the Way to *Nirvana* (i.e., the Four Noble Truths,[6] especially the Fourth, consisting of

---

*dhist Thought in India,* Ann Arbor Paperbacks (Ann Arbor, Mich.: University of Michigan Press, 1968), Part III, "The Mahayana," pp. 195-260; Kenneth W. Morgan, ed., *The Path of the Buddha* (New York: Ronald Press, 1956), pp. 153-400; Alicia Matsunaga, *The Buddhist Philosophy of Assimilation* (Tokyo: Sophia University, 1969), chap. ii, "A New Conception of Divinity in Mahayana," pp. 66-96. This last work offers a fresh and original approach in Buddhology. For the historical approach, see Joshi, *Studies,* chap. i, pp. 1-17, esp. Notes, pp. 12-17.

[4] See Akhilananda, *Modern Problems,* p. 50: "Buddhism is the only religion which can be regarded as ethical idealism"; cf. K. N. Jayatilleke, *Ethics in Buddhist Perspective* (Kandy, Ceylon: Buddhist Publication Society, 1972) and S. B. Shastri, "Buddhist Ethics and Social Ideas in Buddhism," in *Buddhism,* Guru Nanak Quincentenary Celebration Series (Patiala: Punjabi University, 1969), pp. 46-61.

[5] "The Buddhists . . . believe in the state called Nirvana, which is beyond this relative world. It is exactly the same as the Brahman of the Vedantins, and the whole system of the Buddhists is founded upon the idea of regaining that lost state of Nirvana." Vivekananda, *Works,* II, 194-195. Cf. Guy Richard Welbon, *The Buddhist Nirvana and Its Western Interpreters* (Chicago: University of Chicago Press, 1968). Vivekananda also states that according to Buddhism, "man is a succession of waves, and when one goes away it generates another, and the cessation of these wave-forms is what is called Nirvana." *Works,* III, 411. Cf. Patanjali's *Yoga Sutras* 1:2, 13, 41, as follows: "Yoga is restraining the mind-stuff *(Chitta)* from taking various forms *(Vrittis)*." "Continuous struggle to keep them (the *Vrittis*) perfectly restrained is practice." "The Yogi whose *Vrittis* have thus become powerless (controlled) obtains in the receiver, (the instrument of) receiving, and the received (the Self, the mind and external objects), concentratedness and sameness, like the crystal (before different coloured objects)." Then comes "seedless" *samadhi* (sloka 51). In this connection see Swami Abhedananda, *The Thoughts on Sankhya Buddhism and Vedanta* (Calcutta: Ramakrishna Vedanta Math, 1967), chap. iii, "Buddha and Kapila," pp. 37-43. Cf. especially Conze, *Buddhist Thought in India,* "Nirvana," pp. 68-79, and Joshi, "Truth: A Buddhist Perspective."

[6] *Dhammapada* 14:11-14, esp. the following: "He who with clear understanding sees the four noble truths:—suffering, the origin of suffering, the destruction of suffering, and the eightfold noble path that leads to the release from suffering . . . is delivered from all suffering." *The Dhammapada,* trans. by Irving Babbitt, New Di-

the Eightfold Path).[7] This content of his enlightenment is the common factor among the great majority of Buddhist texts, from the early Theravada period to the *Sarvastivada* scriptures, the *Prajnaparamita* corpus, the *Avatamsaka,* the *Sukhavativyuha* corpus, Nagarjuna's works, the Vijnanavada scholastic period *(Mahaparinirvana,* etc.) down to the Buddhist Tantras in India, including the Ceylonese, Tibetan, Chinese, Korean, Japanese and Southeast Asian schools, all of which are ultimately founded on the creative millenia of Buddhist scriptures in greater India following the life of Buddha.

### Buddha's Path as Jnana Yoga

Buddha himself refused to discuss the existence or nonexistence of ultimate Reality.[8] In this regard he was reacting to the abuses of Brahmanical Hinduism of his time.[9] Buddha meant to realize that which would take man beyond suffering,[10] as did the ancient Vedic

---

rections Paperbooks (New York: New Directions, 1965), p. 31. An excellent exposition of *Dukkha, Samudaya, Nirodha* and *Magga* is given by Piyadassi Thera, *The Buddha's Ancient Path* (London: Rider & Co., 1964).

[7] George Appleton, *On the Eightfold Path: Christian Presence amid Buddhism,* ed. by M. A. C. Warren, Christian Presence Series (New York: Oxford University Press, 1961). "The eightfold path consists of right views *(sammaditthi),* right aspirations *(sammasamkappo),* right living *(sammajivo),* right exertion *(sammavayamo),* right speech *(sammavaca),* right actions *(sammakammanto),* right recollection *(sammasati),* and right meditation *(sammasamadhi).* It is called the middle path since it is equally remote from the extremes of superstition and scepticism." *The Dhammapada,* with Pali text, translation and notes by S. Radhakrishnan (London: Oxford University Press, 1966), p. 123. Cf. Patanjali's *Yoga Sutras* 2:29 as follows: "*Yama, Niyama, Asana, Pranayama, Pratyahara, Dharana, Dhyana,* and *Samadhi,* are the eight limbs of Yoga." Vivekananda, *Raja-Yoga* (Mayavati edition), p. 220.

[8] See Edward J. Thomas, *The History of Buddhist Thought* (London: Routledge & Kegan Paul, 1951), p. 96, p. 129, and pp. 124-227.

[9] Govind Chandra Pande, *Studies in the Origins of Buddhism,* Ancient History Research Series No. 1 (Allahabad: Department of Ancient History, Culture and Archaeology, University of Allahabad, 1957), Part II, chap. ix, "Religious Conditions in the Age of Buddha," pp. 310-368; cf. Joshi's controversial *Brahmanism, Buddhism and Hinduism,* The Wheel Publication No. 150/151 (Kandy, Ceylon: Buddhist Publication Society, 1970).

[10] "Philosophy . . . is unknown to Buddhist tradition, which would regard the enquiry into reality, for the mere purpose of knowing more about it, as a waste of valuable time. The Buddha's teaching is exclusively concerned with showing the way to salvation. Any 'philosophy' . . . is quite incidental. . . . Speculation on matters irrelevant to salvation is discouraged. Suffering is the basic fact of life. If a man were

*rishis* before him. His great nobility was that he sought this knowledge not for himself alone, but for all mankind.[11] The method he used in search of his enlightenment can be rightly compared to the *jnana yoga* (path of knowledge) of Hinduism, and his enlightenment itself to *nirvikalpa samadhi*,[12] the ultimate goal of Advaita

struck by an arrow, he would not refuse to have it extricated before he knew who shot the arrow, whether that man was married or not, tall or small, fair or dark. All he would want, would be to be rid of the arrow. The Buddha's last injunction to his disciples ran: *All conditioned things are impermanent. Work out your salvation with diligence.* In their long history, the Buddhists have never lost this practical bent. . . . We can, therefore, say with some truth that Buddhist thinking tends in the direction of what we call *Pragmatism.*" Conze, *Buddhism,* pp. 15-17. Thus the Buddha's approach in taking himself and others beyond suffering was based on *Upayakausalya* or "skill in means."

[11] Swami Vivekananda, who was a lifelong admirer of the Buddha (see his "Buddhistic India," in *Swami Vivekananda Centenary Memorial Volume,* ed. by R. C. Majumdar [Calcutta: Swami Vivekananda Centenary, 1963], pp. xxi-xliv), says the following: "I would like to see moral men like Gautama Buddha, who did not believe in a Personal God or a personal soul, never asked about them, but was a perfect agnostic, and yet was ready to lay down his life for anyone, and worked all his life for the good of all, and thought only of the good of all. Well has it been said by his biographer, in describing his birth, that he was born for the good of the many, as a blessing to the many. He did not go to the forest to meditate for his own salvation; he felt that the world was burning, and that he must find a way out. 'Why is there so much misery in the world?'—was the one question that dominated his whole life." *Works,* II, 350.

[12] Swami Akhilananda and his teacher, Swami Brahmananda, are both fully qualified to discuss the nature of *samadhi.* Swami Brahmananda states: "This mind cannot know Him. He is beyond this mortal mind and far beyond the human intellect. This apparent universe which you see is within the domain of the mind. . . . It cannot go beyond its own domain. Behind the mind of which we are aware is a subtle, spiritual mind, existing in seed-form. Through contemplation, prayer, and *japam* (repetition of the name of God), this mind develops and with its unfoldment a new vision opens. . . . The experience of *samadhi* is indescribable—beyond *is* and *is not.* In this blessed experience there is neither happiness nor misery, neither light nor darkness. All is Infinite Being—inexpressible." *The Eternal Companion,* p. 100. "*Samadhi* is generally classified as of two kinds. In *savikalpa,* the first sort of *samadhi,* there is the mystic vision of a spiritual form of God, while the consciousness of individuality still remains. In *nirvikalpa,* the other type of *samadhi,* a man loses his individuality and goes beyond the vision of the form of God. The whole universe then disappears. There is yet another kind called *Ananda* (blissful) *samadhi.* If an ordinary man reaches this experience, his body and brain cannot bear the supreme ecstatic joy. He does not live more than twenty-one days." *Ibid.,* p. 107. "In the superconscious state of *nirvikalpa samadhi* the individual transcends the limitation

Vedanta.[13] So similar, in fact, are the two paths that the critics of Shankara, who was the champion of Advaita to the Buddhist camp, have often accused him of being a Buddhist himself, or of basing "his Advaita doctrine on Buddhist teachings."[14] That is because not only did Shankara use the dialectic methods of the Buddhists to combat Buddhism, but the practices he advocated in his *jnana yoga* approach were in essence the same as those advocated by Buddha: e.g., ethical conduct, discrimination, renunciation, meditation, and, finally, "conditionless" *samadhi,* or "*samadhi* without support."

## SRI RAMAKRISHNA'S NIRVIKALPA SAMADHI AS NIRVANA

### Support for This Position

This is the path that Sri Ramakrishna travelled in the last stage of his verification of God in Hinduism, which can also be considered his experience of 'God' in Buddhism, for his experience at the end of this path was identical with that of the Buddha. Thus he verified

---

of personality and immediately and directly experiences the Absolute in its integral unity. His soul is completely identified with the Absolute. The knower, known, and knowledge become one *(Triputi Veda).* One of the *Upanishads* says: 'As a result of meditation, the enjoyer, the enjoyed, and the power which brings about enjoyment— all are declared to be the three aspects of Brahman.' (*Svetasvatara Upanishad* 1:12). In other words, all differences and their relations merge into *one.* As Jesus said: 'I and my Father are one.' Hindu teachers say: 'I am Brahman.' These statements are from the depth of the realization of oneness with the Absolute. In that state a man also remains fully unconscious of the objective world, even of his own body, yet inwardly he is one with Consciousness Itself. His whole inner life is changed, and he has identified himself with the whole of existence. All limitations of time, space, and causation and the categories of objective knowledge are completely negated and annulled. What remains then is pure existence, pure knowledge, and pure bliss. All the contents of the empirical self are completely swept away and what remains is the pure Self *(Atma).*" Akhilananda, *Hindu Psychology,* p. 164. Cf. Conze, *Buddhist Meditation,* Ethical and Religious Classics of East and West No. 13 (London: Allen and Unwin, 1956), esp. pp. 106-173; Joshi, "Buddhist Meditation and Mysticism," in *Buddhism,* Guru Nanak Celebration Series; pp. 62-85; and [Sgam.po.pa], *The Jewel Ornament of Liberation,* trans. and annotated by Herbert V. Guenther, The Clear Light Series (Berkeley, Calif.: Shambala Publications, 1971), esp. "The Perfection of Awareness," pp. 202-231 and the following chapters.

[13] *Ashtavakra Samhita,* trans. by Swami Nityaswarupananda (Calcutta: Advaita Ashrama, 1969). Cf. *Gospel of Ramakrishna,* Abhedananda revision, pp. 146-147.

[14] Joshi, *Brahmanism, Buddhism and Hinduism,* p. 39.

the content of Buddha's enlightenment, or *Nirvana,* which the Hindus call *nirvikalpa samadhi.* Swami Nirvedananda states this position unambiguously:

> Advaita Vedanta . . . practically comprehends Buddhism so far as both the method of spiritual discipline and the goal are concerned. The two paths may be equally labelled as the path of knowledge. Both discard the Personal God and all dualistic thoughts and forms of worship with equal emphasis. Both insist on moral perfection, contemplation of the unreality of the objective world and withdrawal of the mind completely from the illusory existence as the cardinal points of spiritual practice. So far they are identical regarding method. Only Advaita Vedanta prescribes meditation on the reality of the human soul and its oneness with the Nirguna Brahman as an additional . . . feature of spiritual practice. Nevertheless, a *jnana-yogin* has to cover all that Buddhism prescribes. Of course, by 'Buddhism' is meant here the purest form of this religion as preached by Lord Buddha. Then regarding the goal, the *nirvana* of the Buddhist . . . corresponds to the *nirvikalpa samadhi* of the Advaitin.
>
> So Ramakrishna, . . . through his Advaita practice . . . had mastered both the method and the aim of Buddhism up to a point of perfection.[15]

### His Guru in Advaita, Tota Puri

The story of Sri Ramakrishna's experiment in the Advaitic approach began with the coming of his new spiritual guide toward the end of 1865. His name was Tota Puri, a staunch *sannyasin* who had realized *nirvikalpa samadhi* after forty years of intense spiritual practices, which consisted of meditation and realization of the formless aspect of God or the Absolute, called *Nirguna Brahman.*[16]

[15] Swami Nirvedananda, *Sri Ramakrishna and Spiritual Renaissance* (Calcutta: Ramakrishna Mission Institute of Culture, 1940), pp. 94-95. Cf. statements by two Buddhist scholars on this point: T. Murti, *The Central Philosophy of Buddhism* (London: Allen & Unwin, 1955), pp. 109-117; and Joshi, "Gaudapada's Rapprochement between Buddhism and Vedanta," *Journal of Akhila Bharatiya Sanskrit Parishad* (Lucknow), I (July, 1969), 11-22. Dr. Joshi communicated orally to this writer in 1970, while a visiting scholar at Harvard Divinity School, that, in his opinion, the innermost content of the Buddhist enlightenment *(Nirvana)* is identical with the *nirvikalpa samadhi* of the Advaita Vedantist. A similar conclusion is set forth by Geoffrey Webster, a practicing Buddhist living in London, in "Some Reflections on Mahayana Buddhism," *Vedanta for East and West* No. 128 (November-December, 1972), pp. 25-30.

[16] "The practice of concentration and meditation in *Jnana Yoga* is very difficult

He was a true *Vedantakesari,* a "lion of the Vedanta"—now wandering about as an itinerant monk after the fruition of his *Advaita sadhana.* Having broken the bonds of illusion *(maya),* he was extremely cautious about forming new attachments to people and places, so he developed the habit of never staying at the same place for more than three days. His temperamental disposition was that of an ultra-radical Shankarite, an extreme Advaitin: for him there was only one Reality, the non-dual Absolute, and this Absolute *(Brahman)* could best be known by realizing It as identical with one's own essence *(Atman).*[17] It was this instruction that he imparted to Sri Ramakrishna.

## *His Preparation for the Advaitic Sadhana*

Sri Ramakrishna had already been prepared for this type of teaching by his *tantric sadhana.* In those *tantric* practices he had raised his level of consciousness successively through the different

---

for an average man or woman as one has to focus the mind on the 'impersonal,' non-bodily, Self-conscious Absolute *(Sat-chid-ananda, Nirguna Brahman).* It is very difficult for an ordinary person who is living on the plane of time-space-causal relationship and name, form, and attributes to conceive anything that is beyond these categories. It is true that certain symbols like sound and light are often given as the objects of concentration; but even such a symbol or substitute of the unconditioned Absolute *(Nirguna Brahman)* is difficult for the beginners of this path to use as an ideal. . . . There are few persons in the world who can start their spiritual practices entirely from the intellectual point of view. They require tremendous discipline and ethical training to begin with this method. . . . Many persons seem to think that they are Absolutists in their philosophy but their actions reveal that they are still functioning on the lower plane of relative existence, or *Maya."* Akhilananda, *Hindu Psychology,* pp. 177-178.

[17] "The highest method of worship is meditation on the unity of the Atman and Brahman." *Eternal Companion,* p. 114. Cf. Vivekananda, *Works,* II, 238-288; Sri Shankaracharya, *Aparokshanubhuti or Self-Realization,* trans. by Swami Vimuktananda (Calcutta: Advaita Ashrama, 1938); Sri Shankaracharya, *Vakyavritti and Atmajnanopadeshavidhi,* trans. by Swami Jagadananda (Mylapore, Madras: Sri Ramakrishna Math, 1967); Sri Shankaracharya, *Brahma-Sutra-Bhasya.* It will be noted that all but the last, while of the school of Shankara, cannot be definitely attributed to Shankara himself. Cf. with the position of the foregoing Raymond Panikkar, *The Unknown Christ of Hinduism* (London: Darton, Longman & Todd, 1968), in which Panikkar develops the Christian Trinity on the foundation of the Advaitic intuition of the *Atman-Brahman* identity. See John Moffitt, review of Panikkar's book in *The Journal of Religious Studies* (Patiala), IV (Spring, 1972), 163-168.

*chakras*[18] or psychic centers through ritualistic worship. In his Advaitic *sadhana,* however, his new *guru* asked him to forsake the form of the Divine Mother (Shakti) in order to have the realization of Brahman without form, qualities or attributes. Like Meister Eckhart, he had to "renounce God for God's sake."[19]

### *His Advaita Realization: Nirvikalpa Samadhi*

After being initiated into *sannyasa* (monasticism)[20] by Tota Puri, Sri Ramakrishna had the following experience, which he describes in his own words:

[18] See Woodroffe, *Serpent Power,* chap v, "The Centres or Lotuses," pp. 103-180. Cf. Vivekananda, *Raja-Yoga,* Mayavati edition, chap. v, "Control of Psychic Prana," pp. 67-74. As Sri Ramakrishna describes, "The six lotuses mentioned in the Science of Yoga correspond to the seven mental planes mentioned in the Vedanta. When the mind is immersed in worldliness, it makes its abode in the lowest lotus at the end of the spine. Sexual desires rise when the mind is in the second lotus, the sexual organ. When it is in the third, the navel, the man is taken up with things of the world—eating, drinking, begetting children. In the fourth mental plane the heart of the man is blessed with the Vision of Divine Glory and he cries out: 'What is all this! What is all this!' In the fifth plane the mind rests in the throat. The devotee talks only on subjects related to God and grows impatient if any other subject comes up in the course of conversation. In the sixth plane the mind is localized between the eyebrows. The devotee comes face to face with God; only a thin glass-like partition, so to speak, keeps him separate from the Divine Person." *The Gospel of Ramakrishna,* Abhedananda revision, pp. 289-290.

[19] "(I renounce the personal God for the Absolute.)"—Akhilananda, *Spiritual Practices,* pp. 87-88. See *Meister Eckhart,* trans. by Raymond B. Blakney, Harper Torchbooks (New York: Harper & Row, 1941); Otto, *Mysticism East and West,* p. 198, p. 204; Suzuki, *Mysticism,* chap. i, pp. 11-33.

[20] For a complete description of Sri Ramakrishna's initiation into *sannyasa* by Tota Puri, his reasons for it, his feelings at the time, etc., see Saradananda, Part II, chap. xv. Note the following by Ghanananda: "In the non-dualistic discipline the aspirant adores and meditates on the Absolute beyond word and thought. In the strictly logical sense such meditation is difficult or rather impossible, for how can one meditate on That which is beyond mind? So the process involved is 'being' and 'becoming.' . . . The non-dualistic discipline is the most difficult of all spiritual practices." *Sri Ramakrishna,* p. 80. In view of the above statement, it is clear that since the *Advaita sadhana* is not simply a mental exercise at abstraction from the notion of plurality but involves an enormous transformation of the total mind and of the very ground of perception itself (see Satprakashananda, *Methods of Knowledge;* cf. Dignaga, *On Perception: Pramanasamuccaya,* trans. by Masaaki Hattori [Cambridge, Mass.: Harvard University Press, 1968]) in an "ontological leap," then all duality and its consequences should be renounced externally as well as internally.

'After the initiation my *guru* began to teach me the various conclusions of the Advaita Vedanta and asked me to withdraw the mind completely from all objects and dive into the Atman (self). But in spite of all my attempts I could not cross the realm of name and form, and bring my mind to the unconditioned state. I had no difficulty in withdrawing the mind from all objects except one, the all too familiar form of the Blissful Mother—radiant and of the essence of Pure Consciousness—which appeared before me as a living reality preventing me from passing beyond the realm of name and form. Again and again I tried to concentrate my mind upon the teachings of Advaita (non-dualism), but every time the Mother's form stood in my way. In despair I said to the *guru,* "It is hopeless. I cannot raise my mind to the unconditioned state and come face to face with the Atman (Self)." He grew excited and sharply said, "What! You can't do it! But you have to." He cast his eyes round, and, finding a piece of glass, took it up; then, pressing the point between my eyebrows, he said, "Concentrate the mind on this point!" Then with a stern determination I again sat to meditate and as soon as the gracious form of the Divine Mother appeared before me, I used my power of discrimination as a sword and with it severed her form in two. There remained no more obstruction to my mind, which at once soared beyond the relative plane, and I was lost in *samadhi* (superconsciousness)!'[21]

Swami Ghanananda comments:

Thus Sri Ramakrishna passed into the unfathomable depths of the *nirvikalpa samadhi* (Contentless Consciousness}. . . . Only existence remained. The soul lost itself in the Self. All idea of duality, of subject and object was effaced. Sri Ramakrishna realized Brahman (the Absolute).[22]

---

This is the reason that monastic vows are recommended as a preliminary qualification for Advaita realization in the Hindu tradition (see Ananda, *Spiritual Practice,* p. 83). It is noteworthy that complete renunciation was also a prerequisite for *Nirvana* in pristine Buddhism; so much so that Buddha institutionalized *sannyasa* in India (the *Sangha*). This institution was then reabsorbed by Hinduism in the form of monastic orders, such as the Puri Order to which Sri Ramakrishna's *guru* belonged. According to Theravada Buddhism, monastic life was superior to household life. But Buddhist as well as Brahmanical traditions also make it clear that an ascetic mode of life or *sannyasa* is not indispensable for attaining Nirvana or realizing the unity of Atman and Brahman. Thus most of the Upanishadic teachers like King Janaka, Yajnavalkya, etc., were married and lived a householder's life. To be sure, they were free from attachment: so is the case in the Mahayana. The *bodhisattvas* need not be monks. Anyone can follow the career of a *bodhisattva* and live in society. The *Vimalakirtinirdesa* makes this clear.

[21] Ghanananda, pp. 82-83.
[22] *Ibid.,* pp. 83-84.

To the astonishment of Tota Puri, his young disciple was able to realize *Nirguna Brahman* in the short period of one day, while he had spent forty years to attain this realization. Sri Ramakrishna remained absorbed in *nirvikalpa samadhi* for three days and nights consecutively, after which his teacher brought him down to normal consciousness by repetition of the appropriate *mantra,* or sound-symbol of the Absolute.

## TOTA PURI'S TRANSFORMATION

### Reliance on Personal Effort

An interesting incident took place with respect to the spiritual development of Tota Puri himself as a result of his encounter with Sri Ramakrishna. As a staunch Advaitin, he favored personal effort over grace, and regarded Sri Ramakrishna's devotion to Divine Mother with a somewhat contemptuous amusement.

> He cared nothing for Mother Kali and her Maya, her divine play. To him, the image in the Kali Temple was just an image; and Ramakrishna was a victim of gross superstition who had somehow mysteriously managed to make great spiritual progress in spite of it. However, Tota did not risk hurting the young man's feelings by saying any of this; for he felt sure Ramakrishna would cast aside his superstitions as soon as he began to practice the non-dualistic *sadhana*.[23]

At their first meeting, when Tota Puri inquired of Sri Ramakrishna if he wished to practice the Advaita Vedanta *sadhana,* for he seemed well qualified to the wandering monk, Sri Ramakrishna replied, "Wait, I'll ask my Mother. It all depends on Her." He returned a little later in a semiconscious state and beaming with joy. He told Tota Puri that Divine Mother had instructed him, "Go and learn—it was to teach you that the monk came here."[24]

23 Isherwood, p. 117.

24 *Ibid.,* p. 116. Saradananda provides an insight to Sri Ramakrishna's motivation to practice Advaita Vedanta after having realized a state of saintly perfection in *bhavasamadhi* as a worshipper of the personal God in various forms. "It is the nature of the devotee that he never tries to realize the states of liberation, . . . and Nirvana, the bodilessness. He always tries to enjoy the glory of the various forms and noble qualities of God with the help of particular devotional moods. [e.g.,] . . . 'I don't want to become sugar, but want to taste it.' . . . Therefore, the Master's effort

*Significance of Tota Puri's Illness*

But Sri Ramakrishna did not cast aside his devotion to Divine Mother and other forms of personal God after his experience of *nirvikalpa samadhi;* rather it was the teacher who was changed. The incident in question took place at the end of Tota Puri's long stay at Dakshineswar—he had remained eleven months instead of his intended three days out of deep spiritual fellowship with Sri Ramakrishna. Unaccustomed to the climate and water of Bengal, Tota Puri developed a severe attack of blood dysentery. He had always been a man of perfect health, so this illness was a new and troubling experience for him. He grew weaker every day. He could no longer meditate nor maintain his mind in *samadhi,* as it would always return to the pain in the intestines. Finally, in disgust for the body which he felt had already served its purpose,[25] i.e., the realization of supreme knowledge of Brahman, he determined to commit it to the river Ganges.[26] He fixed his mind on Brahman, and slowly entered the river at dead of night. But, as Saradananda relates,

> Tota almost reached the other bank but could not get water, deep enough for drowning himself in. . . . Tota was surprised and thought, 'What strange divine Maya is this? Tonight there is not sufficient water in the river even to drown oneself! What strange unheard-of play of God?'

to attain the non-dual state of consciousness beyond all devotional moods may appear to be unnatural to many. But we should remember before we think thus that the Master was not now capable of taking the initiative in doing anything. The child of the divine Mother as the Master was, he now depended entirely and placed full reliance on Her and felt highly delighted in being moved about and guided by Her any way at any time. The divine Mother, on Her part, took upon Herself all his responsibility. . . . The Master launched on practicing the non-dual mood at the hint of the divine Mother" (pp. 249-250).

[25] See Shankaracharya's *Vivekachudamani,* sls. 3 and 4.

[26] According to the Hindu tradition, in which suicide is condemned, this is not considered an act of culpable suicide, for Tota Puri had realized his identity with the Absolute, or Oversoul, so that from his perspective he was not dying, but merely discarding his body. See *Bhagavad-Gita* 2:12-30, esp. 16, 17, 20 and 22. Sri Ramakrishna had the following to say about suicide: "Suicide is a heinous sin, undoubtedly. A man who kills himself must return again and again to this world and suffer its agony. But I don't call it suicide if a person leaves his body after having the vision of God. There is no harm in giving up one's body that way. After attaining knowledge some people give up their bodies. After the gold image has been cast in the clay mould, you may either preserve the mould or break it." *The Gospel of Ramakrishna,* trans. by Nikhilananda, p. 164.

And immediately some one as it were from within pulled off the veil over his intellect. Tota's mind was dazzled by a bright light and he saw 'Mother, Mother, Mother; Mother, the origin of the universe, Mother, the unthinkable Power; Mother in land and Mother in water; the body is Mother, and the mind is Mother; illness is Mother, and health is Mother; knowledge is Mother, and ignorance is Mother; life is Mother, and death is Mother; everything I see, hear, think or imagine is Mother! She makes "nay" of "yes" and "yes" of "nay"! As long as one is in the body one has no power to be free from Her influence, no, not even to die, till She wills! It is that Mother again who is also beyond body, mind and intellect—the Mother, the supreme "fourth," devoid of all attributes. That One whom Tota has so long been worshipping as Brahman . . . was this very Mother! Siva and Sakti in One who was ever existing. . . .

Wading his way through the water in the same manner in which he had gone, Tota began to return, with his heart full of devotion directly experiencing at that dead of night the unthinkable, unmanifest and all-pervading form of the Mother of the universe; all the quarters of the heavens reverberating with the profound cries of 'Mother' having at the same time completely offered himself as an oblation to Her feet. Though there was pain in the body there was now no feeling of it. His heart was now beside itself with an unprecedented bliss. . . .[27]

When morning came Sri Ramakrishna found his teacher an altogether different man. He was smiling blissfully, and his illness had vanished. He told Sri Ramakrishna that the disease had acted as a friend to him.

Tota . . . described slowly all the events of the night. ' . . . I had the vision of the Mother of the universe last night and am freed from the disease by Her grace. Ah! how ignorant I was so long! Well, please persuade your Mother now and allow me to leave this place. . . .' The Master said smilingly, 'Well! you did not accept the Mother before and argued with me saying that Sakti was unreal! But you have now seen Her yourself and direct experience has got the better of your arguments. She has convinced me already of the fact that just as fire and its burning power are not different, so, Brahman and the power of Brahman are not different, but one and the same.'[28]

Tota Puri's experience, which parallels those of Sri Ramakrishna, is significant in that it indicates a cardinal principle of Mahayana Buddhism—especially in such scriptures as the *Prajnaparamita*,

[27] Saradananda, p. 491.
[28] *Ibid.,* p. 492.

*Avatamsaka, Madhyamika karikas, Srimalasinhanada, Mahavairocana, Vajrasekhara,* and others—that one must go beyond Nirvana itself to reach Nirvana; that the world and Nirvana are not different, but only appear so to the untrained mind.[29] Tota Puri was falling prey to the obstacle referred to in these Mahayana texts: he refused to concede the existence of the world and its Creator because they did not exist in his superconscious experience of *nirvikalpa samadhi.* According to Nagarjuna, he did not sunyatize *sunyata* itself.[30]

## SRI RAMAKRISHNA AS AN ADVAITIN

### The State of His Mind

The state of Sri Ramakrishna's mind subsequent to his experience of Advaita Vedanta is described by his biographers in the following manner, quoting his own narration of the episode:

[29] " 'Therefore, Sariputra, the world of beings is not one thing, and the Dharma-body another. The world of beings is just the Dharma-body, the Dharma-body is just the world of beings. Objectively they are not two. The distinction lies in the words only.' " From the *Ratnagotravibhaga Sutra,* as quoted in *Buddhist Texts through the Ages,* ed. by Conze, p. 182.

[30] See Nagarjuna's *Mula madhyamika karikas* 24:7-8 and 24:18 as follows: "We declare that law of *pratityasamutpada* to be voidness *(sunyata).* . . . It is none other than the middle path *(madhyama-pratipad)."* *Sunyata* or voidness is "the fountainhead of all Mahayana philosophies and practical disciplines." D. T. Suzuki, *On Indian Mahayana Buddhism,* chap. iii, "On Emptiness," p. 109. Originating in the *Prajnaparamita* scriptural corpus ca. 200 B.C., it flowered ca. the second century A.D. in Nagarjuna's *Madhyamika karikas.* See Frederick J. Streng, *Emptiness: A Study in Religious Meaning* (Nashville, Tenn.: Abingdon Press, 1967); Conze, *Buddhist Thought in India,* pp. 242-249; Conze, *Thirty Years of Buddhist Studies* (London: Bruno Cassirer, 1967), "The Development of Prajnaparamita Thought," pp. 123-147; *Buddhist Wisdom Books,* containing the Diamond Sutra and the Heart Sutra, trans. by Edward Conze (London: Allen & Unwin, 1958); and especially T. Murti, *The Central Philosophy of Buddhism.* Nagarjuna developed a systematic exposition of the nature of *sunyata* found in the *Prajnaparamita.* This was a methodology rather than a new doctrine: he showed that propositions are refuted by themselves as being self-contradictory, not by other propositions; that any conceptual grasp of reality must depend on its opposite and thereby be annulled; and that even *sunyata* has to be negated by itself. Although he used this negational dialectic to demonstrate *sunyata,* he emphasized the value of meditation to understand it. "The final bliss consists in the cessation of all thoughts in the quiescence of pluralities." From chap. xxv of the *Madhyamika karikas,* trans. by Streng, *Emptiness,* Appendix.

After his *guru* had left Dakshineswar, Sri Ramakrishna was determined to remain in a state of absolute identity with Brahman. He accordingly meditated and entered into *nirvikalpa samadhi* again. Referring to this period of his life, he used to say, 'For six months at a stretch I remained in that state whence ordinary men can never return—the body falling off after twenty-one days like a sear leaf. I was not conscious of day and night; flies would enter my mouth and nostrils just as they do in a dead body, but I did not feel them; the hair became matted with accretions of dust. There was no chance for the body to survive, and it would certainly have perished but for the kind ministrations of a monk who was present at Dakshineswar at the time. He realized the state of my mind and also understood that this body must be kept alive at any cost, since it was to be of immense good to the world. He therefore busied himself in preserving this body. He would bring food regularly to me and try in various ways to bring my mind down to the consciousness of the relative world, even by beating me with a stick. As soon as he found me to be a little conscious, he would press some food into my mouth, only a bit of which reached the stomach; and there were days in which all his efforts would be in vain. Six months passed in this way. At last I received the Mother's command, "Remain on the threshold of relative consciousness *(bhavamukha)* for the sake of humanity." Then I was laid up with a terrible attack of dysentery; an excruciating pain in the stomach tortured me day and night; it went on for six months. Thus only did the mind gradually come down to a lower level and to consciousness of the body. I became a normal man; but before that at the slightest opportunity the mind would take a transcendental flight and merge in the *nirvikalpa samadhi.'* . . .

Sri Ramakrishna . . . had thus gone through the whole range of Hindu disciplines in the course of twelve years, from his eighteenth year to his thirtieth. He had become a Paramahamsa.[31]

## His Knowledge of Oneness

As a result of Sri Ramakrishna's experience of non-duality, whereby he merged his own existence with that of the Absolute and no longer retained a separate identity, he realized his oneness with the universe. He had the knowledge that his existence was inseparable from the existence of all living creation. Not only was he incapable of injuring others, but he went through a period when he actually felt any injury around him on his own person. Consequently, he

[31] Ghanananda, pp. 85-87.

verified empirically another cardinal tenet stressed both by Buddha[32] and his contemporary, Mahavir,[33] (the founder of Jainism), the principle of *ahimsa* or non-injury.

One day, hard stones were thrown down on green blades of grass. Sri Ramakrishna, without knowing what was going on, called out, 'Oh my, they are beating me, they are pressing my heart, they are crushing my chest!' On inquiry it was found that some people were treating the tender blades of growing grass ruthlessly. When they desisted, his pain stopped. Once, at a distance, out of sight of Sri Ramakrishna and unknown to him, a bullock was severely beaten. Scars of assault appeared on the back of Sri Ramakrishna without his knowing the cause. Another time two boatmen were quarreling and came to blows. Sri Ramakrishna felt those blows on his own person. . . . When a man realizes the Oneness of life and existence, then alone does he feel thus. Is not this wonderful love?[34]

*Comparison with Buddhology*

It can reasonably be inferred from these experiences of Sri Ramakrishna that the Buddha himself manifested such universal love because of his own experience of *Nirvana*. This was later translated in Mahayana Buddhism to the *bodhisattva* motif, in which individual *arahantship*[35] was replaced by the principle of universal salvation. It was no longer enough to seek salvation for oneself; a new imperative arose to seek salvation for all mankind. At its apex the *bodhisattva* ideal[36] and the Hindu concept of *avatar*[37] (incarnation

[32] "In all of the Indian stories about Buddha the one central note of that whole life is kept up—sacrifice for others." Vivekananda, *Thoughts on the Gita* (Mayavati, Almora, Himalayas: Advaita Ashrama, 1967), p. 20.

[33] See *Jaina Sutras,* trans. by Hermann Jacobi (2 vols.; New York: Dover Publications, 1968). "Sri Ramakrishna had great reverence for the Tirthankaras, who founded Jainism. In his room at Dakshineswar there was a small statue of Tirthankara Mahavira, before which incense was burnt morning and evening. But he was never heard to speak of the Tirthankaras as Incarnations of God." Ghanananda, p. 93.

[34] Akhilananda, *Sri Ramakrishna and Modern Psychology,* pp. 27-28. Cf. *Saradananda,* p. 266.

[35] *The Path of Purification (Visuddhimagga) of Bhadantacariya Buddhaghosa,* trans. by Bhikku Nyanamoli (2d ed.; Colombo, Ceylon: A. Semage, 1964) deals with this.

[36] See Robinson, *Buddhist Religion,* chap. iii, "The Bodhisattva Path," pp. 54-70. He presents an excellent condensation of the development of the *bodhisattva* ideal

of God) become practically indistinguishable. Sri Ramakrishna's own attitude toward the Buddha, in this connection, is expressed in the following passage:

> Sri Ramakrishna looked upon the Buddha as an Incarnation of God, thus sharing the general notion of the Hindus regarding that Teacher. He used to offer him his sincere devotion and worship, and believed that it was the Lord Buddha's personality that was still worshipped in the holy triad at the Temple of Jagannath. On a certain occasion he remarked, 'There is not the least doubt about the Lord Buddha's being an Incarnation. There is no difference between his doctrines and those of the Vedic *jnanakanda.*' When told that the Buddha was called an atheist, Sri Ramakrishna said, 'Why atheist? He was no atheist—only he could not speak out his realizations. Do you know what "Buddha" means? To become one with "Bodha," the Supreme Intelligence, through deep meditation, to become Pure Intelligence itself.'[38]

through the various Mahayana *sutras,* describing the seven and ten *bodhisattva* stages *(bhumis),* the six perfections *(paramitas)* which are the essential practices of the *bodhisattva* career, and the various *lokas* or Buddha-lands which characterize some scriptural forms. A most complete account of the stages and virtues of a *bodhisattva* is to be found in Har Dayal, *The Bodhisattva Doctrine in Buddhist Sanscrit Literature* (Delhi: Motilal Banarsidass, 1970).

[37] See Akhilananda, *Hindu View of Christ,* chap. i, "Christ, an Incarnation," pp. 15-44. Akhilananda clarifies the concept of *avatar* for the Western reader. Cf. the following passage by Vivekananda: "There are a great many similarities in the teachings of the New Testament and the Gita. . . . in the words of Krishna himself: 'Whenever virtue subsides and irreligion prevails, I come down. Again and again I come. Therefore, whenever thou seest a great soul struggling to uplift mankind, know that I am come, and worship. . . .' (*Gita,* IV: 8; X:41). At the same time, if he comes as Jesus or as Buddha, why is there so much schism? The preachings must be followed! A Hindu devotee would say: these are the great souls; they are already free. . . . They come again and again, take a human embodiment and help mankind. They know from their childhood what they are and what they come for. . . . They do not come through bondage like we do. . . . They come out of their own free will, and cannot help having tremendous spiritual power. We cannot resist it. . . . If He comes to me, I can only recognise Him if He takes a human form. He is everywhere, but do we see Him? We can only see Him if He takes the limitation of man." *Thoughts on the Gita,* pp. 28-30.

[38] Ghanananda, pp. 92-93. The word "doctrine" may be an inappropriate translation here. Cf. Jagadananda's translation of the same passage which reads: "There is no difference between the faith founded by him [Buddha] and the Vedic path of knowledge." Saradananda, p. 301. For an overview of the historical interaction and *mélange* between Hinduism and Buddhism in India, see R. R. Diwakar, *Bhagawan Buddha,* Bhavan's Book University (Chaupatty, Bombay: Bharatiya Vidya Bhavan,

1967), Appendix I, "Hinduism and Buddhism," pp. 146-158. Cf. the following statement by Swami Vivekananda about Buddha with that of Sri Ramakrishna: "He was
the only man who was bereft of all motive power. There were other great men who
all said, they were the Incarnations of God Himself, and that those who would
believe in them would go to heaven. But what did Buddha say with his dying breath?
'None can help you; help yourself; work out your own salvation.' He said about
himself, 'Buddha is the name of infinite knowledge, infinite as the sky; I, Gautama,
have reached that state; you will all reach that too if you struggle for it.' Bereft of all
motive power, he did not want to go to heaven, did not want money; he gave up his
throne and everything else and went about begging his bread through the streets of
India, preaching for the good of men and animals with a heart as wide as the ocean.
He was the only man who was ever ready to give up his life for animals, to stop a
sacrifice. He once said to a king, 'If the sacrifice of a lamb helps you to go to heaven,
sacrificing a man will help you better; so sacrifice me.' The king was astonished. And
yet this man was without any motive power. He stands as the perfection of the active
type [*karma yogi*], and the very height to which he attained shows that through the
power of work we can also attain to the highest spirituality." *Works,* IV, 136. "All
the prophets of the world, except Buddha, had external motives to move them to
unselfish action. The prophets of the world, with this single exception, may be divided into two groups, one holding that they are Incarnations of God come down on
earth, and the other holding that they are Messengers from God; and both draw
their impetus for work from outside and expect reward from outside, however highly
spiritual may be the language they use. But Buddha is the only prophet who said: 'I
do not care to know your various theories about God. What is the use of discussing
all the subtle doctrines about the soul? Do good and be good, and this will take you
to freedom and to whatever truth there is.' He was, in the conduct of his life, absolutely without personal motives; and what man worked more than he? . . . This
great philosopher preached the highest philosophy, and yet had the deepest sympathy for the lowest of animals and never put forth any claims for himself. He is the
ideal karma-yogi. . . . He is the greatest reformer the world has seen. He was the first
who dared to say: 'Believe not because some old manuscripts are quoted; believe not
because it is your national belief, because you have been made to believe it from your
childhood; but reason it all out, and after you have analysed it and found out that it
will do good to one and all, then believe it, live up to it, and help others to live up to
it.'" "The Ideal of Karma-Yoga," *Karma-Yoga and Bhakti-Yoga* (rev. ed.), pp.
110-112.

# CHAPTER V

# Verification of God in Islam

## SRI RAMAKRISHNA'S TRANSITION TO THE PRACTICE OF ISLAM

### His Temperament and Attitude of Mind

Within a very brief period after Sri Ramakrishna descended from his six months' stay in *nirvikalpa samadhi,* he undertook the practice of Islamic mysticism. It was the first time he had ventured outside the boundaries of his Hindu heritage in its manifold aspects, and as such, it represented a radical departure from his traditional Hindu thought-forms and behavioral patterns. For the duration of his worship of God as Allah, the Compassionate Ruler of the Universe, Sri Ramakrishna's immersion in the Muslim attitude was so complete that he underwent a total transformation of his mental structure: he could no longer, in fact, call on the Hindu deities which had become part of his spiritual repertoire through direct experience. This function of his temperament reflected a peculiar facet of Sri Ramakrishna's personality. His devotion to truth, as has been shown, was so dynamic that he could not half-heartedly occupy himself with any enterprise, whether in the spiritual, mental or material universe. Wherever his mind would go, his body and actions would necessarily follow.[1] His personality was wholly integrated, unified. Thus he could not undertake the Islamic experiment without attempting to become fully a Muslim.

A question may be raised with respect to Sri Ramakrishna's adoption of Islamic spiritual practices in order to see God as Allah. Was it because of any dissatisfaction with the religion in which he was born that he did so? Quite the contrary: he had realized the highest goal of Hinduism in his experience of identity with the Absolute: "*Aham Brahmasmi.*"[2] He was fully convinced of the statements in the Vedas, Upanishads, Puranas, Tantras and other Hindu scriptures concerning the nature of Brahman and its manifestations

[1] See Saradananda, p. 170, pp. 360-362; and note the following: "The Master entered upon his life of spiritual practices with the rare possessions of an extraordinary wonderful memory, love of truth and of putting ideas into practice as the very bases of his sadhanas. . . . In the beginning of his sadhana, as soon as the Master discriminated between the real and the unreal and threw into the Ganga a few coins along with lumps of earth, repeating 'rupee-earth, earth-rupee,' the attachment to gold, which spreads its influence down to the very bottom of the human heart, became eradicated for ever from his mind; no sooner had he cleaned with his own hands those abominably filthy places, at whose contamination people could not rest satisfied without a bath, than his mind gave up the egoism due to his Brahmana birth and he became convinced for ever that he was in no way superior to those persons who were regarded in society as untouchables; as soon as he was convinced that he was a child of the divine Mother and 'all the women of the world were parts of Her,' it became impossible for him to look upon any woman as other than the divine Mother Herself, and to have the ordinary conjugal relationship with any. When one ponders these instances one clearly feels that the Master could not have achieved those results if he had not had an extraordinary power of understanding ideas and making them practical" (*ibid.,* p. 211).

[2] *Brihadaranyaka Upanishad,* I, iv, 10. For Shankara's commentary on this sloka, see *The Brhadaranyaka Upanishad,* with the commentary of Sri Sankaracarya, trans. by Swami Madhavananda (4th ed.; Calcutta: Advaita Ashrama, 1965), pp. 145-174. Cf. Shankara's *Vakyavritti,* sl. 49. The distinction between Brahman and Ishvara must be kept clearly in mind, for while the soul can realize its identity with the Absolute or Brahman, it can never do so with respect to the Creator or personal God. (See Vivekananda, "The Philosophy of Ishvara," *Karma-Yoga and Bhakti-Yoga,* pp. 124-131 for further clarification of this point.) Examples of this can be found in the experiences and mystical testimony of Rumi (see A.J. Arberry, *Discourses of Rumi* [London: John Murray, 1961]), al-Hallaj and others in the Sufi tradition; St. John of the Cross; St. Dionysius, Ruysbroeck and Meister Eckhart in the Christian tradition, as well as Plotinus *(The Enneads,* trans. by Stephen MacKenna, rev. by B. S. Page [London: Faber and Faber, 1962]; J. M. Rist, *Plotinus: The Road to Reality* [Cambridge, England: The University Press, 1967]). Shankara and Swami Vivekananda are the foremost examples in Hinduism.

in various aspects because he had verified these statements empirically. It is even reported by his foremost biographer that his experiences went beyond those recorded in the Hindu scriptures.[3] But again reference is made to that mystery of his personality, unprecedented in mystical history, which spurred him on to taste God in other ways. For twelve years he had practiced Hindu *sadhana* with an intensity and comprehensiveness unimaginable to the ordinary mind. Hinduism had satisfied him. Now with the unrestrained catholicity and inclusiveness gained from soaring beyond the finite realm for six months in the non-dual state of *nirvikalpa samadhi*,[4] realizing the oneness of existence in his own experience, he left far behind the old restrictions of caste, creed, form, and ceremony of the traditional Hinduism he had been practicing. While Sri Ramakrishna had broken the bonds of sectarianism of Hinduism *vis-à-vis* Islam and other world religions, and could now embrace Islam, he never renounced Hinduism itself. It was only suspended for a time.

*Social Implications*

It is evident from the foregoing that the rivalry, misunderstanding, discord, and violence which have at times characterized Moslem-Hindu relations on both sides had no place in the mentality of Sri Ramakrishna. His was an attitude of all-inclusive brotherhood on the social level and of free scientific inquiry in the field of religious experience. His attitude toward the Islamic world generally is reflected in the following statement of his disciple-successor, Swami Vivekananda:

[3] Saradananda, p. 242. Although the scope of his spiritual realizations extended beyond the scriptures *(sastras),* they never contradicted them: "Although the Master was almost wholly what we mean by the word 'illiterate,' a study of his life reveals how he maintained the authority of the scriptures all his life. The sadhanas which he undertook . . . even before he was initiated by any spiritual teacher, were all in accordance with the Sastras and never contradicted them. . . . The books that are called the Sastras are nothing but the records of the experiences of hearts like that of the Master, the results of their efforts for the realization of the Truth" *(ibid.,* p. 236; cf. pp. 243-244).

[4] Sri Ramakrishna realized that "non-duality was the ultimate aim of all kinds of sadhanas. For, having performed sadhanas according to the teachings of all the main religious denominations prevalent in Bharata, he had already been convinced that they all took the aspirants towards the non-dual plane. Asked about the non-dual state, he, therefore, said to us over and over again, 'It is the finale, my child, the acme, which comes of itself in the life of all aspirants, as ultimate development of

Mohammed was the prophet of equality, of the brotherhood of man.
. . . each Prophet, each Messenger, has a particular message. . . .

Mohammed by his life showed that amongst Mohammedans there
should be perfect equality and brotherhood. There was no question of
race, caste, creed, colour, or sex. The Sultan of Turkey may buy a Negro
from the mart of Africa, and bring him in chains to Turkey; but should
he become a Mohammedan and have sufficient merit and abilities, he
might even marry the daughter of the Sultan. Compare this with the way
in which the Negroes and the American Indians are treated in this country! And what do Hindus do? If one of your missionaries chance to
touch the food of an orthodox person, he would throw it away. Notwithstanding our grand philosophy, you note our weakness in practice; but
there you see the greatness of the Mohammedan . . ., showing itself in
equality, . . .[5]

. . . practical Advaitism, which looks upon and behaves to all mankind as
one's own soul, is yet to be developed among the Hindus universally.

On the other hand, our experience is that if ever the followers of any
religion approached to this equality in an appreciable degree in the plane
of practical workaday life . . . it is those of Islam and Islam alone.

Therefore we are firmly persuaded that without the help of practical
Islam, theories of Vedantism, however fine and wonderful they may be,
are entirely valueless to the vast mass of mankind. . . .

For our own motherland a junction of the two great systems, Hinduism and Islam—Vedanta brain and Islam body—is the only hope.[6]

## SRI RAMAKRISHNA'S ISLAMIC EXPERIENCE

### His Teacher

Sri Ramakrishna's teacher in Islamic devotion was a Sufi[7] mystic

---

their love of God. Know it to be the last word of all faiths and faiths are paths (and
not the goal).' Having thus had the direct experience of non-duality, the Master's
mind was filled with unbounded catholicity. He had now an extraordinary sympathy
with all the religious communities which taught that the aim of human life was the
realization of God. But, he did not realize at first that the said catholicity and sympathy were his discoveries and that no aspirant, not even the foremost of them, in the
past could attain them as fully as he" (*ibid.,* pp. 261-263).

[5] *Works,* IV, 133-134.

[6] *Works,* VI, 375-376. From a letter written to a Muslim gentleman of Naini Tal,
dated June 10, 1898. Cf. the five chapters on "Practical Vedanta" in *Works,* II,
289-356; Akhilananda, *Modern Problems,* "Practical Vedanta," pp. 129-134. In this
connection, also see Vivekananda, *Lectures from Colombo to Almora* (Calcutta:
Advaita Ashrama, 1963).

[7] While Sufism represented Sri Ramakrishna's point of contact with the Islamic

named Govinda Rai, who had found the hospitality of the Kali temple at Dakshineswar suitable to his spiritual practices and had made it his temporary home. Although he had been born a Hindu of the Kshatriya caste, Govinda Rai had studied various religions in his search after God and had finally found in the Islamic tradition and its community a combination of religious zeal and social liberality which most satisfied his temperament. It was probable that he was learned in Persian and Arabic, and he occupied himself ardently with reading the Qur'an. He had been formally initiated, practiced devotional exercises day and night like the Dervishes, and gave every indication of intense love of Allah.[8]

### Nature of His Islamic Practices and Spiritual Experience

His devotion attracted Sri Ramakrishna, and he felt the spontaneous urge to worship Allah. Accordingly he sought initiation from the Sufi in his tradition, and Govinda Rai complied gladly. Sri Ramakrishna thus became a Muslim, and set his mind and heart completely in the direction of Allah. As his biographers recount:

'I devoutly repeated the name of Allah, wore a cloth like the Arab Moslems, said their prayers five times daily and felt disinclined even to see images of the Hindu gods and goddesses, much less worship them—for the Hindu way of thinking had disappeared altogether from my mind. I spent three days in that mood, and I had the full realization of the sadhana of their faith.' Ramakrishna also said that he had had a vision of a shining impressive personage with a long beard. This figure merged into Ishwara, and Ishwara then merged into Brahman.

Hriday told how, while Ramakrishna was practising the sadhana of Islam, he wanted to eat Moslem food. Mathur begged him not to, because this would include beef. So, as a compromise, a Moslem cook was brought to instruct a Hindu cook how to prepare food in the Moslem manner—more or less. At this time, Ramakrishna never once entered the temple courtyard. He left his own room and slept in the Kuthi.[9]

---

tradition, it is recognized that, while Sufism has affected orthodox Islam by introducing into it the mystical element, it by no means encompasses the totality of normative Islam. Cf. Idries Shah, *The Sufis,* with an Introduction by Robert Graves, Anchor Books (Garden City, N. Y.: Doubleday, 1971).

[8] Saradananda, p. 263.

[9] Isherwood, p. 124.

## ANALYSIS OF SRI RAMAKRISHNA'S ISLAMIC REALIZATIONS

*Threefold Aspect*

It will be noted that a distinctive characteristic of Sri Ramakrishna's Islamic religious experiment was that in it he had the three different types of mystical experiences: personal with form, personal without form, and impersonal. According to Akhilananda:

> Sri Ramakrishna harmonizes the three apparent distinct attitudes and interpretations of God as the different aspects of the same reality: 1) bodily and visible with attributes; 2) invisible yet with qualities and attributes (as the Personalists of America, some Hindus and Mohammedans, and others believe); 3) invisible and beyond qualities and attributes. These aspects of the Reality can be realized by the devotees and seekers of truth in evolutionary stages through spiritual discipline.[10]

*First Aspect: Personal with Form*

It is a matter for speculation only whether the "radiant Person with long beard and grave appearance[11] was the Prophet Muhammad himself, one of his Companions, or a great Sufi saint who had chosen to maintain his separate identity from Allah in a subtle body in order to continue as an instrument of salvation for others, much like the *bodhisattvas,* the Christian saints, or the Sikh Gurus.[12]

*Second Aspect: Personal Without Form*

Regarding Sri Ramakrishna's second experience, that of Allah as Ishvara or *Saguna Brahman,* the reference here is to the formless aspect of God, yet with name, qualities and attributes as contrasted with *Nirguna Brahman,* or the Unconditioned Absolute beyond

---

[10] Akhilananda, *Hindu Psychology,* p. 117.

[11] *Life of Sri Ramakrishna,* p. 208.

[12] "Of the Sikh Gurus Sri Ramakrishna used to say, 'They are all incarnations of the saintly King Janaka. I have heard it said by the Sikhs that just before attaining liberation he was possessed with the idea of doing good to the world. He was therefore born successively as the ten Gurus of the Sikhs, and after founding the Sikh religion was united for ever with the Supreme Brahman. There is no reason to disbelieve this.' " Ghanananda, p. 93. See *Selections from the Sacred Writings of the Sikhs,* trans. by Trilochan Singh *et al.,* rev. by George S. Fraser, UNESCO Collection of Representative Works: Indian Series (London: Allen & Unwin, 1960).

qualification. It is this aspect of God that is predominantly worshipped among Muslims, as well as in the Jewish and Protestant traditions. Akhilananda clarifies this concept in the following statement:

> One can also take God with qualities and attributes yet not with bodily form (*saguna* and *nirakara*). There are many persons in India and the West who prefer a personal aspect of God yet they do not care to think of Him with a physical form. They believe that God has attributes and qualities like 'consciousness' and 'love' without form. We can specially mention the personalistic schools of philosophy in America and Europe, of which the late Professor Bowne, Professor Brightman, Professor Hocking, and others are strong advocates, though they may differ in their interpretation of qualities and attributes. According to Professor Brightman: 'God is a Person supremely conscious, supremely valuable, and supremely creative, yet limited both by the free choices of other persons and by restrictions within his own nature.'[13]

### Third Aspect: Impersonal

COMPARISON WITH SUFI TRADITION

In the final phase of his superconscious experience in Islam, Sri Ramakrishna merged his identity with that of the Absolute, just as the Sufi mystics did who boldly declared, *"Ana 'l-Haqq,"* "I am the Truth."[14] Rumi illustrates this Sufi realization in the following passage:

> When a fly is plunged in honey, all the members of its body are re-

---

[13] *Hindu Psychology,* p. 116. Cf. Edgar S. Brightman, *The Problem of God* (New York: Abingdon Press, 1930), chap. vi, and *A Philosophy of Religion* (New York: Prentice-Hall, 1940), chaps. v-x. Also cf. the following: "It is Hocking's belief that the Idea, the apprehension of the Absolute in immediate human experience, is a partial comprehension of the concept of God. The Absolute of idealism is an aspect of the God of religion. Hocking states: 'I do not say that the Absolute is equivalent to God; I say that God, whatever else he may be, must needs also be the Absolute.' " Andrew J. Reck, "Hocking's Place in American Metaphysics," in *Philosophy, Religion and the Coming World Civilization, Essays in Honor of William Ernest Hocking,* ed. by Leroy S. Rouner (The Hague: Martinus Nijhoff, 1966), p. 39. See William Ernest Hocking, *The Meaning of God in Human Experience* (New Haven, Conn.: Yale University Press, 1912).

[14] A. J. Arberry, *Sufism: An Account of the Mystics of Islam* (London: Allen & Unwin, 1950), p. 59. See Nicholson, *The Mystics of Islam,* chap. vi, "The Unitive State," pp. 148-168.

duced to the same condition, and it does not move. Similarly the term *istighrag* (absorption in God) is applied to one who has no conscious existence or initiative or movement. Any action that proceeds from him is not his own. If he is still struggling in the water, or if he cries out, 'Oh, I am drowning,' he is not said to be in the state of absorption. This is what is signified by the words *Ana 'l-Haqq* 'I am God.' People imagine that it is a presumptuous claim, whereas it is really a presumptuous claim to say *Ana 'l-'abd* 'I am the slave of God'; and *Ana 'l-Haqq* 'I am God' is an expression of great humility. The man who says *Ana 'l-'abd* 'I am the slave of God' affirms two existences, his own and God's, but he that says *Ana 'l-Haqq* 'I am God' has made himself non-existent and has given himself up and says 'I am God,' *i.e.* 'I am naught, He is all: there is no being but God's.' This is the extreme of humility and self-abasement.[15]

LOVE AND THE KNOWLEDGE OF UNITY

It is noteworthy that while the Sufi can say with the Advaita Vedantist, *"Aham Brahmasmi,"* "I am the Absolute," the Sufi's path is, generally speaking, the path of love: "I am He whom I love, and He whom I love is I."[16] Here, devotion is directed to the formless God with attributes, and culminates in the final unitive experience. "That which I was I am no more, for 'I' and 'God' is a denial of the unity of God."[17] As Swami Vivekananda states,

We all begin with love for ourselves, and the unfair claims of the little self make even love selfish. At last, however, comes the full blaze of light, in which this little self is seen to have become one with the Infinite. Man himself is transfigured in the presence of this light of love, and he realizes at last the beautiful and inspiring truth that love, the lover, and the Beloved are one.[18]

[15] *Rumi, Poet and Mystic,* selections from his writings, trans. with introduction and notes by Reynold A. Nicholson (London: Allen & Unwin, 1950), p. 184. Cf. Meister Eckhart's words as quoted in D. T. Suzuki, *Mysticism: Christian and Buddhist* (New York: Macmillan, 1969), *p. 15.*

[16] Nicholson, *Studies in Islamic Mysticism* (Cambridge, England: The University Press, 1921), p. 80, quoting al-Hallaj. See Farid al-Din Attar, *Muslim Saints and Mystics,* trans. by A. J. Arberry (Chicago: University of Chicago Press, 1966).

[17] Nicholson, *The Mystics of Islam,* pp. 17-18, quoting Bayazid of Bistam and the commentary of his biographer. Nicholson draws the connection between the implications of this statement and the position of Vedanta.

[18] Vivekananda, Conclusion to *Bhakti-Yoga,* in *Karma-Yoga and Bhakti-Yoga* (rev. ed.), p. 208. Cf. the following refrain by Ibn al-'Arabi: "When my Beloved appears,/ With what eye do I see Him?/ With His eye, not with mine,/ For none sees Him except Himself." Nicholson, *The Mystics of Islam,* pp. 165-166.

# GOD OF ALL

Sri Ramakrishna had attained that love. Because of his knowledge of unity, he not only had love for God, but for man as well; for he actually saw God in man, and felt his identity with all. At the end of his life, when he was suffering from throat cancer, scarcely able to speak or swallow any food, he declared:

'I am now speaking and eating through so many mouths. I am the Soul of all individual souls. I have infinite mouths, infinite heads, infinite hands and feet. My pure form is spiritual. It is absolute Existence, Intelligence and Bliss condensed, as it were. It has neither birth nor death, neither sorrow, disease nor suffering. It is immortal and perfect. I see the indivisible Absolute Brahman (Sat-Chit-Ananda) within me as well as all around me. You are all like my own parts. The Infinite Brahman is manifesting Itself through so many human forms. Human bodies are like pillow-cases of different shapes and various colors, but the cotton wool of the internal Spirit is one.'[19]

This was the real basis of his liberality. It was the reason he could practice Islam and embrace the Muslim community. Accordingly, he advised his disciples,

'God is the internal ruler of all. . . . When you mix with other people, you should love them all, become absolutely one with them. Do not hate anyone. Do not recognize caste or creed. Do not say that this man believes in a Personal God, that man believes in an Impersonal God; this man worships God with form, that man worships God without form; this man is a Hindu, that one is a Christian or a Mohammedan. Saying this, do not condemn one another. Those distinctions exist because God has made different people understand Him in different ways. The difference lies in the nature of the individuals. Knowing this you will mix with all as closely as possible and love them as dearly as you can.'[20]

---

[19] *Gospel of Ramakrishna* (Abhedananda revision), pp. 421-422.

[20] *Ibid.*, pp. 344-345. It should not be concluded that because of Sri Ramakrishna's great sympathy for other religions and his virtuosity in practicing them he did not recognize their differences. " 'There is, as it were, a mountain of difference between them [Hindus and Muslims]; their thoughts and faiths, actions and behaviour have remained quite unintelligible to one another, in spite of their living together for so long a time.' " Saradananda, p. 265, quoting Sri Ramakrishna. Cf. M. Mujeeb, *The Indian Muslims* (London: Allen & Unwin, 1967). Saradananda expresses the hope that Sri Ramakrishna's practice of Islam may lay the basis for brotherly feeling between Hindus and Muslims, a spiritual brotherhood founded on the commonality of the Advaita Vedanta and Sufi religious experiences *(loc. cit.).*

## EFFECT ON HIS LATER LIFE

It will be noted that while Sri Ramakrishna practiced Islamic devotion for a period of only three days, his Islamic spiritual experiences exerted an abiding influence on his life and teaching career: he had Muslims among his disciples and devotees, he continued to venerate and worship Allah and his prophet in diverse ways and frequently referred to them in his conversations and teachings.[21]

---

Cf. Nirvedananda, p. 91; Isherwood, pp. 124-125. Also cf. Prince Muhammad Dara Shikuh, *Majma'-Ul-Bahrain* ("The Mingling of the Two Oceans"), ed. with trans. and notes by M. Mahfuz-ul-Haq, Bibliotheca India No. 146 (Calcutta: Asiatic Society of Bengal, 1929). The editor states in his Introduction that Shikuh's work, which was written in 1065 (A.H.), clearly expresses his view that "in the higher planes of the realization of Truth there is no essential difference between Hinduism and Islam" (p. 27).

[21] *Sayings of Sri Ramakrishna* and *Gospel of Sri Ramakrishna,* Nikhilananda translation.

# CHAPTER VI

# Verification of God in Christianity

## THE BASIS FOR SRI RAMAKRISHNA'S CHRISTIAN EXPERIENCE

### His Attitude toward Christ's Incarnation

Just as Sri Ramakrishna could never affirm *"la ilha illa 'llah Muhammadur rasulu 'llah"* when he practiced Islam and mean thereby that Allah was the only name of God, or Muhammad his only prophet,[1] so when he practiced Christianity some eight years later he never felt it necessary to assent to the uniqueness of Christ's incarnation, but prayed only for his vision. He shared the common belief among Hindus that the Lord incarnates himself to elevate

[1] See Wilfred Cantwell Smith, *The Faith of Other Men,* Mentor Books (New York: New American Library, 1963), chap. iv, "Muslims," pp. 50-62. Smith takes the position that the Muslim community's "symbol of personal submission to the will of God," the repetition of which is the way formally to become a Muslim, is not so much an assertion of exclusivity as one of ultimate monotheism: "There is no god but God, and Muhammad is his apostle." Smith states, "The Muslims do not themselves call this formula a creed. They call it, rather a 'witness' " (p. 54). The statement, Smith points out, represents an announcement of a spiritual fact, a point of presumed knowledge about the transcendental Creator, rather than a "set of true-or-false propositions" which "become the foreground for intellectual belief" (p. 55). "In the Islamic case, as in the Jewish, the word of God is fundamentally an impera-

man when society is at an ebb,[2] and worshipped Christ accordingly. Thus Sri Ramakrishna fully accepted Jesus as Incarnation of God because this concept already formed an integral part of his own tradition.[3] In this regard he stated,

The Avatara (Incarnation) is always one and the same. Having plunged into the ocean of life, the one God rises up at one point and is

tive. . . . The proclamation of God's oneness is . . . a command to worship Him alone" (p. 56). "It meant in pagan Arabia when it was first proclaimed, a rejection of polytheism and idolatry. . . . From that day to this, Islam has been uncompromising in its doctrine of monotheism, and its insistence on transcendence" (pp. 56-57). "At a subtler level . . . the doctrine has meant at times . . . a rejection of human tyranny. God alone is to be . . . served" (p. 57). Cf. G. Ernest Wright, *The Old Testament and Theology,* chap. iv, pp. 112-113. At another level, one stressed by the Sufis (see al-Ghazali's *'Ihya),* as Smith points out, "to worship God alone is to turn aside from false gods not only in the concrete sense of idols and religious polytheism, but also in the subtler sense of turning aside from a moral polytheism, from false values—the false gods of the heart" (p. 58). Regarding Muhammad himself, Smith posits that the formula identifies his function as opposed to a status he occupies. "The Islamic concept of apostle, or prophet, is quite special" (p. 59). It does not necessarily correspond to Western ideas. "The underlying notion here, and it is tacitly presupposed by the formulation, is that God has something to say to mankind, and has from time to time chosen certain persons in various communities through whom to say it; . . . Muhammad was one of those persons. It too, then, . . . is a statement about God. . . . God takes the initiative. . . . The position differs from the Christian in that it is a revelation *from* God more than *of* God. The apostle or prophet is one who conveys to men the message that God wants them to know; namely, how they live" (pp. 60-61). Cf. Wright, pp. 110-111. In explaining Muhammad's function, Smith states, "The position stands over against the quite different Christian orientation, which sees the person of Christ as central and ultimate, pre-existent and divine. Muslims also posit a central and ultimate truth, pre-existent and divine, namely the *Qur'an*—not a person but a book, or better, what the book says. Muhammad plays in the Islamic scheme the role played in the Christian system by St. Paul or St. Peter; namely, that of an apostle who proclaims among men God's gift to them, which in the Islamic case is the scripture" (p. 61). Cf. Daud Rahbar, "Muhammad and All Men," in Nelson, *No Man Is Alien,* pp. 64-84.

[2] "Whenever, O descendant of Bharata, there is decline of Dharma, and rise of Adharma, then I body myself forth. For the protection of the good, for the destruction of the wicked, and for the establishment of Dharma, I come into being in every age." *Bhagavad-Gita,* IV:7-8. See Vivekananda, "Incarnations," *Karma-Yoga and Bhakti-Yoga* (rev. ed.), pp. 146-149. Cf. Akhilananda, *Hindu View of Christ,* chap. i, "Christ, An Incarnation," pp. 15-44, for a further clarification of the Hindu position *vis-à-vis* the Christian viewpoint.

[3] "Students of Vedanta recognize in the sublime character of the Saviour Christ the manifestation of the universal Logos, or the Word of God, as they do in other

known as Krishna, and when after another plunge, He rises up at another point, He is known as Christ.

The Incarnations are to Brahman (the Absolute) as waves are to the ocean.[4]

A mighty raft of wood floating down a river carries on it hundreds and does not sink. A small piece of wood floating down may sink with the weight of a crow. So when a Saviour incarnates, hundreds find salvation through His grace. The *Siddha* (perfect man) only saves himself with much toil and trouble.[5]

## *Objections from the Christian Perspective*

His position immediately throws Sri Ramakrishna's practice of Christianity as it is generally understood in terms of Western theology into serious question. From this pluralistic viewpoint regarding God's incarnation, could he fully become a Christian? Fundamentally, the tenets of Christianity rest, from its most liberal to the most literal interpretation, on the foundation of the New Testament, which presumes the uniqueness in history of the divinity of Jesus. Can a person become a "partial Christian," and believe in the divin-

---

incarnations of the same almighty Being." Swami Abhedananda, *Great Saviours of the World* (3d ed.; Calcutta: Ramakrishna Vedanta Math, 1966), p. 240. "Though I am unborn, of changeless nature and Lord of all beings, yet subjugating My Prakriti, I come into being by My own Maya." *Bhagavad-Gita*, IV:6. " 'In the beginning was the Word, and the Word was with God, and the Word was God.' The Hindu calls this maya, the manifestation of God, because it is the power of God. (Maya is the Sakti, or power, of the Supreme Lord, which appears to hide His reality and project the names and forms of the relative universe [editor's note]). The Absolute reflecting through maya is what we call nature. The Word has two manifestations: the general one of nature, and the special one of the great Incarnations of God— Krishna, Buddha. Jesus. . . . Christ, the special manifestation of the Absolute, is known and knowable. The Absolute cannot be known. We cannot know the Father; we can only know the Son. We can only see the Absolute through the 'tint of humanity,' through Christ. In the first five verses of John is the whole essence of Christianity; each verse is full of the profoundest philosophy." Swami Vivekananda, *Inspired Talks, My Master and Other Writings* (rev. ed.; New York: Ramakrishna-Vivekananda Center, 1958), pp. 19-20. Vivekananda further comments on the teleological nature of Christ's coming, namely redemption (see John 1:29).

[4] *The Harmony of Religions, A Teaching of Ramakrishna* (London: The Ramakrishna Vedanta Centre, 1965), p. 7. (This is an eight-page collection of sayings of Sri Ramakrishna on this subject.) Cf. *The Gospel of Sri Ramakrishna* (Nikhilananda translation), p. 864.

[5] *Words of the Master*, p. 15.

ity of Christ but not his exclusive divinity? One is a Christian fully, or not at all.

To complicate the matter further, Christianity, like Islam, is eschatological.[6] The aim is salvation through faith at the end of time. A religious aspirant is not expected to bounce in and out of the parameters of the Christian faith merely to experience Christ. What of the rites of baptism, confirmation and, most centrally, the Eucharist?[7] Is it possible even to "practice" Christianity otherwise? Finally, the question of fellowship arises: is it enough to know Jesus personally as the Beloved and Savior, without participating in the fellowship of his Church, the covenant community of the faithful?[8] Can Christian love be practiced without Christian fellowship? While all Christian denominations now extend a universal embrace in *imitatio Dei* to all mankind, which includes the offer of salvation through Jesus Christ, only among the fellowship of Christians can *agape* truly become manifest.[9]

*Response to Objections*

These objections are legitimatized by theology, by scripture, and by the authority of the church. They cannot be refuted by these

---

[6] I Peter 1:3-5.

[7] For an elaboration of the pristine Eucharist, its formation and meaning, see Dom Gregory Dix, *The Shape of the Liturgy* (London: Dacre Press, A. & C. Black, 1945). William D. Maxwell, in *An Outline of Christian Worship, Its Development and Forms* (London: Oxford University Press, 1936), chap. i, pp. 1-25, claims the origin of the Eucharist is the *Kiddush,* which contradicts Luke 22:7-13 (cf. I Cor. 5:7) and the position maintained by Joachim Jeremias in *The Eucharistic Words of Jesus* (New York: Charles Scribner's Sons, 1966), chap. i, "Was the Last Supper a Passover Meal?," pp. 15-88. According to the phenomenological approach to the study of religion, now in vogue among some scholars, it is by participation in the Eucharist that a Christian is identified. See G. van der Leeuw, *Religion in Essence and Manifestation,* and the works of Mircea Eliade, such as *Patterns in Comparative Religion,* trans. by Rosemary Sheed, Meridian Books (Cleveland: World, 1968), *Rites and Symbols of Initiation: The Mysteries of Birth and Rebirth,* also published under the title *Birth and Rebirth,* trans. by Willard R. Trask, Harper Torchbooks (New York: Harper & Row, 1958), *The Myth of the Eternal Return,* trans. by Willard R. Trask, Bollingen Series XLVI, Pantheon Books (New York: Random House, 1954), and finally his recent volume, *The Quest: History and Meaning in Religion* (Chicago: University of Chicago Press, 1969).

[8] I John 1:3; cf. Phil. 1:5.

[9] I John 3:11-18.

methods. They can only be answered by empiricism:[10] the criterion of valid direct experience. May it not be proposed that if the Lord chooses to reveal himself, and that revelation is Jesus Christ, then he who experiences Christ has become a true Christian? Thus applying the standards of empiricism, may it not be said that Sri Ramakrishna was a true Christian, for he had seen Christ?

## SRI RAMAKRISHNA'S INTRODUCTION TO CHRISTIANITY

### His Teacher

He was led to this experience through contact with Sambhu Charan Mallik, a man of great generosity who had studied the scriptures of various religions. Although not a Christian himself, "he was the first to read to Ramakrishna from the Bible and speak to him of Jesus of Nazareth; *Sri Isha,* as the Hindus call him.

---

[10] As a method of knowledge, valid direct experience exerts a *prima facie* primacy over scriptural and ecclesiastical authority, for the latter two are never assumed to be in contradiction with it. Otherwise, there would be no point of contact whatever between the findings of science and the propositions of the Christian faith. The *a priori* datum of normative Christianity is the advent of Christ in human history, a history which itself rests solely on the record of empirical observation and verification. The same approach applies to his resurrection (F. X. Durrwell, *The Resurrection: A Biblical Study,* trans. by Rosemary Sheed [New York: Sheed and Ward, 1960]): if the disciples had not seen the risen Christ (see John 20), there would indeed be no basis of faith for future generations (see John 20:29-31) who had not been thus blessed. The primacy of direct experience is also upheld in religious traditions other than Christianity: in Islam, see al-Ghazali, *'Ihya,* as set forth in Chapter I, p. 13, note 11 herein; in Hinduism see Satprakashananda, *Methods of Knowledge.* Buddha never maintained the authority of any scripture, so that subsequent forms of attesting to such authority as in *Saddharma-Pundarika or The Lotus of the True Law,* trans. by H. Kern, The Sacred Books of the East, Vol. XXI (New York: Dover Publications, 1963) may be considered accretions—the Sangha itself employed *Upayakausalya* rather than any assertion of authority or dogma, as has been mentioned. From the highest viewpoint, direct experience never contradicts the scriptures but confirms them in all religions. Herein lies the power of the life of Sri Ramakrishna. For example, in Christianity he verified the existence of Jesus by experiencing him directly. No amount of theology could do the same, for theology itself as Christology rests on the premise of Christ's verity, and cannot demonstrate it except by faith. The fact that he lived, taught, died on the Cross and was resurrected as the Messiah was itself once a fact of experience as testified to by St. Paul, the original apostles and subsequent Christian saints and mystics (I John 1-4; cf. John 1:14-15; Acts 9:1-9,

Ramakrishna's thoughts began to dwell upon the personality of Jesus."[11]

*The Effect of His Education*

It should be recalled here that Sri Ramakrishna's limited schooling was in the traditional Indian style. His early village school showed little or no influence of the British educational system, which had not then penetrated village life. Thus he had not learned to identify Christianity within the matrix of Western culture. When he received Christ, he received him from within his own culture.

As a result, Sri Ramakrishna was devoid of the explicit reaction to Western influence which is most always present when an Oriental person is confronted with Christian values. The values of religion and the values of culture are usually presented simultaneously to the Indian mind by the Christian missionary activities.[12] These values are frequently indistinguishable, inseparable, and commingled as seen from the Indian standpoint, so that belief in Christ and technological proficiency become identified, salvation and material benefits are made synonymous ("rice Christians"), or, worse,

---

22:6-10, 26:12-19; see esp. I Cor. 15:1-9). Sri Ramakrishna in the modern age reconfirmed the value of normative Christianity, notwithstanding Paul Tillich *(Systematic Theology* [3 vols. in one; New York: Harper & Row, 1967]), Albert Schweitzer *(The Quest of the Historical Jesus* [New York: Macmillan, 1968]), Rudolf Bultmann *(Jesus Christ and Mythology* [New York: Charles Scribner's Sons, 1958], *Primitive Christianity in Its Contemporary Setting,* trans. by R. H. Fuller, Meridian Books [New York: World, 1956], "Primitive Christianity," pp. 175-179, and *Theology of the New Testament,* trans. by Kendrick Grobel, Scribner Studies in Contemporary Theology [2 vols.; New York: Charles Scribner's Sons, 1951, 1955], I, Part I, chap. i, "The Message of Jesus," 1-32), their followers and others who reasoned that the foundations of Christianity did not rest on the historical Jesus. Their conclusions are neither in accord with the Christian scriptures nor with Sri Ramakrishna's verification of the testimony recorded in the Christian scriptures, both of which represent the primacy of direct experience. It is thus noted that Sri Ramakrishna's approach to the dilemma of religious plurality, while in the spirit of the empirical tradition, operated completely from within the parameters of the tradition he was verifying. In this sense he was a true hermeneutician. The imperative which results from the foregoing is that anyone can and therefore must verify by direct experience the truths of scripture in his own religion. This shall be called the *empirical imperative*. It was dynamically practiced by Sri Ramakrishna.

[11] Isherwood, p. 147.

[12] Neill, *Christian Church.*

Christian ethics and empire strategy are equated and often rejected together as inconsistent.[13]

But, in the unusual case of Sri Ramakrishna's encounter with the Bible and the personality of Jesus, the religious component alone was presented to him. Western sensate culture and the language barrier did not intrude on the immediate intimacy he achieved with the teachings and personality of Jesus.

## SRI RAMAKRISHNA'S EXPERIENCE OF CHRIST

### The Nature of His Experience

By the time he reached his thirty-eighth year, Sri Ramakrishna had become an accomplished virtuoso in the field of superconscious experience. This fact made him "bold enough to travel on any road of religion without the help of a spiritual guide. All that he wanted was a map of the road . . . someone who could acquaint him with the contents . . . and ideals of this new faith."[14] He found such a person in Sambhu Charan Mallik, who acted as a conduit for Christ. His biographers relate Sri Ramakrishna's verification of the Christian faith[15] in Jesus Christ in the following manner:

When the desire to realise the Christian ideal arose in his mind, the Di-

---

[13] See Akhilananda, *Modern Problems,* p. 61. Cf. Howard Mumford Jones, *Education and World Tragedy* (Cambridge, Mass.: Harvard University Press, 1946); Pitirim A. Sorokin, *The Crisis of Our Age* (New York: E. P. Dutton, 1941); R. H. Tawney, *Religion and the Rise of Capitalism,* Mentor Books (New York: New American Library, 1954); see Sorokin's *Reconstruction of Humanity,* in which he proposes the remedy.

[14] Nirvedananda, p. 91.

[15] See Wilfred Cantwell Smith, *The Meaning and End of Religion: A New Approach to the Religious Traditions of Mankind* (New York: Macmillan, 1963), chap. vii, "Faith," pp. 170-192, esp. Smith's discussion of "faith in" vs. "faith that," p. 181; esp. note the following: " 'The function of systematic theology is to make clear the meaning and significance of Christian faith. . . . Theology does not determine faith, but analyses Christian faith as it actually exists.' . . . Theology is part of the traditions, is part of this world. Faith lies beyond theology, in the hearts of men. Truth lies beyond faith, in the heart of God" (p. 185). Smith continues, "There is nothing in heaven or on earth that can legitimately be called *the* Christian faith. . . . There is no ideal faith that I ought to have. There is God whom I ought to see, and a neighbor whom I ought to love. . . . The ideal toward which I move is not an ideal of my own faith but is God Himself, and my neighbor himself. Faith is not part of eternity; it is my present awareness of eternity. . . . Men's faith varies. God endures" (pp. 191-192).

vine Mother fulfilled it in a strange way, without any struggle on his part. One day the Master was in the parlour of the garden-house of Jadu Nath Mallik at Dakshineswar, on the walls of which were many beautiful portraits, one of them being Christ's. Sri Ramakrishna was looking attentively at the picture of the Madonna with the Divine Child and reflecting on the wonderful life of Christ, when he felt as though the picture had become animated, and that rays of light were emanating from the figures of Mary and Christ, and entering into him, altogether changing his mental outlook. When he realised that his Hindu ideas were being pushed into a corner by this onrush of new ones, he tried his best to stop it and eagerly prayed to the Divine Mother, 'What is it that Thou art doing to me, Mother?' But in vain. His love and regard for the Hindu gods were swept away by this tidal wave, and in their stead a deep regard for Christ and the Christian church filled his heart, and opened to his eyes the vision of Christian devotees burning incense and candles before the figure of Jesus in the churches and offering unto him the eager outpourings of their hearts. Returning to the Dakshineswar temple he was so engrossed in these thoughts that he forgot to visit the Divine Mother in the temple. For three days those ideas held sway in his mind. On the fourth day, as he was walking in the Panchavati, he saw an extraordinary-looking person of serene aspect approaching him with his gaze intently fixed on him. He knew him at once to be a man of foreign extraction. He had beautiful large eyes, and though the nose was a little flat, it in no way marred the comeliness of his face. Sri Ramakrishna was charmed and wondered who he might be. Presently the figure drew near, and from the inmost recesses of Sri Ramakrishna's heart there went up the note, 'There is the Christ who poured out his heart's blood for the redemption of mankind and suffered agonies for its sake. It is none else but that Master-Yogin Jesus, the embodiment of Love!'

Then the Son of Man embraced Sri Ramakrishna and became merged in him. The Master lost outward consciousness in Samadhi, realising his union with the Brahman with attributes. After some time he came back to the normal plane. Thus was Sri Ramakrishna convinced that Jesus Christ was an Incarnation of the Lord.[16]

## His Own Description of Jesus

The following conversation of Sri Ramakrishna with his disciples at a later date is significant with respect to what some scholars regard as the "problem" of the historicity of Christ:

Long after, in discussing Christ with his disciples who were able to

[16] *Life of Sri Ramakrishna*, pp. 253-255.

speak English, he asked, 'Well, you have read the Bible. Tell me what it says about the features of Christ. What did he look like?' They answered, 'We have not seen this particularly mentioned anywhere in the Bible; but Jesus was born among the Jews, so he must have been fair, with large eyes and an aquiline nose.' Sri Ramakrishna only remarked, 'But I saw his nose was a little flat—who knows why!' Not attaching much importance to these words at the time, the disciples, after the passing away of Sri Ramakrishna, heard that there were three extant descriptions of Christ's features, and one of these actually described him as flat-nosed![17]

## EFFECTS OF HIS EXPERIENCE OF CHRIST

### Devotion Transmitted to Disciples

Based on this vision Sri Ramakrishna maintained an intense devotion to Christ throughout the remainder of his life. In fact, he passed this attitude on to his disciples. After his death, when a dozen or so of them banded together under the leadership of young Narendra, later called Swami Vivekananda, they invoked Christ's name and blessings on Christmas Eve in taking their monastic vows *(sannyasa)*. The account of this episode is related by Swami Vivekananda's biographers:

> It was late in the evening when the monks gathered together before the fire of huge logs. . . . The meditation lasted a long time. When a break was made Naren began to tell the story of the Lord Jesus, beginning with the wondrous mystery of his birth through his death on to the resurrection. Through the eloquence of Narendra, the boys were admitted into the apostolic world wherein Paul had preached the gospel of the Arisen Christ and spread Christianity far and wide. Naren made his plea to them . . . to realise God and to deny themselves as the Lord Jesus had done. Standing there before the Dhuni, with the flames lighting up their countenances and with the crackling of the wood the sole disturbance of their thought, they took the vows of Sannyasa before God and one another. The very air seemed to vibrate with their ecstatic fervour.[18]

### Vivekananda's Personal Testimony

On other occasions Swami Vivekananda remarked that he con-

---

[17] Ghanananda, pp. 91-92.

[18] *The Life of Swami Vivekananda* by His Eastern and Western Disciples (4th ed.; Mayavati, Almora, Himalayas: Advaita Ashrama, 1949), pp. 159-160.

sidered himself the servant of the servants of Jesus, that if he had been present before Christ in the days when he lived in Palestine, he would have washed his feet not with his tears, but with his heart's blood.[19] It has been mentioned that *The Imitation of Christ* was one of two books Vivekananda carried with him during his years of monastic wandering in India. Other disciples of Sri Ramakrishna, like Swami Brahmananda, Swami Saradananda, and Swami Ramakrishnananda also had "exalted experiences of Jesus and the Christian ideals."[20]

### *Attitude of Ramakrishna Order*

Even today, the Swamis of the Ramakrishna Order all over the world regularly celebrate Christmas and Easter with elaborate services, which include meditation and worship. This represents a continuation of the practice which was begun at the inception of the Order. Swami Akhilananda recalls, in the Preface to *Hindu View of Christ:*

> Nearly thirty-five years ago we had the privilege of attending the Christmas celebration in the headquarters of the Ramakrishna Order, a Hindu monastery situated on the bank of the Ganges in Belur, a suburb of Calcutta, India. Swami Brahmananda, our great master, and a few other disciples of Sri Ramakrishna, were celebrating the occasion. It made a deep impression on our youthful minds, and we observed with what reverence and devotion they worshipped Jesus, the Christ, as an incarnation of God. This and successive celebrations of Christmas were so elevating that even now the effect remains with us.[21]

---

[19] Sister Nivedita, *The Master as I Saw Him* (10th ed.; Calcutta: Udbodhan Office, 1966), p. 276.

[20] Akhilananda, *Hindu View of Christ,* p. 13.

[21] *Ibid.,* p. 11. Cf. Swami Prabhavananda's reaction to this same event as told in the Preface to his *The Sermon on the Mount according to Vedanta,* Mentor Books (New York: New American Library, 1963), p. xii.

# CHAPTER VII

# *Universal Moods* (Bhavas) *Inherent In Each Religion*

## BHAKTI

*Predominance of His Bhakti Disposition*

With the exception of Sri Ramakrishna's *Advaita Vedanta* discipline and realization under Tota Puri's guidance, which in this presentation has been made synonymous with Buddha's *Magga*[1] and *Nirvana,* the overwhelming majority of his spiritual practices in all traditions were of the devotional type. *Bhakti* was, from the very beginning, the apparent disposition of his temperament. But even here he was not one-sided. Swami Vivekananda, in contrasting his own nature with that of his teacher, once remarked that "Sri

---

[1] The content of *Magga* or literally the " 'Way' to the cessation of suffering" is the Eightfold Path, which has herein been compared (see Chapter IV, p. 55, note 7) to the eight limbs of Yoga in Patanjali's *Yoga Sutras.* While Patanjali recognizes that devotion to the personal form of God *(Ishvara)* arises out of psychological necessity because the untrained and undeveloped mind cannot conceive of the unconditioned Absolute (cf. *bhakti*-oriented *sutras* in Mahayana Buddhism), and that such devotion to *Ishvara* results in *savikalpa samadhi,* he does not emphasize the devotional path *(bhakti yoga)* as a major vehicle for the ultimate attainment of *nirvikalpa samadhi* (i.e. *Nirvana),* the supreme goal of all *sadhanas.* Nor does Patanjali stress the search after "love of God for love's sake alone" which predominates in many *bhakti* texts, and can lead to a higher state. It can be concluded, then, that as "ethical

Ramakrishna, while seeming to be all *bhakti* was really, within all *jnana;* but he himself, apparently all *jnana,* was full of *bhakti.'*[2]

*Bhakti as Bhava*

The loving attitudes *(bhavas)* which a devotee assumes in relationship to God in order to experience him represent the functional essence of *bhakti.*[3] There are five main classifications of *bhava* according to the Sri Vaishnavite tradition: *santa* (peaceful), *dasya* (servantship), *sakhya* (friendship), *vatsalya* (parent), *madhura* (con-

---

idealism" Buddha's pristine *Magga* or Eightfold Path, which was further condensed to *sila, samadhi, panna,* does not offer a religious aspirant the devotional component as a major factor in the salvific process. This conclusion is fully consistent with Shankaracharya's *jnana yoga* as expounded in his *Vivekachudamani* and other works. *Comment:* It could be said that the Buddha, like Shankara and Meister Eckhart, "renounced God for God's sake," but by that token he also renounced the opportunity to participate in the consuming fire of divine love, which is the aim of a true *bhakta.* Cf. Swami Vivekananda, who was of the same non-dualistic temperament, yet who developed into a universal lover under the influence of Sri Ramakrishna, so that he was able to harmonize the realizations of *Advaita Vedanta* with the most intense devotion. While Buddha manifested the ideals of non-dualism, personal renunciation and self-sacrifice for others, Swami Vivekananda also developed these and added to them that of harmony between heart and intellect, between the diverse paths of *bhakti* and *jnana.* Although such a harmony had been clearly indicated by Sri Krishna in the *Bhagavad-Gita,* it was left for Sri Ramakrishna, Vivekananda and their followers to demonstrate it boldly and unambiguously in their lives. See *Swami Premananda, Teachings and Reminiscences,* ed. and trans. by Swami Prabhavananda (Hollywood, Calif.: Vedanta Press, 1968), pp. 71-72. Also cf. *The Story of a Dedicated Life,* p. 80, 91, 104.

[2] Sister Nivedita, *Notes of Some Wanderings with the Swami Vivekananda* (5th ed.; Calcutta: Udbodhan Office, 1967), p. 44.

[3] In this connection, Akhilananda makes the following observations: "The . . . most natural of all methods is *Bhakti Yoga.* It is, therefore, applicable to the greatest number of people. Sri Ramakrishna describes it: '. . . If once man gains love of God, if once the chanting of His holy "name" begins to thrill the devotee with joy, what effort is needed for the control of passions afterwards? The control comes of itself.' Almost all persons are basically emotional. Even most of those who talk about philosophy and rationalism are primarily emotional. It is amazing to know that in spite of philosophical discussions, a little change in the environment or some emotional reaction can seriously affect the individuals involved. At that time philosophy has no place in their lives. They react just as any person in that state of mind would do. So intellectualism is, after all, nothing but a veneer for most people. There are only a few exceptional individuals who can practice the intellectual method. . . . In *Bhakti Yoga,* the emotions are used for the realization of God. These emotions are the most powerful implements, the most powerful drives found in human beings. So, instead

91

jugal love).[4] These are further refined into more than one hundred subdivisions. In addition, two important attitudes less developed in this tradition are *aptya bhava*[5] (relationship of child to parent) and *satru bhava* (anger),[6] which play a dominant role in other traditions.

## SRI RAMAKRISHNA'S BHAKTI SADHANAS

To recount the events of Sri Ramakrishna's devotional practices

---

of crushing them, the Hindu teachers advocate that they be cultivated and redirected to God. . . . Various emotions are found among the devotees. Some have attachment for the mother or the father, others for the child. In some instances, conjugal love is the most attractive. For some, the friend is the most loved. Such emotions can be directed to God, the devotee regarding Him as parent, child, spouse, or friend, whichever is most suitable. When the emotional relationship is achieved it is called *bhava*, a relationship of intense love. Most people are not aware of the various ways in which one can love God. They are taught that there is only one way to reach Him. A number of years ago an elderly lady attended one of our services. Later she told a friend, 'The Swami talked so nicely, but he did not say anything about God.' The term 'Father in Heaven' had not been used! God is called by various names; but certain names are taught in particular religions. So the people feel that a person using any other name is not worshipping God. This narrow attitude does not help anyone. In fact, it has created serious disturbances in the minds of the people in Europe and America, actually driving many away from the threshold of religion." *Spiritual Practices,* pp. 69-71.

[4] See Bhaktivedanta, *Teachings of Lord Chaitanya,* chap. i, pp. 21-38 and chap. xiii, pp. 113-120; Swami Vivekananda, "Human Representations of Divine Love," *Karma-Yoga and Bhakti-Yoga* (rev. ed.), pp. 199-206; Shishir Kumar Ghose, *Lord Gauranga,* Bhavan's Book University No. 92 (Bombay: Bharatiya Vidya Bhavan, 1961); *Srimad Bhagavatam,* trans. by Swami Prabhavananda; *Narada Bhakti Sutras,* esp. commentaries (both Tyagisananda and Prabhavananda translations); Jadunath Sinha, "Bhagavata Religion: The Cult of Bhakti" in Bhattacharyya, *The Religions,* pp. 146-159; Radha Govinda Nath, "A Survey of the Caitanya Movement," *ibid.,* pp. 186-200; Raj Mohom Nath, "Sankara Deva and the Vaishnava Movement in Assam," *ibid.,* pp. 201-210; Abhedananda, *Human Affection and Divine Love;* Saradananda, *passim;* Singer and Ingalls, *Krishna; The Eternal Companion* (3d ed.), pp. 100-106 and *passim.*

[5] *Aptya bhava* was Sri Ramakrishna's "mood" with respect to Divine Mother. Cf. Christian attitudes toward God as Father.

[6] The attitudes of musing anger, deliberate hostility or even intense hatred toward God have been cultivated and used, odd as it may seem, as effective instruments of salvation in various traditions. Like love, hatred develops an intense form of concentration which when prolonged eventually unifies the mind when the object is God. The effect is quite wonderful. God responds in grace, as in the case of many Muslim

according to the systematic disciplines[7] prescribed in *bhakti* texts would be to portray nearly the entire spectrum of devotional responses by man to God's grace in one life. Two illustrations will suffice: Sri Ramakrishna's *vatsalya bhava* and his *madhura bhava.*

### His Vatsalya Bhava

In the *vatsalya bhava,* a spiritual aspirant assumes the devotional relationship of loving parent to God. This episode in Sri Ramakrishna's *sadhana* recalls to mind the comparable spiritual experi-

---

poet-mystics and even St. Paul, who hated Jesus and persecuted His followers before he had the transforming experience on his way to Damascus. Through *satru bhava* the Lord bestows salvation on his enemies, as Krishna did with Ravana. Vivekananda states, "Buddha set his greatest enemy free because, by hating Buddha so much, he kept constantly thinking of him. That thought purified his mind and he became ready for freedom. Therefore think of God all the time and you will be purified." *Inspired Talks,* p. 146.

[7] It should be clearly pointed out that because *bhakti* uses the emotions as primary implements for superconscious experience, this does not mean that the *bhakti* advocates enjoin a casual or unsystematic approach. Quite to the contrary, the *bhakti* tradition involves a rigorous training process, and is based on the cultivation of ethical precepts as a point of departure (cf. *yama* and *niyama* in Patanjali's *Sutras,* Buddhist *pancha silas* and other ethical principles, the ethics presupposed by Shankara, etc.); see I.C. Sharma, *Ethical Philosophies of India,* ed. and rev. by Stanley M. Daugert, Harper Torchbooks (New York: Harper & Row, 1965); cf. S. C. Thakur, *Christian and Hindu Ethics* (London: Allen & Unwin, 1969); James M. Gustafson, *Christ and the Moral Life* (New York: Harper & Row, 1968). The *sadhana* required for *bhakti* is highly systematic. The methodology according to Sri Chaitanya, for example, is clearly set forth, as are the *rasas* (flavors) of each distinct relationship *(santa, dasya,* etc.), the steps of *rapprochement* in communion with God *(rati, preman, sneha, mana, pranaya, raga, anuraga,* and *mahabhava),* and the correspondence of the relationships to the degrees of attachment or union *(ratis)* with God (see Govinda Nath, "The Chaitanya Movement"; Bhaktivedanta, *Teachings of Chaitanya).* The devotees are grouped, in the school of Sri Chaitanya, into the four classes stipulated according to degrees of intensity of their love. One advances according to his capacity until final identification with Sri Radha in her adoration for Sri Krishna is realized in *mahabhava.* Sri Chaitanya stresses the importance of *sankirtana, japam,* and other devotional exercises as essential ingredients of *sadhana,* along with external observance of the dress, gestures, and mannerisms of the Gopis of Vrindavan to reinforce the aspirant's identification process. Here all men must become like women, with only God as their Lord. A major emphasis that emerges is that for Sri Chaitanya, the Lord's sweetness *(madhurya)* is far more important than His greatness and power *(aisvarya).* If this were not the case, such extreme intimacy with the Lord would not be possible, for the feelings of awe, reverence and fear would create a gulf of "separateness" between the Lord and His devotee deemed

ences in the lives of St. Anthony of Padua and Mira Bai,[8] as well as Sri Chaitanya's practice of the fatherly mood toward Sri Krishna.[9] This type of mood is rare in mystical history compared with other types such as *santa, dasya, sakhya* and *aptya* because in it the Lord is regarded as completely dependent on the devotee, which is an inversion of the more common attitudes. Here, God as the Divine Child looks to the devotee for the fulfillment of his daily needs and wants, much as a child to a parent in real-life circumstances. God, of course, has no needs; it is man who is burdened with countless requirements which he petitions God to fulfill, including the primordial need for salvation itself. This very fact highlights the unique advantage of *vatsalya bhava:* by focusing his emotional life on the daily needs of God as Child, the spiritual aspirant tends to forget his own wants, and eventually develops selfless love for God.[10] This selfless love ripens into complete self-forgetfulness in the thought of God alone, into *prema,* which is the acme and perfection of the devotional life. *Prema* comes

---

intolerable in the love relationship. This "intimacy" is one of the major features of Sri Chaitanya's interpretation of *bhakti.* A comprehensive comparison of the systematic disciplines enjoined by different *bhakti* traditions is given by Swami Tyagisananda in the annotations and commentary to his translation of *Narada Bhakti Sutras.*

[8] For historicity and scriptural authorship, see *Great Women of India,* ed. by Swami Madhavananda and Ramesh Chandra Majumdar (Mayavati, Almora, Himalayas: Advaita Ashrama, 1953), pp. 328-330. Cf. "Gopal Ma," *ibid.,* pp. 448-452.

[9] See Bhaktivedanta. His statement that "Chaitanya is the first to treat God as son" (p. 6) is an unfortunate inaccuracy from the standpoint of this presentation: St. Anthony was born in 1195 and Chaitanya was born in 1486.

[10] See Akhilananda, *Mental Health,* chap. xi, "Power of Love," pp. 129-142. Akhilananda writes, "In life we observe three types of love. The first form of love is immature and childish. . . . This is . . . narcissism or self-love. . . . Many people direct their sentiment to the object of affection but they expect everything in return. Therefore, they are often disappointed. . . . The second form of love includes a sense of mutuality. I give and you give. I worship God and He gives me something. . . . No doubt this form of love is better than the spirit of demanding. . . . In this second form, too, envy and jealousy are often observed. . . . The third form of love has no such elements because the lover gives and gives and demands nothing and expects nothing. . . . Love is unmercenary. There are few persons in the world, who have the sentiment of giving with no thought of return. There are a few, a blessed few, who offer themselves wholly to God, who express love for Him without caring for any reward from Him. The moment a person expects anything in return for his love, that moment the joy of love goes and it deteriorates to the level of the shopkeeper" (pp. 129-133).

. . . unsolicited by the grace of God and by self-sacrifice. Gaining that, man . . . becomes thoroughly contented; . . . has no more desire for anything; is free from grief and hatred; . . . does not exert himself in furtherance of self-interest . . . and becomes intoxicated and fascinated, as it were, . . . completely immersed in the enjoyment of the Bliss of the Atman, the truest and highest self.[11]

*Prema* is the goal of *bhakti yoga*.[12]

Sri Ramakrishna's teacher in the *vatsalya bhava* was an accomplished mystic of the Sri Vaishnava tradition named Jatadhari. He came to Dakshineswar in 1864, and carried with him a small metallic image of Ramlala[13] (Child Rama) whom he worshipped. As a

[11] *Narada Bhakti Sutras,* trans. by Tyagisananda, sls. 3-6. It is clearly evident here that the objective of *bhakti yoga* is the same as that of *jnana yoga*—the Atman is realized in both cases. The major difference from the epistemological viewpoint is that sometimes the *bhakta* desires to maintain his separate identity for the sake of perpetuating the bliss that arises from communion with the Beloved (i.e., "I don't want to become sugar, but to taste it"), while the *jnanin* merges his identity from the very beginning with the Atman in the Advaitic intuition, *"Aham Brahmasmi."* To illustrate, cf. the spiritual practices and realizations of the two foremost monastic disciples of Sri Ramakrishna: Swami Brahmananda *(bhakta)* and Swami Vivekananda *(jnanin);* see *The Disciples of Ramakrishna* (Mayavati, Almora, Himalayas: Advaita Ashrama, 1955), chap. i, "Swami Brahmananda," pp. 3-36; and Swami Nikhilananda, *Vivekananda: A Biography* (Mayavati: Advaita Ashrama, 1953). It is significant that by the application of Sri Ramakrishna's principle of harmony, the development of each mutually overlapped to a point where Brahmananda also fully realized the Advaitic goal, and Vivekananda became filled with *prema.* It was this intense love for God and God's children that transformed itself into the root motive power behind Vivekananda's tremendous activities of service which literally burned out his life by age thirty-nine. Correspondingly, it was through the knowledge of Advaita that Brahmananda gained the breadth of vision to carry out the training of subsequent generations of monastic disciples and the administration of the Order as its first president. These two spiritual personalities stand as living examples that the paths of *bhakti* and *jnana,* which appear so widely different in form and practice, can be fully harmonized in substance not only among individuals with different temperaments but within the same person. Such harmony represents an original application of existing spiritual ideals in the teachings of Sri Ramakrishna.

[12] *Prema* and *parabhakti* are virtually synonymous. Akhilananda, in *Mental Health,* quotes the following statement by Sri Ramakrishna: "The stage of devotion called *Bhava* is like an unripe mango; *Prema* is like the ripe fruit. Prema is like a string in the hands of the *Bhakta* (lover of God), binding him to that Sachchidananda (Existence-Knowledge-Bliss) which is God. The devotee holds the Lord, so to speak, under his control. God comes to him whenever he calls' " (p. 134).

[13] D. S. Sarma, *The Prince of Ayodhya* (Madras: Sri Ramakrishna Math, 1946); K. M. Munshi, *Bhagawan Parashurama,* Parts I and II, Bhavan's Book University Nos. 61 and 62 (Bombay: Bharatiya Vidya Bhavan, 1965).

result of a lifetime spent in single-minded devotion to this form of God, Jatadhari actually felt the constant presence of the deity. He spent his time in offering service to the Child Rama, nursing and feeding him, playing with him, and even chastising him when he would act like a spoiled child. A *sannyasin* who had completely renounced worldly enjoyment, Jatadhari would beg for food and cook it for the deity, who would actually take it, and on occasion demand something else, as children do. He kept his extraordinary experiences a secret, but Sri Ramakrishna quickly recognized them and began to participate in them. Thus Ramlala became the common object of devotion of the two saints. The following account is given by Sri Ramakrishna in his own words about his experience of the *vatsalya bhava,* as related by his biographers:

'Jatadhari was engaged day and night in serving Him and was in a state of constant bliss. I could see the actions of Ramlala; so I used to spend the whole day with the Babaji in order to watch Him. Days passed in this way and Ramlala became more and more intimate with me. As long as I remained with Jatadhari, Ramlala was cheerful; but the moment I left, He followed me to my room. No argument would move Him. At first I thought that it might be an hallucination, for how could Ramlala prefer me—practically a stranger—to Jatadhari whose life had been spent in serving Him? I argued that I might be deceived once or twice, but this scene was repeated every day. I saw Ramlala as vividly as I see you all—now dancing gracefully before me, now springing on my back, or insisting on being taken up in my arms. Sometimes I would hold Him on my lap. He would not remain there, but run to the fields in the sun, pluck flowers from thorny bushes, or jump into the Ganges. I would remonstrate saying, "Don't run in the sun; your feet will get blistered;" or "Don't remain so long in water; you will catch cold and get fever." But Ramlala would turn a deaf ear. He would fix his beautiful eyes on me and smile, or, like a naughty boy, He would go on with His pranks, or pout His lips or make faces at me. Sometimes I would lose my temper and cry, "Wait, you naughty boy, I am going to beat you black and blue." I would drag Him away, and diverting Him with various toys, ask Him to play inside the room. But sometimes I lost patience and slapped Him; with tearful eyes and trembling lips He would look at me. Oh, what pain I would feel then for having punished Him! I would take Him on my lap and console Him. All these things actually happened.

'One day,' Sri Ramakrishna continued, 'I was going to bathe. Ramlala insisted on accompanying me, so I took Him with me. But He would not come out of the water, nor did He heed my remonstrances. Then I got angry and pressing Him under the water said, "Now play in it as much as you like.". Ah! I saw Him struggling for breath; then, repenting of my act, I took Him up in my arms. Another incident pained me greatly, and I wept bitterly over it. He insisted on having something which I could not supply. To divert Him I gave Him some parched rice not well husked. As He was chewing it, I found His tender tongue was scratched. This sight was too much for me. I took Him on my lap and cried out, "Mother Kausalya used to feed you with cream or butter with the greatest care, and I was so thoughtless as to give you this coarse stuff."[14]

. . . 'Sometimes the Babaji,' Sri Ramakrishna went on, 'after cooking his food, could not find Ramlala. Being sorely distressed he would run to my room, and find Ramlala playing with me. In wounded pride the *sadhu* would say, "The food is ready; I have been searching for You, and here You are, playing at ease! Well, that is Your nature. You do whatever You like. You have no feelings. You are hard-hearted and unkind. You left your parents and went to the forest. Your father died of a broken heart, but You did not return even to see him on his death-bed." Scolding thus he would take Ramlala away and feed Him. The Babaji stayed here for a long time, because Ramlala would not go away from me, and the Babaji could not leave behind his dearly beloved Ramlala.

'One day Jatadhari, weeping, came to me and said, "Ramlala out of His infinite grace has fulfilled my desire. He has revealed Himself to me in the form I prefer. Also He has told me that He will not go and leave you behind; but I am not distressed on that account: I am filled with joy to see Him live here happily and play with you. I am satisfied when He is happy; I shall gladly leave Him and go my way. It gladdens my heart to think that He is happy in your company." With these words Jatadhari left Ramlala with me and bade adieu to Dakshineswar. Ever since, Ramlala has been here.'[15]

---

[14] "When he retold this incident many years later to his young disciples, Ramakrishna would burst into tears. Saradananda, who was one of them, records this, and adds that he and the other boys used to exchange glances of utter bewilderment as they listened to this story of Ramlala. It sounded to them, even in their youthful faith, absurd and impossible—and yet it was Ramakrishna who told it, and they could not think him capable of the smallest falsehood. The mature Saradananda, in his book, makes good-humoured allowances for the incredulity of the reader: 'Accept as much of this story as you can digest,' he writes. 'Omit the head and the tail, if you like.' But at the same time, Saradananda makes it clear that he himself has come to believe every word of it." Isherwood, p. 108.

[15] Ghanananda, pp. 71-73. It will be noted that many of Sri Ramakrishna's spiritual experiences are presented in identical form by his biographers, when quoting his own statements verbatim. Cf. *Life of Sri Ramakrishna,* pp. 166-169, Isherwood, pp. 107-109, etc.

It was during this period that Sri Ramakrishna underwent an unusual transformation of his nature: in his attitude toward God he felt himself to be a woman. This particularly well suited his *sadhana* of the *vatsalya bhava,* of the *madhura bhava* which followed, and certain forms of worship of the Divine Mother which he practiced at that time. His sense of personal identity completely changed. The thought patterns, habits, mannerisms and gestures of the masculine gender were swept from his nature and were replaced by those of a woman, and for the time being he no longer regarded himself as a man. This transformation was spontaneous, prompted by the intense love for the Child Rama that possessed Sri Ramakrishna.

> The form of Ramachandra that he now saw in the image of Ramlala was . . . the embodiment of spiritual love. It is, therefore, no wonder that his mind was now filled with . . . that wonderful love and attraction which a mother feels toward her young child.[16]

Jatadhari formally initiated Sri Ramakrishna into the *vatsalya sadhana* before he left Dakshineswar. Sri Ramakrishna subsequently realized, after a few days' intense concentration and worship in this mood, that the Divine Child who appeared before him "also pervaded every being, that He projected the universe and transcended it in His aspect of Pure Brahman, the One without . . . name, form, or attribute."[17]

### His Madhura Bhava

By far the most extraordinary spiritual discipline in Sri Ramakrishna's career, both from the perspective of his spiritual attainment and its incomprehensibility to the vast majority of people, is his practice of the *madhura bhava. Madhura bhava,* the sweet relation between a woman and her lover, represents the synthesis[18] of the

---

[16] Saradananda, p. 214.

[17] *Life of Sri Ramakrishna,* p. 172.

[18] "The *madhura* or the relationship between lovers . . . is the most intense form of attachment in which the least idea of separation becomes unbearable—God is the Sweetheart, a part and parcel of one's being. . . . It is higher than all the foregoing methods of worship and includes them all; it is the consummation of all the other forms of devotion. The votary on this path serves his Beloved like a servant, counsels Him, rejoices and sympathizes in His joys and sorrows like a friend, and watches over His mental and physical comforts like a mother. The perfect devotee of this type is obviously one who looks only to the comfort of the Beloved, regardless of his

other *bhavas* in the Sri Vaishnavite tradition, and is regarded as the most intimate, deepest form of union between the devotee and God. Here God is the only Male Principle in the universe, and all embodied creatures are female.[19] This attitude is personified in the Gopis (cowgirls of Vrindavan who carried on a love-relationship with Sri Krishna). Radha was foremost among them. She loved Sri Krishna with the greatest intensity and became merged in him in *mahabhava.* Thus exponents of the *madhura bhava,* such as Sri Chaitanya, recommend that the devotee emulate Sri Radha's wholehearted, selfless love for Lord Krishna in order to experience him. For this, the devotee assumes the role of a woman—first that of one of Radha's companions, a Gopi, then finally by degrees that of Radha herself, who achieved identity with Sri Krishna.[20] While the images and language are unquestionably sensual, the drama is enacted strictly on the transworldly plane, and requires perfect self-control and subjugation of the senses for spiritual realization.[21]

---

own personal happiness or convenience." Ghanananda, pp. 67-68. Also see Saradananda II, xiii, 24 (p. 232).

[19] "Meera Bai . . . on reaching Brindavana . . . sent for a certain famous *sadhu* (Sanatana, the Sannyasin disciple of Sri Chaitanya). He refused to go, on the ground that women might not see men in Brindavana. When this had happened three times, Meera Bai went to him herself saying that she had not known that there were such beings as men there, she had supposed that Krishna alone existed. And when she saw the astonished *sadhu* she . . . [uttered] the words 'Fool, do you call yourself a Man?' And as he fell prostrate before her with a cry of awe, she blessed him as a mother blesses her child." Nivedita, *Notes of Some Wanderings,* p. 123. Also see Saradananda, II, xiii, 22 (p. 231).

[20] It is noted that here again *bhakti* and *jnana* are in harmony: "I and Brahman are one. . . . This conclusion you will find has not only been reached through knowledge and philosophy, but parts of it through the power of love. You read in the *Bhagavata,* when Krishna disappeared and the Gopis bewailed his disappearance, that at last the thought of Krishna became so prominent in their minds that each one forgot her own body and thought she was Krishna, and began to decorate herself and to play as he did. We understand, therefore, that this identity comes even through love. There was an ancient Persian Sufi poet, and one of his poems says, 'I came to the Beloved and beheld the door was closed; I knocked at the door and from inside a voice came, "Who is there?" I replied, "I am." The door did not open. A second time I came and knocked at the door and the same voice asked, "Who is there?" "I am Thyself, my Love," and the door opened.' " Vivekananda, *Works,* III, 282.

[21] " 'What is this idea of *bhakti* without renunciation? . . . It is most pernicious!' " Swami Vivekananda, as quoted in Nivedita, *Notes of Some Wanderings,* p. 41. Also see Saradananda, II, xiii, 19 (pp. 228-229); cf. *Swami Premananda, Teachings and*

Whereas sexual transformation has historically occurred in *madhura bhava,* as in the cases of Sri Chaitanya and Sri Ramakrishna, the spiritual aspirant ultimately rises beyond the plane of sex-consciousness, since neither gender exists in that superconscious state. The remarkable events of Sri Ramakrishna's practice of the *madhura bhava* are recounted fully in Saradananda's *The Great Master.* The following abbreviated account is presented here:

In the same year in which he practised the *vatsalya bhava,* Sri Ramakrishna, prayed to the Divine Mother for permission to practise the *madhura bhava* and attain success in realizing Sri Krishna as his Beloved. He then began to devote all the energy of his soul to the practice of this *sadhana.* The burning sensation, which he experienced all over the body twice before, appeared again. Minute drops of blood began to ooze from the pores of his skin. At times the joints of his body seemed to be loosened. Owing to the intensity of his anguish, his senses would stop functioning and he looked like a corpse. The world had seldom seen such zeal. According to tradition, which tells of the need of propitiating Radha, who is the Beloved of Krishna and nearest to Him, Sri Ramakrishna prayed to her with fervour and devotion. Within a short time she revealed herself to him. This time also he felt the figure vanish into his own body. He used to say, 'It is impossible to describe the heavenly beauty and sweetness of Radha. Her very appearance showed that she had forgotten all personal considerations in her passionate love for Sri Krishna. Her complexion was light yellow.'

Subsequent to this experience Sri Ramakrishna began to feel himself to be Radha. His constant meditation on her obliterated his own personality and transformed him. Bhairavi Brahmani, his Tantrik *guru,* and learned devotees who were with him, were amazed at this and found it to be the same as the unique state of Radha described in the Puranas and the same as that of Sri Chaitanya, hundreds of years later. Sri Ramakrishna referring to this period of his *sadhana* said, 'The manifestation in the same individual of nineteen different kinds of emotion towards God is described in the books on *bhakti* as *mahabhava.* An ordinary man takes a whole lifetime to realize even a single one of these. But in this body (meaning himself) there has been a perfect manifestation of all the nineteen.' His complete identification with Sri Radha and meditation with passionate attachment upon Sri Krishna brought him in a short time to the consummation of his practices. Sri Krishna revealed Himself

---

*Reminiscences,* p. 70; also *Narada Bhakti Sutras,* trans. by Swami Tyagisananda, p. 104.

to him in His exquisitely graceful form, and fulfilled the longing of his soul. Then He merged Himself in the person of Sri Ramakrishna, who remained for three or four months in a state of divine felicity. At times, forgetting his own identity he looked upon himself as Krishna, at others, he saw Him manifested in all creatures, sentient and insentient. Sri Krishna appeared blue in complexion.

There was one particularly significant vision that Sri Ramakrishna had during this period: One day he was seated in the verandah of the Vishnu Temple listening to the reading of *Srimad Bhagavatam,* when he fell into an ecstatic mood and saw the resplendent form of Krishna. Next he found that luminous rays issuing from His feet in the form of a stout rope touched first the *Srimad Bhagavatam* and then his own chest, connecting for some time all three. Sri Ramakrishna used to say, 'After this vision, I came to realize that God, His devotee and the Scriptures which are His words, though they appear to be distinct entities, are in reality one and the same.'[22]

## EVALUATION AND ANALYSIS

The generalization which immediately emerges from Sri Ramakrishna's spiritual realizations through the practice of *bhavas* is this: it is suggested that *bhavas* are in fact trans-traditional, universal, and inherent in every religion in which love of God forms an essential part. Although these devotional forms had their origin in India as systematic disciplines, there appear to be no limitations as to dogma or creed in this methodology which prevents its complete application to the paths of devotion in other religious traditions. They were an outgrowth of the recognition of the vast differences in emotional temperament and mental structure among individuals struggling for spiritual experiences, and of the power in efficiently directing the emotions to God to attract his grace.[23]

The following statement of Saradananda summarizes the historical occurrence of *bhavas* in the Indian tradition:

When we study the history of religion, as embodied in the Sastras, it becomes clear that a particular mood became the principal prop of the

[22] Ghanananda, pp. 76-78; see also Saradananda, pp. 220-244. Cf. Muslim reverence for the Qur'an as described by W. C. Smith in note 1 of Chapter VI herein. Cf. Benjamin B. Warfield, *The Inspiration and Authority of the Bible* (Grand Rapids, Mich.: Baker, 1948).

[23] Akhilananda, *Hindu Psychology,* pp. 178-180.

human minds during meditation in a particular age; . . . We meet mainly with the final development of the Santa mood in the Vedic and Buddhistic ages; with the non-dual mood, as the ultimate development of the Santa, and the moods of the Dasya and the Apatya in the Upanisadic age; with the moods of the Santa and of the Dasya mixed with motiveless action in the age of the Ramayana and Mahabharata; with the Apatya and the partial Madhura in the Tantric age, and with the moods of the Sakhya, the Vatsalya and the Madhura in the Vaishnava age.[24]

A careful study of world religions, especially the study of their mystical history, reveals that a comparable spectrum of divine moods was manifest among the other religious traditions. As in the case of Hinduism, the different *bhavas* have not necessarily arisen simultaneously in all traditions, nor did they occur with the same degree of intensity in each particular tradition, reflecting the power of historical and cultural variants in the religious life of man. A few examples will suffice to illustrate this point.

The songs of King Solomon which express the friendly and sweet moods in relation to God represent an integral part of the Jewish, Christian, and Muslim communities, despite the fact that they have often been misunderstood. It is apparent that both *sakhya* and *madhura bhavas* have been widely practiced among Sufi Islamic saints, although many orthodox Muslims regard such forms of worship as contrary to the precepts of the Qur'an. The manifestations of *santa, dasya,* and *aptya bhavas* are most commonly observed in these three traditions, and examples of their mature development are plentiful in their mystical history.[25] *Vatsalya bhava,* which is much less common, can best be illustrated by St. Anthony of Padua.[26] It is entirely possible that many other mystics practiced *bhavas* leaving no testimony for future generations. The biographies of saints often do not record their spiritual experiences and practices, but emphasize their external lives. In the case of Sri Ramakrishna, fortunately, his biographers and immediate follow-

[24] Saradananda, pp. 224-225.

[25] *Ibid.,* II, xiii, 12 (p. 225). See Chap. III, p. 39, note 9 herein for the development of *dasya bhava* in the Old Testament concept of servantship to Divine Suzerain.

[26] Cf. the experiences of Mama Ndona Beatrice, a Christian Kongolese prophetess, who had a similar experience of the Divine Child. See R. Batsikama, *Ndona Beatrice.*

ers left a detailed account of his spiritual moods, a religious catalogue from the life of one man.[27]

Sri Ramakrishna's dynamic application of the power of love in
order to experience God through the different *bhavas* illustrates
that these *bhavas* are effective instruments for that experience. His
versatility in practicing the path of divine love has shown the value
of comparable paths of love of other mystics throughout religious
history in all traditions. Thus it may be suggested, on the basis of
these experiences, that these divine moods or *bhavas,* which express
variously man's relationship with God, are inherent in each religion. As such, *bhavas* may be considered universal, and represent
an important aspect of Sri Ramakrishna's approach to the dilemma
of religious plurality. He stated: "Whoever performs devotional exercises, in the belief that there is but one God, is bound to attain
Him, no matter in what aspect, name or manner he is worshipped."[28]

---

[27] Swami Nirvedananda quotes the following statement by Swami Saradananda,
Sri Ramakrishna's foremost biographer, concerning his own spiritual attainments:
" 'Nothing beyond my spiritual experience has been recorded in the book, *Sri Rama-
krishna Lila-prasanga* [*The Great Master*]' " (p. xxiv).

[28] Sri Ramakrishna, as quoted in Ghanananda, p. 138.

# CHAPTER VIII

# *The Harmony of Mysticism and Everyday Life*

## THE WORLD AND GOD

Sri Ramakrishna's spiritual experiences resulted in a profoundly practical philosophy, applicable to the everyday life of all individuals and their society. While "one of the most important contributions of Sri Ramakrishna is the verification of the existence of God"[1] by means of diverse religious paths, no less important a contribution is the harmony which pervades his teachings between the dimensions of superconscious experience and life in this world. Akhilananda reflects this attitude in the following statement:

Real religion and mystical experience are identical.

............................................................................................................

. . . Very little of religion can be understood without practicing it, just as the value of scientific discoveries cannot be understood without experimentation in the laboratory. So it is that religion cannot be properly evaluated until those principles are applied in everyday life.

............................................................................................................

The objective of religion is the awareness of God in our everyday life. . . . This very statement implies that our life must be saturated with religious ideas and ideals. The substance of religious ideals is conscious-

---

[1] Akhilananda, *Modern Problems,* p. 147.

ness of the presence of God, as experienced by Brother Lawrence. As Sri Ramakrishna tells us, we must live in this world in the awareness of God.

............................................................................................................................

. . . History reveals that humanism of the materialistic or pragmatic type cannot sustain the stability of an individual in human fellowship and brotherhood. That is the reason why in this modern age Sri Ramakrishna declared that we must install God in our lives and then perform our duties. . . .

Human beings are interrelated and related to God, just as the rays of the sun have a relationship to each other and to the sun. This very ideal is the basis of happiness in our everyday life. Swami Vivekananda's principle of *Karma-Yoga* (Path of action for God-realization) shows us that we should cultivate the presence of God in and through our activities, regardless of their nature. It is essential that we have the awareness and knowledge of God; then we may perform our duties, and our lives will be harmonious. The type of work we do is not so important, religious or otherwise; it is our attitude that counts. When we have the knowledge of God, all work, no matter what it may be, is converted into worship. . . . The real spirit of religion is not in negating life and the world, but in perceiving God in and through the world. . . .[2]

Let us consider the life of Sri Ramakrishna . . . He was constantly in a superconscious state. It was difficult for him to come down to an ordinary state of consciousness. His mind would soar to the plane of the Absolute where there is no relativity, no time, space, or causal relationships. When he came down to this plane of existence, he would find the manifestation of that Absolute in all.[3]

---

[2] *Spiritual Practices*, pp. 115-119.

[3] *Modern Problems*, p. 123. In the sayings and parables of Sri Ramakrishna, this last point becomes a recurring theme, as illustrated by the following: " 'God dwells in all beings; without Him nothing can exist. . . . Know that God resides in all things animate and inanimate. Hence everything is an object of worship, be it men, beasts or birds, plants or minerals. . . .' The Bhagavan continued: 'In the sacred scriptures it is written, "God dwells in water"; but some water can be used for divine service, or for drinking purposes, some for bathing or washing, while dirty water cannot be touched even. In the same manner, although God resides in all human beings, still there are good men and bad men, there are lovers of God and those who do not love God.' " Abhedananda, *Memoirs of Ramakrishna* (3d ed; Calcutta: Ramakrishna Vedanta Math, 1967), pp. 37-39. " 'Revered sir, can the world exist for the mind which is fixed on God?' Ramakrishna: 'Of course it will exist; otherwise where will it go? I see that wherever I remain, I am in the Kingdom of God. Verily I say unto you, this world is the Kingdom of God. Ramachandra, the Divine Incarnation and the hero of the epic *Ramayana,* said to his father that he would renounce the world and go to a spiritual *Guru* in order to attain spiritual wisdom. The father summoned the

This experience mentioned above by Akhilananda, the fact that Sri Ramakrishna perceived that same Reality or God which he had known directly in the superconscious state as present in the phenomenal universe, especially in the form of man, provides the basis for his harmony between mysticism and everyday life. Rather than being poles apart and unreconcilable, God, the world, and man became empirically unified for Sri Ramakrishna, and this was reflected in his life and teachings.

In fact, this realization that man was a manifestation of God was so vivid and pervasive a part of his spiritual experience that he transmitted it as a major tenet of his teachings to his disciples, especially to Swami Vivekananda, who in turn had this realization himself and then placed special emphasis on it in his lectures in England, India, and America. According to Swami Ashokananda,

> Swami Vivekananda used to call the application of Vedanta in its highest form 'practical Vedanta.' I sometimes think that this, if it was not the most central, was next to the central teaching of Swami Vivekananda. I regard his central teaching as the divinity of man. . . . He wanted every person to become aware of his spiritual, divine nature; he thought that was the most important thing for man in the present age, in the West as well as in the East. Probably next in importance was the worship of God in man.[4]

---

great sage Vashishta to reason with his son. Vashishta saw that Rama had intense dispassion for the world; he then said to him: "O Rama, first discriminate with me, then renounce the world." By right discrimination Rama realized that God manifests Himself in the form of *jiva* or the individual soul and the world. Everything lives and exists in and through His Being. Then Rama kept silent. Some time ago Vaishnava Charan said that perfect knowledge of God is attained when one perceives Him in all human beings. I have now come to a stage of realization in which I see that God is walking in every human form and manifesting Himself alike through the sage and the sinner, the virtuous and the vicious. Therefore, when I meet different people, I say to myself: "God in the form of the saint, God in the form of the sinner, God in the form of the unrighteous and God in the form of the righteous." He who has attained to such realization goes beyond good and evil, above virtue and vice, and realizes that the divine will is working everything.' " *Ibid.,* pp. 66-67. Cf. pp. 70-71.

[4] Ashokananda, *Spiritualizing Everyday Life* (San Francisco: Vedanta Society of Northern California, 1969), pp. 1-2. Ashokananda was particularly well qualified to interpret the life and teachings of Swami Vivekananda. Although he never met Vivekananda and was a disciple of Brahmananda, he had some profound spiritual experiences which included direct personal instruction from Swami Vivekananda. See Ashokananda, *My Philosophy and My Religion* (San Francisco: Vedanta Society of Northern California, 1970) and *Memories of Swami Shivananda* (San Fran-

## The Harmony of Mysticism and Everyday Life

Swami Vivekananda had absorbed his central teachings, the divinity of man and the worship of God in man, at the feet of his master during his period of spiritual training as a young man. They were based squarely on Sri Ramakrishna's experiences, as is shown by the following illustrations: Once, while discussing a subtle philosophical point in reply to young Vivekananda's questions, Sri Ramakrishna exclaimed, "I see that Being as a Reality before my very eyes! Why should I reason? I do actually see that the Absolute has become all things about us. It appears as the individual soul and the phenomenal world."[5] On another occasion, during the last year of Sri Ramakrishna's life when he was dying of throat cancer, he said in Vivekananda's presence,

'Do you know what I see right now? I see that it is God Himself who has become all this. It seems to me that men and other living beings are made of leather, and that it is God Himself who, dwelling inside these leather cases, moves the hands, the feet, the heads. . . . Ah! What a vision.'[6]

---

cisco: Vedanta Society of Northern California, 1969), p. 4 ff. It is necessary to point out here that the terms "Vedanta" and "practical Vedanta" as used by Ashokananda in this quotation denote religion in the generic sense rather than the particular Advaitic Vedantic school, so that Dvaita and Vishishtadvaita as well as Advaita can be classified under it, thus including all religious approaches. Synonymous terms for Vedanta and practical Vedanta as used above, then, would be "Religion" and "practical Religion." It was in this sense that Vivekananda himself developed and used the term Vedanta. See *Works,* II, 357-394, also pp. 298-356; Marie Louise Burke, *Swami Vivekananda in America: New Discoveries* (Calcutta: Advaita Ashrama, 1958), chap. xiii, pp. 537-616; Satis Chandra Chatterjee, *Classical Indian Philosophies: Their Synthesis in the Philosophy of Sri Ramakrishna* (Calcutta: University of Calcutta, 1963).

[5] *Gospel of Ramakrishna* (Abhedananda revision), p. 372. Sri Ramakrishna added the significant comment, " 'One must have an awakening of the spirit within to see the Reality. . . . It is not in mere words such as "I see that God has become everything"; mere saying is not enough' " (*ibid.*).

[6] *Gospel of Sri Ramakrishna* (Nikhilananda trans.), p. 942. This experience occurred on Monday, March 15, 1886, at a time when Sri Ramakrishna could barely speak—"sometimes in a whisper, sometimes by signs" (p. 941). He also stated that he had "had a similar vision once before," at which time he "saw houses, gardens, roads, men, cattle—all made of One Substance" (p. 942). After Sri Ramakrishna reported that vision, he went immediately into *samadhi*. After coming down from *samadhi*, he cast his glance at one of his disciples, and said, " 'There is Loto. He bends his head, resting it on the palm of his hand. I see that it is God Himself who rests His head on His hand' " (*ibid.*).

## WORSHIP OF GOD IN MAN

Such experiences revealing the nature of man as inseparably connected with God represented the acme of Sri Ramakrishna's spiritual pilgrimage. He indicated this to Swami Vivekananda on January 2, 1886, in the following episode, as related two days later to Mahendranath Gupta (known as "M") by Vivekananda:

'I was meditating here last Saturday when I suddenly felt a peculiar sensation in my heart. It was probably the awakening of the kundalini. I clearly perceived the ida and pingala nerves. Yesterday, I told the Master about it. I said to him, "The others have had their realization, please let me have it too. Am I the only one who has to stay unsatisfied?" He said, "Why don't you settle your family affairs first? Then you can have everything. . . . What is it you want?" I said, "I want to remain in samadhi for three or four days, only coming down to the sense-plane once in a while, to eat a little." Then he said to me, "You're a fool—there's a much higher state than that! You are fond of singing the song, 'All that exists art Thou'—well, after coming down from samadhi, one may see that it is God himself who has become the universe and all that exists. Only an ishwarakoti can reach that state. An ordinary man can only reach samadhi, at best. He can't go any farther." '[7]

## DEIFICATION OF EXPERIENCE: WORK AS WORSHIP

The mystical experiences as described by Sri Ramakrishna in the foregoing illustrations are those in which the world and man himself are perceived as God. From this vantage point all experience,

---

[7] As quoted in Isherwood, pp. 297-298. Swami Vivekananda was considered by Sri Ramakrishna to be an *ishwarakoti* (see *ibid.,* p. 223; cf. Akhilananda, *Hindu View of Christ,* p. 27). For Vivekananda's own explanation of the awakening of the kundalini, see his *Raja-Yoga* (Mayavati edition), chap. v, "The Control of Psychic Prana," pp. 66-74. Another incident which reinforces the point in this passage, i.e., that to see God in all is the pinnacle of mystical life according to Sri Ramakrishna, is related in his *Life*: "One day the Master asked Sarat, 'How would you like to realise God? What divine visions do you prefer to see in meditation?' Sarat replied, 'I do not want to see any particular form of God in meditation. I want to see Him as manifested in all creatures of the world. I do not like visions.' The Master said with a smile, 'That is the last word in spiritual attainment. You cannot have it all at once.' 'But I won't be satisfied with anything short of that,' replied the boy, 'I shall trudge on in the path of religious practice till that blessed state arrives' " (p. 475). Sarat later became Swami Saradananda.

no matter how ordinary, is deified.[8] All acts are acts of worship.[9] Here mysticism of the highest type becomes harmonized with everyday life. Sri Ramakrishna uses the data of his spiritual experience as a pedagogical tool, showing that the means and the end are one:[10] as God is in man, man should be worshipped as God; as all experience is in God, it should be deified to experience God. His teachings stress that daily life become an instrument for God-realization, that work become worship, and that every person is to be looked upon as a veritable expression of God.[11] The following event highlights this point.

## "THE SERVICE MOTIVE"

One day in 1884 Sri Ramakrishna, in the presence of Vivekananda and others, was commenting on the teachings of Sri Chaitanya. Explaining that the whole universe is the household of God,

[8] Cf. Vivekananda, "God in Everything," *Works,* II, 144-145, esp. the following: "It really means deification of the world—giving up the world as we think of it, as it appears to us—and to know what it really is. Deify it; it is God alone. . . . 'Whatever exists in this universe, is to be covered with the Lord.' . . . See God in the wife . . . see God in your children. . . . It is He who is in the child, in the wife and in the husband; it is He who is in the good and in the bad. . . . A tremendous assertion indeed!" (p. 146). Cf. Ashokananda, *Spiritualizing Everyday Life,* pp. 9-27.

[9] See Vivekananda, *Karma-Yoga, Works,* I, 23-116. Cf. Brother Lawrence, *The Practice of the Presence of God* (London: A. R. Mowbray, 1965).

[10] Cf. Vivekananda, *Works,* I, 68-69; Oliver Lacombe, "Swami Vivekananda and Practical Vedanta," in *Swami Vivekananda Memorial Volume* (Calcutta: Swami Vivekananda Centenary Committee, 1963), pp. 283-286.

[11] Akhilananda, *Modern Problems,* chap. ix, "Practical Vedanta," pp. 129-134. In this connection, Akhilananda states, "True social service, philanthropic work, and love of neighbor are practiced and taught by the people who are well established in these higher experiences and love of God. So the refutations of some religious groups and scientific thinkers are far from the truth. The real mystic who has spiritual realization of superconscious experiences becomes extremely interested in his fellow beings as he finds the expression of God in them. A mystic feels the presence of God everywhere and so he takes a loving interest not only in human beings but also in other beings. St. Francis of Assisi, after having his mystic realization, saw first the presence of God in every object; and secondly, he could feel universal brotherhood everywhere. . . . When you study the lives of Christian, Hindu, Buddhist and Mohammedan mystics, and other religious personalities, you will find that the secret of their loving service lies in the depth of their mystic superconscious experiences" (pp. 152-153).

and that therefore one should have compassion for all beings, he suddenly went into *samadhi*. When he regained partial consciousness, he declared, "Who are you to bestow compassion on anyone? Not compassion, but service! service! service! Service to *jiva* as Shiva. Service to man as God Himself."[12]

Swami Vivekananda's reaction to this statement is set forth in the following passage from Saradananda:

All went on listening to those words of the Master in Bhavasamadhi; but none could detect and understand their hidden import at that time. It was Narendranath [Vivekananda] alone who, coming out of the room at the end of the Master's samadhi, said, 'Ah! what a wonderful light have I got today from the Master's words! In synthesizing the Vedantic knowledge, which was generally regarded as dry, austere and even cruel, with sweet devotion to the Lord, what a new mellowed means of experiencing the Truth has he revealed today! In order to attain the nondual knowledge, one, we have been told so long, should have to renounce the world and the company of men altogether and retire to the forest and, mercilessly uproot and throw away love, devotion and other soft and tender emotions from the heart. Formerly when the sadhaka used to try to attain that knowledge in the old way, he used to regard the whole universe and each person in it as obstacles to the path of religion and, contracting, therefore, a hatred for them, he more often than not used to go astray. But from what the Master in Bhavasamadhi said today, it is gathered that the Vedanta of the forest can be brought to human habitation and that it can be applied in practice to the work-a-day world. Let man do every thing he is doing; there is no harm in that; it is sufficient for him, first, to be fully convinced that it is God that exists, manifested before him as the universe and all the beings in it. Those, with whom he comes in contact every moment of his life, whom he loves, respects and honours, to whom his sympathy and kindness flow, are all His parts—are all He Himself. If he can thus look upon all the persons of the world as Siva, how can there be an occasion for him to regard himself as superior to them or cherish anger and hatred for them or an arrogant attitude to them, yes, or to be even kind to them? Thus serving the Jivas as Siva, he will have his heart purified and be convinced in a short time that he himself is also a part of Isvara, the eternally pure, awake and free, and Bliss absolute.

'We get a great light on the path of devotion too from those words of the Master. Until he sees God in all beings, the sadhaka has not the

12 *Sayings,* p. 260; Saradananda, p. 821.

remotest chance of realizing true transcendental devotion. If the devout sadhaka serves the Jivas as Siva or Narayana, he, it is superfluous to say, will see God in all, attain true devotion and have the aim of his life fulfilled in a short time. Those sadhakas who adopt the yoga of action or the royal road to the realization of God, will also get great light from those words. For, as embodied beings can never rest for a moment without doing work, it goes without saying that it is only the work of the service of Jivas as Siva that should be performed and action done in that spirit will enable them to reach the Goal sooner than otherwise. If the divine Lord ever grants me an opportunity, I'll proclaim every where in the world this wonderful truth I have heard today. I will preach this truth to the learned and the ignorant, to the rich and the poor, to the Brahmanas and the Chandalas.'[13]

## SYNTHESIS

The "service motive" as enunciated by Sri Ramakrishna and interpreted by Swami Vivekananda provides a realistic, workable synthesis among the paths to God of *karma yoga* (action), *bhakti yoga* (devotion), and *jnana yoga* (knowledge). It brings mysticism down from its inaccessible and dizzy heights to the workaday world of ordinary human contacts, and transforms everyday experience into the mystic's reality. Its practice is non-sectarian: a Christian, Muslim, Jew or Hindu can regard his fellow-being as a child of God, a part of God, or as God Himself depending on his temperamental or philosophical disposition, and serve him accordingly.[14] This attitude of service itself becomes, then, a dynamic spiritual practice leading to the vision of God.

---

[13] Saradananda, pp. 821-822. Cf. Ashokananda, *Swami Vivekananda in San Francisco*, pp. 36-43. Akhilananda states, "The new spirit of the service of man was introduced by Sri Ramakrishna. Charity and philanthropy, as known ordinarily, had no spiritual meaning for him, as he saw that they stimulated the feeling of superiority in the giver with a consequent corresponding feeling of inferiority in the receiver. So both giver and receiver were demoralized by such charity." *Modern Problems*, pp. 144-145.

[14] Akhilananda, *Modern Problems*, p. 129.

# CHAPTER IX

# The Harmony of Marriage and Monasticism

Monasticism and marriage are the two basic ways of life by which a person may develop spiritually. While marriage as such is sanctified by most religious traditions, only Hinduism, Buddhism, and Christianity among the world religions have institutionalized monasticism.[1]

## MEANING OF SRI RAMAKRISHNA'S DUAL ROLE

Sri Ramakrishna showed by his life and teachings that the ideal of both the householder and monk represent workable paths to the experience of God,[2] and by harmonizing both these ideals in his own life, he showed that they need not be mutually exclusive. His example in the modern age furnishes a reaffirmation of the divine purpose regulating the holy union between husband and wife. His complete renunciation re-establishes the legitimacy of the monastic vow for God-realization. At a time when neither marriage nor mo-

---

[1] This is not to say that monasticism as a spiritual way of life has not existed in other traditions at various times during religious history on an individual or collective basis (viz., some Sufi saints, the Essenes, Therapeutae, etc.).

[2] Cf. Vivekananda, Karma-Yoga, chap. ii, "Each is Great in His Own Place," Works, I, 34-49.

nasticism has preserved its spiritual vitality, at a time when both are disintegrating as institutions of society as well as of God, the examples of such singular men encourage others to uphold rather than denounce or ignore these primary ideals of religious life.

## MARRIAGE TO SRI SARADA DEVI

Sri Ramakrishna's marriage to Saradamani Devi occurred after he had experienced God, at age twenty-three. According to Indian custom,[3] his family searched for an appropriate bride, but it was not until he himself said, in a mood of absorption in God-consciousness, " 'It is useless to try here and there. Go to Jayrambati, and there you will find the bride providentially reserved for me in the house of Ram Chandra Mukhopadhyaya.' "[4] Although the girl was considered somewhat young, being five years of age, she was accepted by the family and the betrothal ceremony took place. From this event it is clear that not only did Sri Ramakrishna fully consent to his marrying, which had been at the insistence of his mother and relatives, but he had a direct role in the choice of his bride. On the surface, this attitude appears paradoxical in the light of his indifference to worldly and domestic concerns at that time resulting from his total commitment to spiritual practices.

Sri Ramakrishna spent several months with Sarada Devi following this occasion and then again on his return to Kamarpukur in

---

[3] "The Hindus, to keep up a high standard of chastity in the race, have sanctioned child-marriage, which in the long run has degraded the race. At the same time, I cannot deny that this child-marriage makes the race more chaste. What would you have? If you want the nation to be more chaste, you weaken men and women physically by child-marriage. On the other hand, are you in England any better off? No, because chastity is the life of a nation. Do you not find in history that the first death-sign of a nation has been unchastity? When that has entered, the end of the race is in sight. Where shall we get a solution of these miseries then? If parents select husbands and wives for their children, then this evil is minimised. The daughters of India are more practical than sentimental. But very little of poetry remains in their lives. Again, if people select their own husbands and wives, that does not seem to bring much happiness. The Indian woman is generally very happy; there are not many cases of quarrelling between husband and wife. On the other hand, in the United States, where the greatest liberty obtains, the number of unhappy homes and marriages is large." Vivekananda, *Our Women* (Calcutta: Advaita Ashrama, 1965), pp. 22-23.

[4] *Life,* pp. 101-102.

1867, when she was thirteen years old. His young bride was sweet, pure-hearted[5] and, even at that young age, extremely devoted to her new husband. In his presence, as she recalled later, " 'I used to feel always as if a pitcher full of bliss were placed in my heart—the joy was ineffable.' " Sri Ramakrishna's biographer states that "as a result of this inward bliss her character was completely transformed."[6]

When Sarada Devi came to Calcutta to join her husband in 1872, Sri Ramakrishna resumed the task, begun five years before, of instructing her in a "wide range of subjects from house-keeping to the knowledge of Brahman."[7] With regard to conjugal love, "he was prepared to allow her to exercise her right as a wife and yet he

---

[5] One of the chief characteristics of Sri Sarada Devi's personality was the purity she manifested throughout her life. "I used to pray in the moon-lit night," she once said, " 'O Lord, there is stain even in the moon. Let there be no stain in my mind.' " *Thus Spake The Holy Mother,* comp. by Swami Suddhasatwananda (Mylapore, Madras: Sri Ramakrishna Math, 1953), p. 52. On other occasions she made the following statements relative to this point: "Everything depends on the mind. Nothing can be achieved without purity of mind. . . . What else does one obtain by the realization of God? Does he grow two horns? No, his mind becomes pure, and through a pure mind one obtains knowledge and awakening. . . . He who has a pure mind sees everything pure. . . . It is in the mind alone that one feels pure and impure" *(ibid.,* pp. 40-41). Cf. Matt. 5:8. "When a man sees defects in others, his mind first gets polluted. What does he gain by finding fault in others? He hurts himself by that. From my childhood I could not find faults in others. That one thing I have never learnt in life" (p. 48). "One should work hard for the realization of God. What a wonderful mind I had at that time! Somebody used to play on flute at night at Dakshineswar. As I listened to the sound my mind would be extremely eager for the realization of God. I thought that the sound was coming directly from God, and I would enter into *Samadhi.* . . . The mind is rendered pure as a result of much austerities. God who is purity itself cannot be attained without austerities" (pp. 44-45). "Sri Sarada Devi['s] . . . last statement before passing away was . . . 'There is no one who is your enemy. Make everyone your own by love.' This is the true spirit of religion." Akhilananda, *Modern Problems,* p. 107.

[6] *Life,* p. 246.

[7] *Ibid.,* p. 249. "She used to say that in those days the Master taught her everything—beginning with such details of domestic life as how a lamp was to be trimmed, how she was to behave with the different members of her family according to their different natures, and how she should conduct herself while visiting, up to the highest spiritual subjects such as prayer, chanting of the Lord's name, meditation, Samadhi and even realisation of the Brahman. How different from the married life of the ordinary man!" *(ibid.,* p. 251).

paused—and frank as a child he asked her once, in her early days at Dakshineswar, " 'Do you want to drag me down into Maya?' 'Why should I do that? I have come only to help you in the path of religious life,' was her prompt reply. And she lived true to her word."[8] The following passage from his most recent biographer puts this issue in sharp relief from Sri Ramakrishna's perspective:

Ramakrishna regarded Sarada's coming as a test of purity; and it was not for him, but for God, to decide when it should take place. This test was to be, in fact, the last of his sadhanas. During the eighteen months that now followed, Ramakrishna and Sarada lived together in the closest intimacy. Often they slept together in the same bed. When Sarada spoke of this period later in her life, she would describe it as one of continuous ecstasy; a state of married bliss which was nevertheless absolutely sexless. Such a relationship is so unthinkable to most of us that we can do nothing but take it on trust.

'If she had not been so pure,' Ramakrishna used to say of Sarada, 'if she had lost her self-control and made any demand on me—who knows? Perhaps my own self-control would have given way. Perhaps I should have become sex-conscious. After I got married, I implored the Divine Mother to keep Sarada's mind absolutely free from lust. And now, after living with Sarada all that time, I know that the Mother granted my prayer.'

One day, while Sarada was massaging Ramakrishna's feet, she asked him, 'How do you think of me?' And he answered, 'The same Mother who's in the temple, and the same Mother who gave birth to me and is now living in the music-tower—that same Mother is rubbing my feet. That's the truth; I always see you as a form of the blissful Divine Mother.'

Once, at night, as he watched Sarada lying asleep beside him, Ramakrishna addressed his own mind, in a mood of discrimination: 'Oh, my Mind, this is the body of a woman. Men look on it as an object of great enjoyment; something to be highly prized. They devote their lives to enjoying it. But, if one possesses this body, one must remain confined within the flesh; one can't realize God. Oh my Mind, don't be thinking one thing in private and outwardly pretending another! Be frank! Do you want this body of a woman, or do you want God?' The mere idea of touching Sarada's body with lust made Ramakrishna's mind recoil and lose itself so deeply in samadhi that he did not regain normal consciousness all night.[9]

---

[8] Kalpalata Devi, "The Life Divine (A Tribute to Sri Sarada Devi)," *Prabuddha Bharata,* The Holy Mother Birth Centenary Number, LIX (March, 1954), 122.
[9] Isherwood, pp. 145-146.

## THE PROBLEM OF CONTINENCE

### Evaluation of Sexual Continence

The rationale for sexual continence as a means for God-realization is clear: sexual energy is stored and transformed into psychic or spiritual energy.[10] This energy strengthens the mind, which is the

[10] See Ananda, *Spiritual Practice, passim,* esp. chap. xiii, "Brahmacharya," pp. 130-140; Gonda, *Change and Continuity,* chap. ix, "Brahmacharya," pp. 284-314; *Spiritual Teachings of Swami Brahmananda, passim;* and the following passage from Vivekananda's *Raja-Yoga* (Mayavati edition): "The *Yogis* claim that of all the energies that are in the human body the highest is what they call *'Ojas.'* Now this *Ojas* is stored up in the brain, and the more *Ojas* is in a man's head, the more powerful he is, the more intellectual, the more spiritually strong. One man may speak beautiful language and beautiful thoughts, but they do not impress people; another man speaks neither beautiful language nor beautiful thoughts, yet his words charm. Every movement of his is powerful. That is the power of *Ojas.* Now in every man there is more or less of this *Ojas* stored up. All the forces that are working in the body in their highest become *Ojas.* You must remember that it is only a question of transformation. The same force which is working outside as electricity or magnetism, will become changed into inner force; the same forces that are working as muscular energy will be changed into *Ojas.* The *Yogis* say that that part of the human energy which is expressed as sex energy, in sexual thought, when checked and controlled, easily becomes changed into *Ojas,* and as the *Muladhara* guides these, the *Yogi* pays particular attention to that centre. He tries to take up all this sexual energy and convert it into *Ojas.* It is only the chaste man or woman who can make the *Ojas* rise and store it in the brain; that is why chastity has always been considered the highest virtue. A man feels that if he is unchaste, spirituality goes away, he loses mental vigour and moral stamina. That is why in all the religious orders in the world which have produced spiritual giants you will always find absolute chastity insisted upon. That is why the monks came into existence, giving up marriage. There must be perfect chastity, in thought, word and deed; without it the practice of *Raja-Yoga* is dangerous, and may lead to insanity. If people practise *Raja-Yoga* and at the same time lead an impure life, how can they expect to become *Yogis?"* (pp. 72-74). Cf. Thomas à Kempis, *The Following of Christ; Spiritual Talks* by the First Disciples of Sri Ramakrishna (Mayavati, Almora: Advaita Ashrama, 1955); *The Spiritual Exercises of St. Ignatius,* trans. by Anthony Mottola, Image Books (Garden City, N. Y.: Doubleday, 1964); *The Confessions of St. Augustine;* Peter Brown, *Augustine of Hippo;* Eugene Portalie, *A Guide to the Thought of St. Augustine,* trans. by Ralph J. Bastian (Chicago: Henry Regnery Co., 1960); Jean Leclerq, *The Love of Learning and the Desire for God, A Study of Monastic Culture,* trans. by Catharine Misrahi, Mentor Omega Books (New York: New American Library, 1961); Jorgensen, *St. Francis of Assisi; The Works of St. John of the Cross;* Barban, *St. Anthony of Padua; The Sutra of the Sixth Patriarch on the Pristine Orthodox Dharma,* trans. by Paul F. Fung and George D. Fung (San Francisco: Buddha's Universal Church, 1964); Thera, *The Buddha's Ancient Path;* Buddhaghosa, *The Path of Purification;* Swami Atmananda, *The Four Yogas* (Bombay:

instrument of perception, making it possible for it to experience subtler and subtler realities through prayer and meditation, until the subtlest of all reality—God—reveals Itself. It was with this understanding that Sri Ramakrishna chose to maintain, even during married life, the vow of monasticism *(sannyasa)* into which he was initiated by Tota Puri in 1864. For him, continence and God-realization were inseparably related. Additionally, Sri Ramakrishna's choice to maintain continence during married life was fully consistent with his perception of the Divine Mother in all women.[11] The following incident, related by Sri Ramakrishna's biographers, representing the culmination of his twelve years of spiritual practices, highlights this fact:

> In the spring of 1872, Ramakrishna confirmed, by one of the most memorable acts of his life, the truth of the answer he had given to Sarada's question, 'How do you think of me?' It was May 25, a day of the new moon which is set aside for a special worship of the Goddess Kali.[12]

Sri Ramakrishna made special arrangements for it [the worship] in his

---

Bharatiya Vidya Bhavan, 1966); Swami Abhedananda, *True Psychology* (3d rev. ed.; Calcutta: Ramakrishna Vedanta Math, 1965), his *The Yoga Psychology* (Calcutta: Ramakrishna Vedanta Math, 1967), and his *Yoga, Its Theory and Practice* (Calcutta: Ramakrishna Vedanta Math, 1967); W. Y. Evans-Wentz, ed., *Tibetan Yoga and Secret Doctrines* (2d ed.; London: Oxford University Press, 1958); Ghose, *Lord Gauranga,* and Joan Mowat Erickson, *Saint Francis and His Four Ladies* (New York: W. W. Norton, 1970). In considering the Vedantic viewpoint, note the following statement: *"Brahmacharya* (continence) . . . is the very basis of spiritual progress. . . . The root of sex-consciousness goes deep into our mind and life. It may almost be said to be contemporaneous with the very beginning of individual life. The idea of duality is in a sense the prop of the sexual consciousness. Therefore, Sri Ramakrishna said that until a man has realized God, he cannot completely rid himself of lust. To recognize sexual difference in men and women is a kind of sexuality. When one has completely eradicated lust, one will not feel that difference. Only the Atman will be apparent, existing in all, beyond all distinction of sex and body." Ananda, pp. 129-130.

[11] Cf. the following statement by Vivekananda: "In my opinion, a race must first cultivate a great respect for motherhood, through the sanctification and inviolability of marriage, before it can attain to the ideal of perfect chastity. The Roman Catholics and the Hindus, holding marriage sacred and inviolate, have produced great chaste men and women of immense power. . . . As you have come to see that the glory of life is chastity, so my eyes also have been opened to the necessity of this great sanctification for the vast majority, in order that a few lifelong chaste powers may be produced." *Our Women,* p. 11.

[12] Isherwood, p. 146.

own room, instructing the Holy Mother to be present. She went there at 9 P.M. Sri Ramakrishna took the seat of the priest. After the preliminaries were over, he beckoned the Holy Mother to the seat which was reserved for the Goddess. Sarada Devi was in a semi-conscious state as she reverently watched the proceedings, and . . . took the seat as she was told. Sri Ramakrishna with the help of an assistant, went through the regular form of worship, in which the Holy Mother took the place of the Deity. During the ceremony she went into Samadhi. The Master, too, when he had finished the Mantras, went into the superconscious state. Priest and Goddess were joined in a transcendental union in the Self. Hours passed. At dead of night the Master partially recovered consciousness; then with the appropriate Mantra he surrendered himself and the fruits of his lifelong Sadhana, together with his rosary, at the feet of the Holy Mother and saluted her.

With this sacred ceremony, called in the Tantras the Shodasi Puja or the worship of the Woman, was finished the long series of Sri Ramakrishna's spiritual practices. It was the consummation of his Sadhana, in which he dedicated his all to the Mother of the universe, manifested through the living symbol of Sarada Devi. To his illumined vision everything in the universe became the symbol of God. His sweeping glance encompassed both Absolute and Manifestation.[13]

### Sanctification of Marriage

Thus did Sri Ramakrishna "consummate" his marriage to Sarada Devi, known as the Holy Mother.[14] Contrast this with contemporary sensate culture,[15] in which lack of sexual union in a marriage is considered legal grounds for divorce or annulment, marriage itself being a legal convenience for procreation and property rather than a path to God.[16] Sri Ramakrishna's wife had a radically different kind of union, one in which she was made fully aware of the indwelling presence of God. Sister Nivedita[17] makes the following observation in this connection:

[13] *Life,* pp. 249-250.

[14] Swami Gambhirananda, *Holy Mother, Shri Sarada Devi* (Madras: Sri Ramakrishna Math, 1955); *Sri Sarada Devi, The Holy Mother* (Madras: Sri Ramakrishna Math, 1949); *At Holy Mother's Feet (Teachings of Shri Saradi Devi),* by Her Direct Disciples (Mayavati, Almora: Advaita Ashrama, 1963); *Prabuddha Bharata,* LIX (March, 1954).

[15] See Sorokin, *Reconstruction of Humanity;* Akhilananda, *Modern Problems.*

[16] Cf. Nivedita, *The Master as I Saw Him,* p. 332.

[17] Sister Nivedita (Miss Margaret Noble) was an Englishwoman who became one

Sri Ramakrishna, it was said, had always referred to marriage as a special, and to the monastic life as a universal service. In this he was, one supposes, alluding only to marriage of the very highest type. And this was clearly the determining concept of celibacy or Brahmacharya.[18]

All the disciples of Ramakrishna believe that marriage is finally perfected by the man's acceptance of his wife as the mother; and this means, by their mutual adoption of the monastic life. It is a moment of the mergence of the human in the divine, by which all life stands thenceforward changed. The psychological justification of this ideal is said to be the fact that, up to this critical point, the relation of marriage consists in a constant succession of a two-fold impulse, the waxing followed by the waning, of affection. With the abandonment of the external, however, impulse is transcended, and there is no fluctuation. Henceforth the beloved is worshipped in perfect steadfastness of mind.[19]

This steadfastness of mind, in which both husband and wife worshipped each other as embodiments of the ultimate Reality, did not abate with the end of the formal worship in which both had become absorbed in *samadhi*. "Months passed in this way, but not once did the minds of this divine couple come down to the plane of sense. This was possible, because both husband and wife had their minds attuned to the Infinite."[20] Sri Ramakrishna's biographer makes the following comment relative to the termination of his strenuous twelve-year period of spiritual practices:

---

of Vivekananda's foremost disciples. She had the opportunity of knowing the Holy Mother intimately some time after Sri Ramakrishna's passing away. See Pravrajika Atmaprana, *Sister Nivedita of Ramakrishna-Vivekananda* (2d ed.; Calcutta: Sister Nivedita Girls' School, 1967); see Nivedita's letter to Holy Mother in *Thus Spake The Holy Mother*, pp. xiv-xviii.

[18] Nivedita, *The Master as I Saw Him*, p. 331.

[19] *Ibid.*, pp. 337-338.

[20] *Life*, p. 252. Not only on the plane of the Infinite, but in common everyday contact with her, Sri Ramakrishna treated Sarada Devi with the utmost respect and tenderness as the following passage illustrates: "I was married to such a husband who never so much as spoke to me slightingly. Once at Dakshineswar I carried some food to his room. Thinking it was Lakshmi and not I, he said to me as I was coming away, 'Close the door as thou goest,' using the familiar second person singular (i.e. thou) as is the custom (in Bengal) when addressing juniors or inferiors. I answered, 'Yes, I am doing so.' He was embarrassed when he recognized my voice and said, 'Oh, it is you! I thought it was Lakshmi. Please do not mind my addressing you that way.' Even the next day he came before my room and said, 'Look, my dear, I could not sleep last night, wondering how I could speak so rudely to you.' " *At Holy Mother's Feet*, p. 142.

When even after the lapse of a year or more Sri Ramakrishna felt not the least trace of body-idea in his mind, and continued to look upon Sarada Devi sometimes as the manifestation of the Divine Mother and sometimes as the Atman or Brahman, he understood that the Mother had brought him successfully through the ordeal, and that, through Her grace his mind was able to remain without any effort on his part on the highest plane of spiritual realisation. He felt that the grace of the Divine Mother had brought him to the end of his Sadhanas.[21]

## HIS WIFE AS FIRST DISCIPLE

Sarada Devi not only represented Sri Ramakrishna's final test in his struggles as a spiritual aspirant, but she also became his first disciple as a spiritual teacher. She would later be instrumental in guiding the young monks of the Order after his passing away. Her purity, modesty, simplicity of life and spiritual attainments would set the example for men and women of diverse religious paths and temperaments who would come to her for spiritual blessings, guidance and consolation.[22]

Having conquered lust with God's grace, and having lived, sought and realized the truth, Sri Ramakrishna could then, as a spiritual teacher, insist uncompromisingly on the two cardinal virtues which he deemed necessary for the experience of God: truth and continence.[23] In these, according to this viewpoint, lay the harmony between monasticism and marriage. While he recognized poverty, chastity, and obedience as the universal ideals of the monastic life, he would advocate mental detachment to "woman and gold" (his characteristic expression for sex and wealth) for his householder disciples, so that their married life in the world might itself become a path to God, and thereby be transformed into a life of God-consciousness.[24] Truth was at the root of all his teachings to householder and monk alike.

---

[21] *Life, ibid.*

[22] See *Sri Sarada Devi, The Holy Mother.*

[23] *Spiritual Life* (Madras: Sri Ramakrishna Math, n.d.), p. 12.

[24] See *Gospel of Ramakrishna,* both Abhedananda and Nikhilananda versions; cf. Vivekananda, *Karma-Yoga,* chap. vi, "Non-Attachment is Complete Self-Abnegation," *Works,* I, 79-91.

## ANALYSIS OF HIS MOTIVES IN MARRYING

In considering Sri Ramakrishna's personal motives for marriage after having renounced worldly enjoyments for the sake of the experience of God, Isherwood makes the following comments based on Saradananda's interpretation:

> Saradananda, in his book, anticipates the reader's question: why, if Ramakrishna had dedicated himself to a monastic life, did he get married?
>
> Certainly, says Saradananda, Ramakrishna was not bullied into marriage by his family. Anyone who has read his story even up to this point will know that nobody ever made Ramakrishna do anything against his will—or, to put it more accurately, against what he believed was the will of the Divine Mother. It is obvious that he married willingly, since it was he who chose the bride.
>
> After dismissing some other possible reasons, Saradananda concludes that Ramakrishna married in order to show the world an ideal. The Hindu practice of marriage had become degraded at that time. The wife was a mere servant of her husband's domestic convenience and his lust. But Ramakrishna educated his wife in many ways and watched over her like a father. He did not even treat her as an equal; he worshipped her, as an embodiment of the Mother. If Ramakrishna had never married, his lay disciples might have said to themselves, 'It's very easy for him to talk about continence; he has never known the temptations of sex.' But Ramakrishna . . . preserved unbroken continence, while living with his wife in the closest intimacy at a time when she was a beautiful young woman.
>
> It is not that Ramakrishna held up the ideal of a sexless marriage for all to follow; he was not proposing to put an end to the human race. 'Whatever I do,' he used to say, 'is done for all of you. If I do all the sixteen parts'—referring to the sixteen annas which make up the whole rupee—'you may possibly do one.'[25]

## EVALUATION OF HIS CONTRIBUTION TO SPIRITUAL PRACTICES

For traditions in which chastity is regarded as a primary ideal for

[25] Isherwood, pp. 82-83. Cf. Gonda, chap. iv, "The Number Sixteen," pp. 115-130; Nivedita, *The Master as I Saw Him*, chap. xxi, pp. 324-343; see esp. *The Saint Durgacharan Nag (The Life of An Ideal Householder)* (Madras: Sri Ramakrishna Math, 1951); Akhilananda, *Mental Health*, chap. xii, "Love, Marriage and Religion," pp. 143-159.

spiritual life, Sri Ramakrishna's special contribution to spiritual practices is the *method* by which chastity can be achieved. He demonstrated in his relation with his wife that when a man or woman is regarded as a veritable manifestation of God, man as "Father" and woman as "Mother," lower propensities are automatically subdued and nobler, uplifting thoughts replace them. In this way a man aspiring to the higher life of God-consciousness looks upon every woman, including his own wife, as the embodiment of the Divine Mother of the universe. When this attitude is practiced regularly and systematically in conjunction with other aspects of mental and spiritual training as advocated by the great teachers of all religions, lust itself becomes transformed into the desire to know and experience God. According to Sri Ramakrishna,

'So long as these passions are directed towards the world and its objects, they behave as enemies. But when they are directed towards God, they become the best friends of man; for then they lead him to God. The lust for the things of the world must be changed into a hankering for God; the anger that man feels in relation to others should be turned towards God for His not manifesting Himself to him. One should deal with all passions in the same manner. These passions cannot be eradicated, but they can be educated.[26]

Sri Ramakrishna transmitted this attitude, which was based on his own life and practices, to his householder and monastic disciples alike. At the same time, he treated each individually with deep insight into the mental structure of each person, administering spiritual instruction according to his or her temperament and character. But Swami Vivekananda, who had been imbued with a thoroughly rationalistic Western education, was unable to understand or accept Sri Ramakrishna's worship of God as Mother for the first few years. This became a focal point in his dramatic discipleship under Sri Ramakrishna's spiritual guidance.

[26] *Spiritual Life,* pp. 11-12.

# CHAPTER X

# *Vivekananda: Seeker Becomes Teacher*

## LINE OF SUCCESSION

Swami Vivekananda was Sri Ramakrishna's spiritual successor with respect to the mission of broadcasting and interpreting his life and teachings both to India and the West, while Swami Brahmananda was regarded as Sri Ramakrishna's spiritual son, and as such became the first President of the Ramakrishna Order. While Swami Vivekananda founded the religious order bearing Sri Ramakrishna's name, it was left to Swami Brahmananda to carry out the work of training a generation of young monks under the guiding principles of Sri Ramakrishna's teachings. Swami Vivekananda, the first missionary of Hinduism to the West, was a man of extraordinary dynamism whose ten-year career of service to "God in man" burned out his life at age thirty-nine on July 4, 1902. This key to his nature, service to God in man, was inspired by profound spiritual realizations at the feet of his master, and guided all his subsequent activities. Akhilananda comments on his temperamental disposition and early questing spirit:

> In contemporary history, Swami Vivekananda demonstrated that he was a universal lover of mankind, even though he was originally a monist.[1]

[1] *Spiritual Practices,* p. 107.

His mind was predominantly rational. He followed that path primarily, but he was also a lover of God. His love cannot be measured by ordinary people. He attained various types of *samadhi* (superconscious experience) even though he started first with the monistic attitude.[2]

Swami Vivekananda was brought up in the Western system of education in Calcutta. He was thoroughly acquainted with the philosophy of John Stuart Mill, Herbert Spencer, and such others. He was acquainted with the philosophical and scientific thinking of his time; consequently, he can be regarded as representative of contemporary thinkers. In his quest for the truth, he went to various religious men and asked the challenging question, 'Sir, have you seen God?' No one could give him a satisfactory answer. Then he met Sri Ramakrishna and put the question to Him. He answered, 'Yes, I see Him more vividly than I see you, and you can see Him too.' We can safely say that this was the beginning of Swami Vivekananda's experimentation in the field of mysticism.[3]

## EARLY TRAINING

Vivekananda's versatility in superconscious experience reflected that of his teacher. As Akhilananda points out, his spiritual life began with a thoroughly monistic attitude through his experience of the impersonal aspect of God, *Nirguna Brahman,* but his spiritual development led to various exalted experiences of the personal God in different forms, including that of Divine Mother. The first instance of *samadhi* in the life of Vivekananda was communicated by a touch from Sri Ramakrishna, and is described as follows by Saradananda, using Vivekananda's own words:

'No sooner had he seen me than he called me joyfully to him and made me sit on one end of the bedstead. He spoke indistinctly something to himself, looked steadfastly at me and was slowly coming towards me. . . .

[2] *Ibid.,* p. 34.

[3] *Ibid.,* p. 101. On that occasion, Sri Ramakrishna also said, as D. S. Sarma narrates: " 'God can be realized. One can see and talk to Him as I am doing with you. But who cares to do so? People shed torrents of tears for their wives and children, for wealth or property, but who does so for the sake of God? If one weeps sincerely for Him, He surely manifests Himself.' This impressed Narendra at once. In later years he used to say referring to this incident, 'For the first time, I found a man who dared to say that he had seen God, that religion was a reality to be felt, to be sensed, in an infinitely more intense way than we can sense the world. As I heard these things from his lips, I could not but believe that he was saying them not like an ordinary preacher, but from the depths of his own realizations.' " *The Master and the Disciple,* p. 73.

He came to me and placed his right foot on my body, when, immediately, I had a wonderful perception. I saw with my eyes open, that all the things of the room together with the walls were rapidly whirling and receding into an unknown region and my "I"-ness together with the whole universe was, as it were, going to vanish in the all-devouring great void. I was then overwhelmed with a terrible fear; I had known that the destruction of "I"-ness was death and that death was before me, very near at hand. Unable to control myself, I cried out loudly and said, "Ah! what is it you have done to me? I have my parents, you know." Giving out a hoarse laugh to hear those words of mine and touching my breast with his hand, he said, "Let it then cease now; it need not be done all at once; it will come to pass in course of time." I was amazed to see that extraordinary perception of mine vanish as quickly as it had come when he touched me that way and said those words. I came to the normal state and saw things inside and outside the room standing still as before.'[4]

The second such experience was told to Saradananda both by Vivekananda and Sri Ramakrishna, and is recounted as follows:

The Master walked with Narendra for some time in the garden on the bank of the Ganga that day. Talking with Narendra, he came to that parlour, sat down there and went into samadhi shortly afterwards. Narendra sat near at hand, and was calmly observing that state of the Master, when the latter suddenly approached and touched him as before. Although he exercised great caution because of his previous experiences, Narendra became completely overwhelmed at that powerful touch. He lost external consciousness completely that day, unlike what had happened on the previous occasions. When he regained consciousness, after some time, he saw that the Master was passing his hand on his chest and, on seeing him come to the normal state, smiled gently and sweetly.

Narendra did not tell us anything of the nature of the experience he had after he had lost his external consciousness. We thought he did not express it to us because it was a secret. But we realized later that it was natural for Narendra not to have remembered it, from what the Master told us one day in course of his conversation on this event. The Master said:

'When Narendra had lost his external consciousness I asked him that day many questions, such as who he was, where he came from, why he came (was born), how long he would be here (in this world) and so on and so forth. Entering into the depth of his being, he gave proper answers to all these questions. These answers of his proved what I thought

[4] Saradananda, p. 737.

and saw and knew in my visions about him. It is forbidden to say all those things. But I have known from all these that on the day when he will know who he is, he will no more remain in this world; he will, with a strong power of will, immediately give up his body through yoga. Narendra is a great soul perfect in meditation.'[5]

## Skepticism

Despite these extraordinary experiences and the loving, kind manner in which Sri Ramakrishna treated him, Vivekananda had considerable difficulty in fully accepting Sri Ramakrishna as his *guru*. He was drawn to him by love, yet "because of his exposure to scientific skepticism and Western philosophy in school . . . he maintained a skeptical attitude until the very end of his association with the Master."[6] This very attitude, however, paralleled that of Sri Ramakrishna, for whom the test of the existence of God was the experience of God.

---

[5] *Ibid.,* pp. 739-740. This was indeed the manner of his passing away. See Letter of August 20, 1902, from Swami Premananda to Swami Abhedananda, describing the details of Vivekananda's *mahasamadhi,* in *Swami Premananda, Teachings and Reminiscences,* pp. 128-132. It is a curious fact that the doctor who later examined Swami Vivekananda "could not diagnose the cause of his death" (p. 132). Cf. Isherwood, p. 327.

[6] E. R. Marozzi, "The Making of Swami Vivekananda," in *Swami Vivekananda in East and West,* ed. by Swami Ghanananda and Geoffrey Parrinder (London: The Ramakrishna Vedanta Centre, 1968), p. 18. In connection with his schooling he displayed a prodigious mental capacity which he himself described as follows: " 'It so happened that I could understand an author without reading his book line by line. I could get the meaning by just reading the first and the last line of a paragraph. As this power developed I found it unnecessary to read even the paragraphs. I could follow by reading only the first and last lines of a page. Further, where the author introduced discussion to explain a matter and it took him four or five or even more pages to clear the subject, I could grasp the whole trend of his arguments by only reading the first few lines.' " *Life of Swami Vivekananda,* p. 23. Further regarding his schooling, D. S. Sarma writes: "Mr. Hastie, the Principal of his college, once remarked about him thus:—'Narendranath is really a genius. I have travelled far and wide, but I have never yet come across a lad of his talents and possibilities, even in German universities amongst philosophical students. He is bound to make his mark in life.' It is interesting to note that it was from this Englishman, Mr. Hastie, that Narendranath first heard of Sri Ramakrishna. Explaining to his class Wordsworth's experience described in his 'Excursion,' Mr. Hastie once said, 'Such an experience is the result of purity of mind and concentration on some particular object, and it is rare indeed, particularly in these days. I have seen only one person who has experienced that blessed state of mind, and he is Sri Ramakrishna Paramahamsa of

Sri Ramakrishna in his method of training Swami Vivekananda encouraged him to adopt the attitude of a monist, an ultra-radical Advaitist, one for whom no difference exists between the Absolute and the individual soul. He was asked to renounce God for God's sake, as did Meister Eckhart, and to conduct his spiritual practices accordingly. But young Vivekananda resisted this training, reflecting his previous association with the Brahmo Samaj, which advocated dualistic worship of the formless aspect of God with attributes. When Sri Ramakrishna gave him highly nondualistic books to read, such as the *Ashtavakra Samhita,* he would scoff at such ideas, as the following passage illustrates:

> As soon as he read a little, at the request of the Master, he blurted out, 'What is the difference between this and atheism? Should the created Jiva think of himself as the Creator? What can be more sinful than this? What ideas can be more unreasonable than, "I am God, you are God, all things that are born and die are God." The brains of the Rishis and Munis, the authors of such books, must have been deranged; how otherwise, could they have written such things?' The Master smiled to hear those words of the plain-speaking Narendra but, instead of suddenly attacking his spiritual attitude, he said, 'You may not accept them now; but why do you condemn the Munis and Rishis, because of that? And why do you put a limit to the nature of God? Go on calling on Him who is Truth itself, and then believe that to be His true nature, in which He will reveal Himself to you.' But Narendra did not give ear to those words of the Master. For, whatever was not established by reason then appeared to him to be untrue and it was his nature to stand against all kinds of untruth. He, therefore, did not hesitate to adduce reasons against the doctrine of nondualism to many besides the Master, and use even sarcastic words from time to time.[7]

---

Dakshineswar. You can understand it, if you go there and see for yourself.' . . . Narendranath took his advice." *The Master and the Disciple,* pp. 71-72. With regard to his scientific skepticism, Swami Vivekananda can be taken as a "representative of contemporary thinkers" because "his doubt was his passion" (Isherwood, p. 192). "He *had* to doubt in order to know. He dared not take anything that was told him on trust" *(ibid.,* p. 189). Sri Ramakrishna recognized this tendency, and used to say to him, "You must test me as the money-changers test their coins. You mustn't accept me until you test me thoroughly" *(ibid.,* p. 209). Thus young Vivekananda "was determined to test for himself everything that Ramakrishna taught him. . . . We cannot be too grateful for this attitude of Naren's. His skepticism makes him one of the most reliable of all the witnesses to Ramakrishna" *(ibid.,* p. 200).

[7] Saradananda, p. 767.

Vivekananda's reluctance to accept the Advaitic principle of the non-duality of existence is fully understandable, as it denies the evidence of sense experience. It apparently contradicts all the categories which give the human mind support, such as the notions of time, space, and causal relationships, individuality of the personality, and so forth. In addition, the path to its realization (*jnana yoga*) requires a spirit of dedication, strength of mind, and personal renunciation, of which few are capable without considerable preparation.[8] If it were not for the fact that this principle of Advaita can be experienced, and in this way unify all other experience, it would be relegated to mere philosophical speculation, providing little scientific confirmation for its support. Young Vivekananda's attitude was precisely this: as a seeker after truth, he could be satisfied only by direct experience; he could not accept second-hand knowledge.

*Advaitic Experience*

Aware of his strong-minded disciple's disposition, Sri Ramakrishna acted accordingly, and one day instructed him in Advaita of the purest type, with a full-blown experience of the Absolute, again transmitted by his touch:

> Thus one day the Master told Narendranath many things indicating the oneness of Jiva and Brahman of the non-dual philosophy. He heard those words, undoubtedly with attention, but he could not comprehend them and went to Hazra at the end of the Master's talk. Smoking and discussing those things again with Hazra, he said, 'Can it ever be possible that the waterpot is God, the cup is God, whatever we see and all of us are God?' Sri Hazra also joined Narendra in thus ridiculing the idea and both of them burst into laughter. The Master was till then in the state of partial external consciousness. Hearing Narendra laugh, he came out of his room like a boy with his wearing cloth in his armpit and, coming to them smiling, said affectionately, 'What are you both talking about?' He then touched Narendra and went into samadhi.
>
> Narendra said to us afterwards, 'There was a complete revolution in the state of my mind in a moment at the wonderful touch of the Master. I was aghast to see actually that there was nothing in the whole universe except God. But I remained silent in spite of seeing it, wondering how long that state would last. But that inebriation did not at all diminish

[8] *Vedantasara of Sadananda,* trans. by Nikhilananda, chap. i, "Preliminaries," pp. 1-20.

that day. I returned home; it was all the same there; it seemed to me that all that I saw was He. I sat for my meal when I saw that all—food, plate, the one who was serving as well as myself—were nothing but He. I took a mouthful or two and sat quiet. My mother's affectionate words—"why do you sit quiet; why don't you eat?"—brought me to consciousness and I began eating again. Thus, I had that experience at the time of eating or drinking, sitting or lying, going to the college or taking a stroll. I was always overwhelmed with a sort of indescribable intoxication. When I walked along the streets and saw a carriage coming along before me, I did not feel inclined, as at other times, to move away, lest it should collide with me. For, I thought, "I am also that and nothing but that." My hands and feet always remained insensible at that time. I felt no satisfaction whatever when I took my food. It seemed to me as if some one else was eating the meal. . . . When that overwhelming intoxication diminished a little, the world appeared to me to be a dream. Going for a walk on the bank of the Hedua tank, I knocked my head against the iron railings round it to see whether what I saw were dream-rails or actual ones. On account of the insensibility of my hands and feet I was afraid whether I was not going to have paralysis. I could not escape that terrible intoxicating mood and overwhelming condition for some time. When I came to the normal state, I thought that that was the indication of non-dual knowledge. So what is written in the Sastras about it is by no means untrue. Since then I could never doubt the truth of non-duality.[9]

The extraordinary love manifested by Swami Vivekananda in his adult life, which has been compared to that of St. Francis in the Christian tradition,[10] and which provided the motive power behind his activities of service, was based on this unitive spiritual experience which Sri Ramakrishna imparted to him. Having perceived his own identity with the Absolute, he had that same knowledge with respect to others: thus, seeing God in man, he worshipped God in man. This perception also formed the basis of his preaching activities later on. As he then declared, "I am bringing Vedanta from the forest to the marketplace. The time has come when this truth should be spread broadcast.' "[11]

[9] Saradananda, pp. 768-770.

[10] "When the presence of God is seen in the world, a person will serve the world. The servants of the world are those who are thoroughly established in the knowledge of God. Can you find better servants of the world than St. Francis and Swami Vivekananda?" Akhilananda, *Mental Health*, p. 203; see also p. 204.

[11] Ashokananda, *Spiritualizing Everyday Life*, p. 16.

## FURTHER TRAINING

*A Test*

Vivekananda's spiritual training by no means ended here. Sri Ramakrishna's method of teaching was based on "the power to see into a person and at once know his thoughts, impressions, and *karma* 'as in a glass case' (as he himself said)," so that "he could readily determine what kind of instruction was needed at any given moment in order to effect the desired development."[12] He used direct and indirect methods, including play and merriment,[13] as well as highly subtle methods of instruction.[14] At one point he tested his foremost disciple by ignoring him completely for one month. At the end of that period Ramakrishna asked the young Vivekananda,

'Why do you keep coming here, when I don't speak a single word to you?' 'Do you think I come here just to have you speak to me?' Naren answered. 'I love you. I want to see you. That's why I come.' Ramakrishna was delighted. 'I was testing you,' he told Naren, 'to see if you'd stop coming when you didn't get love and attention. Only a spiritual aspirant

---

[12] Marozzi, p. 23.

[13] "The disciple's training at Dakshineswar went on not only as *sadhana* of meditation and spiritual exercises but also by means of play and merriment—running about, climbing trees, swinging on creepers, picnicking and cooking their own meals, etc. Recalling this Narendra said, 'It is difficult to explain to others how blissfully I spent my days with the Master. There is no limit to our astonishment when we think how, through play, merriment and other ordinary daily activities, he gave us high exalted spiritual education and moulded our lives without our knowledge. Just as a powerful wrestler, at the time of teaching a boy, keeps his skill in reserve and, displaying a part only of his power, as suits the purpose of teaching the boy, produces self-confidence in him by defeating him sometimes with great effort, and sometimes allowing himself to be defeated by him; so, on many occasions, the Master assumed that attitude in behaving with us at that time." *Ibid.,* p. 24.

[14] "A remarkable incident is narrated by Narendra and shows how the Master would instruct him not only when he was present in the gross body but, miraculously, also in the subtle body when the gross body was absent. 'He (Ramakrishna) is bestowing love, devotion, divine knowledge, liberation and whatever he may desire on whomever he likes. Oh! the wonderful power! I was lying on my bed at night with the door of my room bolted from within, when he suddenly attracted and took me—the one that lives within this body—to Dakshineswar. Giving a great deal of instruction to me and talking on various subjects, he allowed me to return. He can do anything he likes; this *Gora Rai* of Dakshineswar can do anything.' How often this happened is known only to the unique Master and his wonderful disciple." *Ibid.,* p. 22.

of your quality could put up with so much neglect and indifference. Anyone else would have left me long ago.'[15]

## Vivekananda's One-sidedness

While experience of the Absolute, revealing the non-duality of existence, was the real point of departure for Vivekananda's spiritual life, Sri Ramakrishna, by contrast, first realized the personal form of God in different aspects before he had the direct knowledge of Advaita. This reflected a basic difference in their religious temperaments, the former being predominantly rational and the latter predominantly emotional. During Vivekananda's discipleship, this temperamental difference became the focal point of an ongoing controversy between teacher and student, during which Vivekananda was unable to concede the reality of a personal God. In fact, he would openly ridicule Sri Ramakrishna's child-like reliance on Divine Mother. Vivekananda's earlier affiliation with Ram Mohan Roy's Brahmo Samaj which regarded image worship as primitive, his Western education, his thoroughly rationalistic approach, and now the experience of Advaita Vedanta all seemed to take the student in a path opposite to that of his teacher.

A basic requirement for *bhakti* is the worship of a personal aspect of God. In the non-dual state of existence there is neither love nor Beloved, but only One: who is to love whom? That is, for *bhakti* to exist, non-duality must be put aside, if only temporarily, so that a worshipper and his God can emerge to permit the flow of devotion. In the case of Swami Vivekananda, the personal aspect of God did not appeal to him, particularly in the form of Kali. Not only was there lack of affinity, but he actively rebelled against Her worship.

## The Remedy

### EXPERIENCE OF DIVINE MOTHER

A profound experience under Sri Ramakrishna's guidance enabled Vivekananda to overcome his one-sidedness and fully understand the reality of *bhakti* in his own life. His father died in 1884, some time before the results of his B.A. examination were released. Although his father had been a successful lawyer, and Vivekanan-

---

[15] Isherwood, pp. 207-208.

da was raised in comfort, his father died leaving only debts, and Vivekananda's mother, sisters and brothers were about to be ejected from their home. Six persons now depended on him, so that a boy once used to philosophical inquiry and religious search was faced with the unfamiliar prospect of going from place to place searching for a job. He suffered terribly. For three or four months, going from office to office, barefoot in the midday sun, he sought work without success. He and his family experienced grinding poverty, lack of food, and the abandonment of friends. He remarks of that occasion:

> From that very first worldly experience of mine I felt keenly that selfless sympathy was very rare in this world—there was no place here for the weak and the poor. Those who deemed it, only a day or two previously, a piece of good fortune to be able to help me now found an opportunity to do the contrary and made a wry face at me and, although able, were reluctant to help me. When I had such experiences, the world seemed to me, very often, to have been created by a demon.[16]

He then yielded in his misery to the most terrible forms of atheism and nihilism, discounting all that he had felt, learned and experienced about things spiritual in the face of his anguish. Evil and pain seemed the only things real. He regarded his search after abiding truth as a meaningless mockery, as he did all pretense of order and justice in a world which he saw universally permeated with human suffering. Rather than conceal these feelings, he broadcast them. Vivekananda stopped seeing his teacher. Everyone thought he had fallen, but he cared little for their opinions. One day during the rainy season, when he was drenched, famished, and completely exhausted, the following took place:

> 'I cannot say whether external consciousness left me. . . . I remember that thoughts and pictures of various colors, one after another, arose and vanished of themselves in my mind. I had no power to drive them away or to concentrate on one particular thought. I suddenly felt as if within my mind many screens were raised one after another by some providential power and saw in the innermost recesses of my heart the solutions of the problems which so long had baffled my intellect and distracted my mind:—the problems such as "Why are there malignities in the creation of the Benign? Where is the harmony between the stern justice and the

16 Saradananda, p. 806.

infinite mercy of God?" I was beside myself with joy. Afterwards, when I resumed my walk home, I found that there was not an iota of fatigue in my body and that my mind was filled with infinite strength and peace.'[17]

He subsequently went to Sri Ramakrishna, thinking that in some way his teacher's prayers on behalf of his family's sorry condition would be answered. He asked Sri Ramakrishna to supplicate the Divine Mother on behalf of his family's wants, but Sri Ramakrishna refused, saying he could not bring himself to pray for worldly benefits, even for others, but only for spiritual grace. He suggested that Vivekananda pray himself, but the latter replied that he had no knowledge of the Mother. Sri Ramakrishna answered, " 'You don't accept the Mother; that is why you suffer so much.' "[18] Thereupon Vivekananda went to the temple that night to pray to Kali. He relates:

'As I was going, a sort of profound inebriation possessed me; I was reeling. A firm conviction gripped me that I should actually see Mother and hear her words. I forgot all other things, and became completely merged in that thought alone. Coming in the temple I saw that Mother was actually pure Consciousness, was actually living and was really the fountain-head of infinite love and beauty. My heart swelled with loving devotion; and, beside myself with bliss, I made repeated salutations to Her, praying, "Mother, grant me discrimination, grant me detachment, grant me divine knowledge and devotion; ordain that I may always have unobstructed vision of you." My heart was flooded with peace. The whole universe completely disappeared and Mother alone remained filling my heart.

'No sooner had I returned to the Master than he asked, "Did you pray to Mother for the removal of your worldly wants?" Startled at his question, I said, "No, sir; I forgot to do so. So, what should I do now?" He said, "Go quickly again and pray to Her." I started for the temple once more, and, coming to Mother's presence, became inebriated again. I forgot everything, bowed down to Her repeatedly and prayed for the realization of divine knowledge and devotion.'[19]

---

[17] *Ibid.,* p. 810.

[18] *Ibid.,* p. 811.

[19] *Ibid.,* pp. 811-812. Vivekananda's acceptance of Divine Mother paralleled that of Tota Puri, Sri Ramakrishna's *guru* in Advaita Vedanta. See Chapter IV herein. Cf. Robert Linssen, "The Ideal of Love-Energy of Teilhard de Chardin and the Bhakti-Yoga of Swami Vivekananda," *Vedanta for East and West,* CXVIII (March-April, 1971), 25-32.

The same thing happened once more: Sri Ramakrishna sending him back, saying, "Silly boy, could you not control yourself a little and make that prayer?," Vivekananda again leaving the temple without accomplishing his task, too ashamed to ask for anything but knowledge and devotion. Sri Ramakrishna finally assured his young disciple that since he had experienced the reality of Divine Mother and accepted her, his family would never be in want of plain food and clothing.

EVALUATION OF THIS EXPERIENCE

This experience was a landmark for Vivekananda. The hidden meaning of the Motherhood of God and of her worship in symbols and images had been revealed to him. He was allowed a glimpse into the mystery of suffering in the universe, and its relation to the divine. His spiritual life became immensely richer. He had acquired *bhakti*, yet it was built on the foundation of his initial experience of Advaita, one not denying but supplementing the other.[20] Now he possessed the beginning of a more universal perception of religious life, a harmony which was to be expressed in his message during the last decade of his life.

As a result of that experience, Vivekananda's intense love for his *guru* became extended to an attitude of complete surrender, which now included his teacher's spiritual ideal, Kali.[21] Having fully accepted the personal form of God in the aspect of Divine Mother, Vivekananda's reverence for other forms of God blossomed. But he felt increasingly that the Mother Herself had taken hold of his life. This feeling is expressed in his poem, "Kali the Mother,"[22] which he

[20] See Claude Alan Stark, "Swami Vivekananda as a Devotee," *Journal of Religious Studies*, IV (Spring, 1972), 89-106.

[21] That he felt Sri Ramakrishna's love for him is shown by the following statement: " 'Ever since our first meeting, it was Master alone, and no one else, not even my own mother and brothers who always had uniform faith in me. That faith and that love of his, have bound me to him for ever. It was the Master alone who knew how to love and he did love; while others of the world but feign love for the satisfaction of their self-interest.' " Saradananda, p. 814.

[22] *In Search of God and Other Poems*, p. 25. Cf. "A Hymn to the Divine Mother," pp. 58-60. Vivekananda's conversations and letters are replete with exalted references to the Divine Mother. See *Letters of Swami Vivekananda* (Mayavati, Almora: Advaita Ashrama, 1964), *passim; Inspired Talks*. As his biographer states, "His idea of the Divine Motherhood, the Power behind all manifestation, was as poetic as it was impersonal." *Life of Swami Vivekananda*, p. 609.

wrote at a later date in a state of devotional intoxication, after which he collapsed on the floor in *bhavasamadhi*. In this poem Vivekananda expressed his perception of Kali as a reality representing the highest philosophical reading of the Absolute by the human mind, yet transcending all the categories of the mind. He saw in Kali a form of God which encompassed both good and evil, yet was beyond both.

The intense devotion felt by Swami Vivekananda for Divine Mother may be documented by other incidents in his life. While wandering as an itinerant *sannyasin* in Kashmir some time after his teacher had passed away, he came across an abandoned temple of Kali, evidently destroyed partially by a wave of invaders, but whose image was strangely beautiful. He stood at the entrance. Anger welled up and he thought how terrible it was that Mother's temple should come to this. A voice from the image rang out, "My child, it is through my will that temples in my name are built, and also by my will that they are destroyed."[23] He came away intoxicated with the vividness of this experience and a thoroughly changed outlook. Later, he said to Sister Nivedita, referring to this experience, " 'There must be no more of this anger. Mother said, "What even if the unbeliever should enter My temples and defile My images, what is that to you? *Do you protect me? Or do I protect you?"* ' "[24]

## VIVEKANANDA'S UNIVERSALITY

Sri Ramakrishna had led his foremost disciple through various experiences of the impersonal and personal aspects of God to a point where, having gained an appreciation for many facets of spiritual life, he paralleled Sri Ramakrishna's own universality.[25] This was a prerequisite for one who would preach the message of his

[23] *Life,* p. 611.

[24] Nivedita, *The Master as I Saw Him,* p. 55.

[25] "Swami Vivekananda's universality is rooted in his experience of the spiritual oneness of existence. It is not due simply to his intellectual comprehension, extensive knowledge, keen interest in human values, and world-wide sympathy or fellow-feeling. It is different in character from humanism, humanitarianism, and universalism. All these value man as man irrespective of creed, colour, rank or position. . . . But Swami Vivekananda sees God dwelling in human forms." Satprakashananda, "Swami Vivekananda's Universality," in *Swami Vivekananda in East and West,* pp. 186-187.

master, the harmony of religions, who would "participate in every form of spiritual worship."[26] Vivekananda later declared, " 'I shall go to the mosque of the Mohammedan; I shall enter the Christian's church and kneel before his crucifix; I shall enter the Buddhist temple where I shall take refuge in the Buddha and his law.' " [27] Not only was this universality derived from Sri Ramakrishna's influence, but it was based on Vivekananda's direct knowledge of God both as unmanifested and as the power behind all manifestation. As Sister Nivedita observes, "He who has sounded the depths of both of these . . . opposite conceptions of God . . . will be capable of understanding the significance of every possible human symbol of the divine, since all must be included in one or other of the two."[28]

The zenith of Vivekananda's discipleship came one evening in the summer of 1886 at the Cossipore garden-house, where Sri Ramakrishna lay dying:

> The greatest moment in the period of Narendra's discipleship is perhaps that during which he attained to the state of Nirvikalpa-samadhi like his Master. Ever since he had been initiated, he had been longing for this great experience. But it came suddenly and unexpectedly one evening, a few days before the death of Sri Ramakrishna. He was meditating, as usual, according to the instruction of his Master, when suddenly he felt a light at the back of his head. The light grew larger and larger and seemed to burst, and his mind became merged in it. One of his brother disciples observed his rigid body and ran to the Master for help. But the Master, who seemed to know what was happening in Narendra's room, which was adjacent to his, replied, 'Let him stay in the state for a while. He has teased me long enough for it.' After some hours, Narendra returned to normal consciousness and was full of ecstasy, because he had reached the goal of his sadhana and all his doubts had vanished. When he went to his Master, the latter said to him, 'Now then, the Mother has shown you everything. Just as a treasure is locked up in a box, so will this realization you have just had be locked up, and the key shall remain with me. You have work to do. When you will have finished my work,

---

[26] Sidney Spencer, "Vivekananda and the Unity of Churches and Religions," in *Swami Vivekananda in East and West,* p. 181.

[27] Vivekananda, *Works,* II. 372.

[28] Nivedita, *The Master as I Saw Him,* pp. 127-128. Cf. *The Use of Symbols in Religion,* ed. by Satprakashananda (St. Louis: The Vedanta Society, 1970); Akhilananda, *Spiritual Practices,* chap. vi, "The Psychological Aspects of Religious Symbols," pp. 76-84.

the treasure box will be unlocked again, and you will know everything, just as you do now.'[29]

## VIVEKANANDA'S CONTRIBUTION TO RELIGIOUS UNDERSTANDING

Vivekananda's contribution to religious understanding after the death of his master was considerable. As the first *sannyasin* ever to leave the shores of India, he boldly set forth his teacher's ideals. The harmony of religions was his theme at the Parliament of Religions in Chicago in 1893, where he spoke as a representative of Hinduism. His last speech aptly illustrates his position:

The Christian is not to become a Hindu or a Buddhist, nor a Hindu or Buddhist to become a Christian. But each must assimilate the spirit of the others and yet preserve his individuality and grow according to his own law of growth.

If the Parliament of Religions has shown anything to the world it is this: It has proved to the world that holiness, purity, and charity are not the exclusive possessions of any church in the world and that every system has produced men and women of the most exalted character. In the face of this evidence, if anybody dreams of the exclusive survival of his own religion and the destruction of the others, I pity him from the bottom of my heart, and point out to him that upon the banner of every religion will soon be written, in spite of their resistance: 'Help and not Fight,' 'Assimilation and not Destruction,' 'Harmony and Peace and not Dissension.'[30]

In a lecture delivered in Pasadena, California, in 1900, he stated:

Our watchword, then will be acceptance, and not exclusion. Not only toleration, for so-called toleration is often blasphemy, and I do not believe in it. I believe in acceptance. Why should I tolerate? Toleration means that I think that you are wrong and I am just allowing you to live. Is it not a blasphemy to think that you and I are allowing others to live? I accept all religions that were in the past, and worship with them all; I worship God with every one of them, in whatever form they worship Him. . . . Not only shall I do all these but I shall keep my heart open for all that may come in the future.[31]

---

[29] Sarma, *Master and Disciple,* pp. 77-78.
[30] *Works,* I, 22.
[31] *Ibid.,* II, 371-372.

During his lecture tours in the United States, in which he often gave as many as fourteen lectures per week in different cities, he continued to propagate Sri Ramakrishna's message according to his own unique style.[32] He writes of his activities in America in a letter from India to a Western friend: "I had to work till I am at death's door and had to spend nearly the whole of that energy in America, so that the Americans may learn to be broader and more spiritual."[33] Labeled the "cyclonic monk," Vivekananda became well known to many of the intellectual leaders of the period in America, England, and Europe. He attracted both men and women as disciples in the West, and trained them according to his teacher's guidelines. Harvard University offered him the Chair of Eastern Philosophy,[34] which he turned down as a violation of the sacred work entrusted to him by his master.

An essential part of that work was to clarify for his Western audiences the principles of his own tradition. "He spoke little about the Hindu cults of Rama, Kali, Vishnu, or Shiva,"[35] and rarely mentioned the personality of Sri Ramakrishna.[36] Not only was the subject of his *guru* highly charged with emotion for him, but he did not intend to create another cult out of Sri Ramakrishna's life and teachings.[37] "Instead I preached Ramakrishna's principles,"[38] he said when he returned to India. Vivekananda's objective of presenting Hinduism's spiritual ideals in a form which appealed to the

[32] Marie Louise Burke's *Swami Vivekananda in America: New Discoveries* carefully documents Vivekananda's activities and personal experiences in America. Her thorough research includes newspaper articles of the period on Vivekananda.

[33] *Works*, V, 105.

[34] *Life of Swami Vivekananda*, p. 396.

[35] Isherwood, p. 322.

[36] An exception to this was the lecture, "My Master," delivered in New York. See *Inspired Talks, My Master and Other Writings*, pp. 149-201. Also see *Inspired Talks*, pp. 43-46, for conversations with his intimate Western disciples about Sri Ramakrishna at Thousand Island Park, N. Y.

[37] In the words of Swami Premananda, a brother disciple who followed closely the spiritual leadership of Vivekananda: "Sri Ramakrishna did not come to found another sect. He came to bring new life, new impetus, into the spirit of all religions. And it was to produce young men of selfless character and purity to broadcast the Master's ideal of universality that Swamiji founded this monastery." *Swami Premananda, Teachings and Reminiscences*, p. 76.

[38] Isherwood, p. 322.

West yet did no damage to its authenticity is stated in a letter to an Indian disciple written from America in 1896:

> To put the Hindu ideas into English and then make, out of dry philosophy and intricate mythology and queer startling psychology, a religion which shall be easy, simple, popular, and at the same time meet the requirements of the highest minds—is a task only those can understand who have attempted it. The abstract Advaita must become living—poetic—in everyday life; out of hopelessly intricate mythology must come concrete moral forms; and out of bewildering yogi-ism must come the most scientific and practical psychology—and all this must be put in a form so that a child may grasp it. That is my life's work.[39]

## EVALUATION OF HIS ATTITUDE OF SERVICE

Through all the personal adulation he received he remained loyal to his teacher and humble to the core.[40] His renunciation was unsullied despite the temptations set in his path by sudden fame, by the large amounts of money that passed through his hands from lecture tours and Western contributors, and by the personal power he had to assume as founder of the Ramakrishna Order of monks. In fact, so complete was his renunciation that toward the end of his life he had to beg two *annas* from Swami Brahmananda, the President of the Order, for the price of the fare to cross the Ganges in a ferryboat. His attitude is illustrated in the following passage from a letter written in California to a Western disciple two years before his death:

> After all, Joe, I am only the boy who used to listen with rapt wonderment to the wonderful words of Ramakrishna under the banyan at Dakshineswar. That is my true nature—works and activities, doing good and so forth, are all superimpositions. Now I again hear his voice, the same old voice thrilling my soul. . . . Now only the voice of the Master calling.

[39] Swami Ranganathananda, *Swami Vivekananda: His Life and Mission* (Calcutta: The Ramkrishna Mission Institute of Culture, 1963), p. 11.

[40] Swami Turiyananda, a brother disciple, states in this connection: "Swamiji really had the power to help others. He had no jealousy. But that's where we are put into difficulties. We are always afraid lest anybody tops over us. But he was too great for that sort of fear. He had not the least bit of jealousy. He used to say, 'Help everyone forward from where he is, and if you can, supply his particular deficiency. But if you can't don't try to drag him to your own level." *Spiritual Talks*, p. 223.

... Yes, I come. Nirvana is before me. I feel it at times, the same infinite ocean of peace, without a ripple, a breath.

I am glad I was born, glad I suffered so, glad I did make big blunders, glad to enter peace. I leave none bound, I take no bonds. Whether this body will fall and release me or I enter into freedom in the body, the old man is gone, gone for ever, never to come back again!

The guide, the guru, the leader, the teacher, has passed away; the boy, the student, the servant is left behind.

... The sweetest moments of my life have been when I was drifting. I am drifting again—with the bright warm sun ahead and masses of vegetation around—and in the heat everything is so still, so calm—and I am drifting, languidly—in the warm heart of the river. I dare not make a splash with my hands or feet—for fear of breaking the wonderful stillness, stillness that makes you feel sure it is an illusion!

Behind my work was ambition, behind my love was personality, behind my purity was fear, behind my guidance the thirst for power. Now they are vanishing and I drift. I come, Mother, I come, in Thy warm bosom, floating wheresoever Thou takest me, in the voiceless, in the strange, in the wonderland, I come—a spectator, no more an actor.[41]

Swami Vivekananda died prematurely at thirty-nine years of age, having given his life in the spirit of service. Swami Shivananda, a brother disciple, later said,

The right kind of service is possible only when one sees God in the person served. ... Swamiji [Vivekananda] ... propounded this doctrine of service. The Master's life is the aphorism, as it were, and Swamiji's is the commentary on it.[42]

Vivekananda expressed this love, manifested in his life as service to God in man, in a poem, "To a Friend":

Listen, friend, I will speak my heart to thee:
I have found in my life this truth supreme—
Buffeted by waves, in this whirl of life,
There's one ferry that takes across the sea.

Formulas of worship, control of breath,

---

[41] *Inspired Talks,* pp. 244-245.

[42] *Spiritual Talks,* pp. 342-343. On numerous occasions Vivekananda stated that he taught nothing which he had not learned from Sri Ramakrishna. Cf. *ibid.,* pp. 195, 281, and 292.

Science, philosophy, systems varied,
Relinquishment, possession, and the like,
All these are but delusions of the mind—
Love, Love—that's the one thing, the sole treasure.

......................................................................................................................

Aye, born heir to the Infinite thou art,
Within the heart is the ocean of Love,
'Give,' 'Give away'—whoever asks return,
His ocean dwindles down to a mere drop.

From highest Brahman to the yonder worm,
And to the very minutest atom,
Everywhere is the same God, the All-Love;
Friend, offer mind, soul, body, at their feet.

These are His manifold forms before thee,
Rejecting them, where seekest thou for God?
Who loves all beings, without distinction,
He indeed is worshipping best his God.[43]

[43] *In Search of God and Other Poems,* pp. 41-45. Cf. this poem with the familiar "Prayer of St. Francis" and his "Canticle of Brother Sun" ("Laudes Creaturarum"), *The Writings of St. Francis of Assisi,* pp. 127-131. Cf. also "St. Francis and Sri Ramakrishna," in *Vedanta for the Western World,* ed. by Christopher Isherwood (New York: Viking Press, 1969), pp. 253-260. Vivekananda postulates that the realization of spiritual oneness is a basis of ethics: "We have always heard it preached, 'Love one another.' What for? That doctrine was preached, but the explanation is here. Why should I love everyone? Because they and I are one. Why should I love my brother? Because he and I are one. There is this oneness, this solidarity of the whole universe. From the lowest worm that crawls under our feet to the highest beings that ever lived all have various bodies, but are the one Soul. Through all mouths you eat; through all hands you work; through all eyes you see. You enjoy health in millions of bodies, you are suffering from disease in millions of bodies. When this idea comes and we realize it, see it, feel it, then will misery cease, and fear with it. How can I die? There is nothing beyond me. Fear ceases, and then alone come perfect happiness and perfect love. The universal sympathy, universal love, universal bliss, that never changes, raises man above everything." *Works,* II, 412-413. "The infinite oneness of the Soul is the eternal sanction of all morality, that you and I are not only brothers—every literature voicing man's struggle towards freedom has preached that for you—but that you and I are really one. This is the dictate of Indian philosophy. This oneness is the rationale of all ethics and spirituality." *Ibid.,* III, 189. Cf. Leviticus 19:18; Matthew 19:19.

# CHAPTER XI

# Sri Ramakrishna as a Spiritual Teacher

## HIS ATTITUDE

*Humility*

Sri Ramakrishna's career as a spiritual teacher, which lasted from 1879 to 1886, was characterized by the same simplicity of manner and humility which he had maintained during his earlier years as a spiritual seeker. So complete was his self-effacement, in fact, that he could not even bear to be called by the titles *babu* (father) or *guru.* " 'It is God who does all these things,' " he would say, " 'I do not know anything.' "[1] The following dialogue between

---

[1] *Gospel of Sri Ramakrishna,* Nikhilananda trans., p. 505. "His teaching and preaching were peculiar: he would never take the position of a teacher. In our country a teacher is a most highly venerated person; he is regarded as God Himself. We have not even the same respect for our father and mother. Our father and mother give us our body, but the teacher shows us the way to salvation. We are his children; we are born in the spiritual line of the teacher. All Hindus come to pay respect to an extraordinary teacher; they crowd around him. And here was such a teacher. But the teacher had no thought whether he was to be respected or not; he had not the least idea that he was a great teacher; he thought that it was the Mother who was doing everything, and not he." Vivekananda, "My Master," in *Inspired Talks,* pp. 170-171. Further, with regard to Sri Ramakrishna's humility as a spiritual teacher, Gnaneswarananda states: "The 'I and my' dropped off from his consciousness. So vivid was the Divine Presence within, that the Master was unable to use any declension of the

142

Sri Ramakrishna and "M," a householder disciple who recorded his conversations,[2] typifies this attitude:

> Master: 'Does what I say in the state of ecstasy attract people?'
>
> M: 'Oh yes. Very much.'
>
> Master: 'What do people think of me? Do they think anything in particular about me when they see me in that condition?'
>
> M: 'We feel in you a wonderful synthesis of knowledge, love, and renunciation, and on the surface a natural spontaneity. Many divine experiences have passed, like huge steamboats, through the deep of your inner consciousness; still you maintain outwardly this utter simplicity. Many cannot understand it, but a few are attracted by this state alone.'
>
> Master: 'There is a sect of Vaishnavas known as the Bhoshpara, who describe God as the "Sahaja," the "Simple One." They say further that a man cannot recognize this "Simple One" unless he too is simple. *(To M.)* Have I any ego?'
>
> M: 'Yes, sir. A little. You have kept it to preserve your body, and to enjoy divine love in the company of the devotees and impart spiritual knowledge to them. Further, you have kept this trace of ego by praying to the Divine Mother for it.'
>
> Master: 'No. I have not kept it. It is God Himself who has left it in me.'[3]

### Function of a Spiritual Teacher

Sri Ramakrishna regarded the function of a teacher in spiritual life as one who shares the fruits of his experiences. This ideal of a spiritual teacher[4] places primary emphasis on the empirical as com-

---

personal pronoun I, even in his ordinary conversation. 'The Mother here,' indicating his heart, or 'the One here' took the place of the 'I.' *Ramakrishna: The Man and the Power,* pp. 83-84.

[2] In a letter dated November 24, 1897, Vivekananda writes to "M" with regard to his manuscript of the *Ramakrishna Kathamrita,* later translated into English as *The Gospel of Ramakrishna:* "Never the life of a great teacher was brought before the public untarnished by the writer's mind as you are doing. . . . Strange, isn't it? Our teacher . . . was so original and each one of us will have to be original or nothing. I now understand why none of us attempted his life before. It has been reserved for you, this great work. . . . Socratic dialogues are Plato all over. You are entirely hidden." *Gospel,* Abhedananda rev., p. viii.

[3] *Gospel,* Nikhilananda trans., p. 505.

[4] Sri Ramakrishna's ideal of a spiritual teacher is elaborated in the following: Akhilananda, *Spiritual Practices,* chap. ii, "Requirements of a Spiritual Teacher," pp. 25-36; Vivekananda, *Works,* III, 45-52; *Spiritual Teachings of Swami Brahmananda, passim;* Ananda, *Spiritual Practice,* chaps. xv and xvi, pp. 151-168;

pared with the conceptual value of what is transmitted between teacher and student: a teacher evokes in the disciple that which he has himself experienced, not merely what he knows to be true by other sources of knowledge.[5] The clear implication is that not only must a spiritual teacher have direct knowledge of God, but his effectiveness depends on the depth and scope of that knowledge, and on the degree of spiritual power *(shakti)* he has accumulated in the course of his spiritual practices *(sadhanas)*. The fact that his spiritual instruction is devoid of pride, possessiveness, egotism, or desire for any reward other than the religious development of his disciple is a natural consequence of his own superconscious experiences. Sri Ramakrishna expressed his attitude in the following passage:

'After attaining samadhi some souls of their own accord keep the "ego of Knowledge." But that ego does not create any attachment. It is like a line drawn on the water.

'Hanuman kept the "servant ego" after realizing God in both His Personal and His Impersonal aspects. He thought of himself as the servant of God. The great sages, such as Narada, Sanaka, Sananda, Sanatana, and Sanatkumara, after attaining the Knowledge of Brahman, kept the "servant ego" and the "ego of Devotion." They are like big steamships, which not only cross the ocean themselves but carry many passengers to the other shore.

'There are two classes of paramahamsas, one affirming the formless Reality and the other affirming God with form. Trailanga Swami be-

---

*Words of the Master,* pp. 24-25; *Sayings of Sri Ramakrishna,* pp. 213-219; Saradananda, Part III, p. 325 ff. Cf. Woodroffe, *Introduction to Tantra Sastra,* pp. 66-68; Gonda, chap. viii, "The Guru," pp. 229-283.

[5] In this connection Akhilananda writes: "A man of spiritual personality is he who lives the ideal and not he who talks about it. There are many intellectual giants who beautifully explain philosophy, art, science, and religion. There are many persons who can give wonderful descriptions of religion and mysticism, yet those talks do not affect people because those ideals are not lived by the speakers. Their words may satisfy our intellect; but, on the other hand, the simple unsophisticated statements of a man of religious experience change the thought current and life of men, bringing out the inner perfection of innumerable persons. He does not utter a single word that he does not live. . . . We have seen again and again how a few simple words of great spiritual personalities changed the thought current of many disintegrated and disrupted men and women, who were transformed by the magnetic touch of such personalities." *Hindu Psychology,* pp. 99-100. Cf. Akhilananda, *Hindu View of Christ,* chap. ix, "Teaching and Preaching," esp. pp. 227-230.

lieved in the formless Reality. Paramahamsas like him care for their own good alone; they feel satisfied if they themselves attain the goal.

'But those paramahamsas who believe in God with form keep the love of God even after attaining the Knowledge of Brahman, so that they may teach spiritual truth to others. They are like a pitcher brimful of water. Part of the water may be poured into another pitcher. These perfected souls describe to others the various spiritual disciplines by which they have realized God. They do this only to teach others and to help them in spiritual life. With great effort men dig a well for drinking-water, using spades and baskets for the purpose. After the digging is over, some throw the spades and other implements into the well, not needing them any more. But some put them away near the well, so that others may use them.

'Some eat mangoes secretly and remove all trace of them by wiping their mouths with a towel. But some share the fruit with others.'[6]

### His Pedagogical Method

This attitude of sharing spiritual experience, rather than one in which a teacher has something to give and a disciple has something to receive, is quite in keeping with Sri Ramakrishna's realization of man as a manifestation of God. With this assumption, if teacher and student are both divine, who is to teach whom?[7] Thus Sri Ramakrishna's pedagogical method was to unfold each individual student's unique religious potential along the path best suited for him, rather than attempt to cast all in the same mold.[8] Because he respected each person's inherent divinity, he never sought to impose his own ideas on them but allowed each to learn by experience as he had done.

Sri Ramakrishna . . . could fit in with everybody. But what we do is to try to mould all according to our own ideas. Whereas he used to take everybody where he was and push him forward. He never disappointed anybody by failing in the attempt to mould him according to his own light. He had a distinct relation with each devotee and maintained that

[6] *Gospel,* Nikhilananda trans., p. 500.

[7] As Woodroffe explains, "So long as Sakti is not fully communicated . . . so long the conventional relation of the guru and sisya exists. A man is sisya only so long as he is sadhaka. When, however, siddhi is attained, both Guru and Sisya are above this dualism. With the attainment of pure monism, naturally this relation, as all others, disappears." *Introduction to Tantra Sastra,* p. 68.

[8] Gnaneswarananda, *Man and the Power,* p. 80.

throughout. Through humor he would teach them a good deal. Ah, what a teacher he was! Where can one get a teacher like him?[9]

How wonderfully Shri Ramakrishna taught each man so as to remove his particular wants! He used to illustrate it saying, 'A mother has made various curries out of a fish. She doesn't give all her boys the same thing. She gives to each what would exactly suit his stomach.' The Master followed this in practice also.[10]

In commenting on Sri Ramakrishna's disposition as a teacher, Swami Vivekananda stated:

> Do not try to disturb the faith of any man. If you can give him something better, if you can get hold of a man where he stands and give him a push upward, do so; but do not destroy what he has. The only true teacher is he who can convert himself, as it were, into a thousand persons at a moment's notice. The only true teacher is he who can immediately come down to the level of the student and transfer his soul to the student's soul and see through the student's eyes and hear through his ears and understand through his mind. Such a teacher can really teach, and none else. . . .
>
> In the presence of my Master I found out that a man could be perfect even in this body. Those lips never cursed anyone, never even criticized anyone. Those eyes were beyond the possibility of seeing evil, that mind had lost the power of thinking evil. He saw nothing but good. That tremendous purity, that tremendous renunciation, is the one secret of spirituality.[11]
>
> Teaching is not talking, teaching is not imparting doctrines; it is communicating. Spirituality can be communicated just as directly as I can give you a flower. This is true in the most literal sense.[12]

### Content of His Teaching

That which Sri Ramakrishna communicated to his disciples was the experience of God. Herein lay his peculiar genius, his true effectiveness as a spiritual teacher: the ability completely to transform the minds of diverse souls from various religious backgrounds with "a touch, a word, a wish, or even a glance,"[13] and bring them face to

[9] Swami Turiyananda, in *Spiritual Talks,* pp. 221-222.

[10] *Ibid.,* pp. 223-224.

[11] "My Master," in *Inspired Talks,* p. 177.

[12] *Ibid.,* pp. 171-172.

[13] *Hindu Psychology,* pp. 195-196. Cf. Vivekananda, *op. cit.,* p. 173: "I actually saw that religion could be given. One touch, one glance, can change a whole life."

face with the ultimate Reality or God by transmitting superconscious experience. The statements of his disciples concerning their spiritual experiences with Sri Ramakrishna are adequate testimony regarding the efficacy of this approach. The quality of their lives subsequent to these experiences points to their authenticity.[14] Akhilananda writes:

> A great spiritual personality who is perfectly established in higher realizations can transmit this knowledge to a disciple even if the disciple has not undergone vigorous spiritual practices. Sri Ramakrishna . . . could transmit spiritual power and various experiences immediately and directly to his disciples. . . . One day when Swami Brahmananda was rubbing oil on the body of Sri Ramakrishna, he . . . entered into superconscious realization spontaneously and immediately. He not only lost the consciousness of the external and objective world but he experienced the Ultimate Reality. On another occasion, this great Master wrote a name of God on the tongue of another disciple, who then had the realization of the personal aspect of God, his chosen Deity. We know from the history of that period that this great man had a peculiar power of awakening the latent possibilities of his disciples, and that innumerable men and women had their highest realization from him. . . . One of the greatest disciples of the Master, Swami Shivananda, told us that all of the disciples had the highest realization *(samadhi)* during the lifetime of the Master. Their lives prove to us without the least shade of doubt that they were well established in God either through realization of the personal (bodily) aspect or through the Impersonal (formless) aspect of God. . . . Even the disciples of these great teachers can awaken latent spiritual power and give the higher realizations when they are in that particular mood. We know definitely that Swami Vivekananda, Swami Brahmananda, and others transmitted this power on certain occasions to their disciples and devotees.[15]

## Disposition toward Seeking Disciples

Sri Ramakrishna never went out in search of disciples. "He waited for those who wanted his teachings to come to him"[16] at the temple of Mother Kali on the banks of the Ganges. In consequence,

The Master's modest room became the 'parlor of devotees,' many of

---

[14] "The real criterion is the effect on the character of the person." Akhilananda, *op. cit.*, p. 148.

[15] *Ibid.*, pp. 195-196.

[16] Vivekananda, *Inspired Talks,* p. 46.

whom came even from distant parts of India. Orthodox Hindus, modernized Brahma [*sic*] Samajists, Christians, Mohammedans, Free Thinkers and Atheists assembled with equal zeal under the all-embracing shelter of Ramakrishna's universality.[17]

Long before his disciples began to arrive, he had been shown in a vision those who were to be his intimate followers, so that he knew them when they came.[18]

## SWAMI BRAHMANANDA (RAKHAL)

### *His Temperament*

Among these was Rakhal Chandra Ghosh (later Swami Brahmananda), with whom Sri Ramakrishna developed a most interesting relationship. Rakhal, who had already known Naren (Swami Vivekananda) as a close boyhood friend,[19] met Sri Ramakrishna while still in his teens. He had a gentle, affectionate nature and was devoted to the personal form of God. Because of his religious tem-

---

[17] Gnaneswarananda, p. 83.

[18] Of the period before his devotees began to come, Sri Ramakrishna's biographers record the following: "At this time there arose a tremendous longing in his mind to meet his devotees—the pure souls whom the Mother had already shown him in spiritual forms during his transcendent visions. The time had come to train the instruments that were to give his message to the world, and he was burning with desire to pass on his realisations to the favoured children of the Mother. About this he would say later, 'There was no limit to the yearning I had then. During the daytime I managed somehow to control it. The secular talk of the worldly-minded was galling to me, and I would look forward wistfully to the day that my beloved companions would come. I hoped to find solace in conversing with them and unburdening my mind by telling them of my realisations. Every little incident would remind me of them, and thoughts of them wholly engrossed my mind. I was already arranging in my mind what I would say to one and give to another, and so on. But when the day came to a close, I could not curb my feelings. The thought that another day had gone and they had not come, oppressed me! When during the evening service the temple rang with the sound of bells and conch-shells, I would climb to the roof of the building in the garden, and writhing in anguish of heart cry at the top of my voice, "Come, my boys! Oh, where are you? I cannot bear to live without you!" A mother never longs so intensely for the sight of her child, nor a friend for his companion, nor a lover for his sweetheart, as I did for them! Oh, it was indescribable. Shortly after this yearning the devotees began to come in." *Life of Sri Ramakrishna,* pp. 295-296.

[19] *The Disciples of Ramakrishna* (Mayavati, Almora: Advaita Ashrama, 1955), p. 5.

perament, he was ideally suited to be Sri Ramakrishna's spiritual companion, which the latter had sought:

> Some time before the coming of Rakhal, Ramakrishna had prayed to the Divine Mother for a companion: 'Bring me a boy who is like myself, and is pure-hearted and devoted to you.' A few days later, he saw in a vision a boy standing under a banyan tree in the temple grounds. Later, in a second vision, the Divine Mother placed a boy, recognizably the same but much younger, on his lap and told him, 'This is your son.' Ramakrishna was dismayed at first, supposing that he would have to beget this son by an act of sex, but the Mother reassured him; this would be his spiritual, not his physical child.[20]

At their first meeting Sri Ramakrishna "recognized in Rakhal the boy of his visions."[21] Rakhal himself felt an intense attraction for Sri Ramakrishna and a peculiar joy in his presence. Subsequently, "Rakhal began to go to Dakshineswar as often as he could. . . . sometimes to stay there. Though a young man of eighteen or nineteen, in the presence of the Master he felt like a child of four or five, and he actually behaved that way," often sitting on his lap, or at other times acting petulant and pouting. Sri Ramakrishna in turn "also treated him exactly as his child."[22]

## *Relationship with Sri Ramakrishna*

Their relationship had all the "spontaneity and naturalness"[23] of father and son, with the added dimension of spiritual servantship to the *guru*. Among other forms of service, Rakhal "would carefully guard the body of the Master when the latter's mind was lost in Samadhi."[24] Sri Ramakrishna, for his part, would nourish his spiritual son's religious development with the daily example of his own life, with jokes and laughter, admonitions, scoldings, and especially with various superconscious experiences. On one occasion,

> Rakhal was in deep meditation in front of the Kali temple when the Master arrived on the spot. Finding him seated in meditation, the Master accosted him and said, 'This is your sacred Word and this is your

[20] Isherwood, p. 179.
[21] *Ibid.*
[22] *The Disciples of Ramakrishna,* p. 6.
[23] *Ibid.,* p. 7.
[24] *Ibid.*

Chosen Ideal.' Rakhal looked up and was vouchsafed the vision of his Chosen Deity.[25]

## His Potential and Later Role

During those days in the company of Sri Ramakrishna, "Rakhal would be constantly in communion with God,"[26] a way of life which prepared him for the work which was to come. " 'Rakhal has the wisdom and capacity to administer a vast kingdom,' "[27] Sri Ramakrishna once said of him. Several decades later this statement proved literally true.[28] Isherwood writes that "under his direction the Ramakrishna Math and Mission were shaped and Vivekananda's plans translated into action."[29] Concerning Swami Brahmananda's effectiveness, Isherwood continues,

> Brahmananda was a great administrator of the Mission's activities, but he constantly reminded his disciples and fellow-workers that spirituality comes first, social service second. 'The only purpose of life is to know God,' he would tell them. 'Attain knowledge and devotion; then serve God in mankind. Work is not the end of life. Disinterested work is a means of attaining devotion. Keep at least three fourths of your mind in God. It is enough if you give one fourth to service.'

[25] *The Apostles of Shri Ramakrishna,* comp. and ed. by Swami Gambhirananda (Calcutta: Advaita Ashrama, 1967), pp. 85-86.

[26] *Ibid.,* p. 88.

[27] *Ibid.* His biographer further states that "the young disciples held Rakhal in great esteem, because he was so much loved and admired by the Master. One day Narendra suggested to his brother-disciple, 'Henceforward let us address Rakhal as "Raja" (meaning King).' Everyone gave a spontaneous assent to the proposal. . . . Thus Rakhal became Swami Brahmananda. But his brother-disciples preferred to address him as 'Raja,' as a mark of deep love and respect, and in subsequent years, he was known in the order as Raja Maharaj or simply Maharaj." *Ibid.,* pp. 88-89.

[28] During the intervening years between Sri Ramakrishna's passing away and his assuming the presidency of the Order, Swami Brahmananda practiced severe spiritual austerities and went on arduous pilgrimages. Swami Prabhavananda writes of this period, "By constant practice throughout these years of pilgrimage, Maharaj had at last achieved his aim. The state of samadhi was now his own possession. He had won it for himself and he dwelt in it continually. Even in the periods of his normal consciousness, there was, as he said, 'a fullness of God' in his heart. All around him, wherever he went, nature seemed to vibrate with joy." *The Eternal Companion: Brahmananda,* Teachings and Reminiscences with a Biography by Swami Prabhavananda (3d ed.; Hollywood, Calif.: Vedanta Press, 1970), p. 48. Cf. Swami Ashokananda, *Swami Brahmananda* (San Francisco: Vedanta Society of Northern California, 1970).

[29] Isherwood, p. 328.

..........................................................................................................

As head of the Order he was of course empowered to make the final decision whether or not to expel a monk who had been guilty of serious misbehaviour. But he never made such decisions. Often he did not deal directly with the offense itself; instead, he would send for the culprit and have him meditate daily in his presence and render him personal service. On such occasions, the effect of his immense spiritual power and love would be witnessed by all. The culprit would become transformed. Brahmananda's care for others extended far beyond the ordinary human limits of compassion; indeed it was supernatural, for, as he occasionally admitted, he was at all times in mental communication with everybody in the Order and aware of all their problems. He knew that he could give spiritual help whenever it was needed, even at a long distance; and this knowledge made him magnificently unanxious and serene.

However, it should not be supposed that he was overlenient with his disciples. He would even subject a monk to public humiliation and dismissal from his presence; especially if he regarded that monk as having exceptional qualities and if he wished to train him for some difficult duty.... 'These experiences were painful at the time but they were later treasured among the disciple's sweetest memories. It often happened that even while the disciple was being rebuked by Maharaj he would feel a strange undercurrent of joy.'

..........................................................................................................

Brahmananda did not have the eloquence of a Vivekananda. He inspired people by his silences quite as much as by his words. It is said that he could change the psychological atmosphere in a room, making the occupants feel talkative and gay and then inclining them to silent meditation, without himself saying anything.[30]

Although Brahmananda, or "Maharaj," as he was called, was characteristically reserved and indrawn, his mind pitched on a higher plane, he was also fond of humor and joking, especially practical jokes.[31] "M" once told one of Brahmananda's disciples, " 'Observe how Maharaj acts and you will have some idea of what Sri Ramakrishna was like. When his mind came down to the finite plane, his sense of humor was very keen.' "[32] "Often he would make us roar with laughter," Prabhavananda relates. "Maharaj would sometimes

---

[30] *Ibid.,* pp. 328-330. Cf. *Spiritual Teachings of Swami Brahmananda; The Eternal Companion* (3d ed.), pp. 107-288.

[31] Some of these practical jokes are documented in *The Eternal Companion* (3d ed.), pp. 76-81.

[32] *Ibid.,* p. 78.

remark: 'It is good to laugh every day. It relaxes the body and the mind.' "[33]

### Brahmananda as Guru

In his role as a spiritual teacher, however, Swami Brahmananda represented a reservoir of spiritual power which, along with the other direct disciples of Sri Ramakrishna, enabled a second generation of disciples to mold their religious lives around the ideals established by Sri Ramakrishna. The following occurrence highlights Brahmananda's dynamic personality as a *guru:*

Once Akhilananda, who was then a very young boy, was told by Swami Vijnananda to say to Maharaj when he met him: 'There is something within me that needs awakening—please give me your help.' Akhilananda repeated these words to Maharaj, who replied: 'Why didn't you ask Vijnananda to do this awakening for you?' Akhilananda answered that he had, but that Swami Vijnananda had said: 'I have very little spiritual power within me, but Maharaj lives in the powerhouse. He can easily do what you ask.' Maharaj looked very serious and said: 'Yes, the awakening will come. Don't be impatient. For this awakening one needs initiation.' 'Then please initiate me.' 'That will be done,' Maharaj promised.

To quote Akhilananda's own words: 'Maharaj made us feel that spiritual awakening and God-realization are not difficult to achieve. He made us understand that if only we will struggle a little, tremendous help will be given us, and that we shall easily reach the goal.'[34]

Despite his many devotees and disciples—most of the Swamis of the Ramakrishna Order who came to America were trained by him —Brahmananda reflected the same exalted though humble attitude that prevailed in Sri Ramakrishna's disposition as a spiritual teacher. In this connection, Prabhavananda writes,

Maharaj once told me: 'There are times when it becomes impossible for me to teach anyone. No matter where I look, I see only God, wearing many masks. Who am I, the teacher? Who is to be taught? How can God teach God? But when my mind comes down again, to a lower level, I see the ignorance in man and I try to remove it.'

Maharaj spent most of his later life in a state of high spiritual consciousness, coming down only in order to teach and help us. His aware-

---

[33] *Ibid.*
[34] *Ibid.*, p. 96.

ness of God had become so habitual that he would experience mystical visions even while conscious of the external world around him. . . .

Vijnanananda, a disciple of Sri Ramakrishna, said of Maharaj and his visions: 'The gods and goddesses are not myths, they are real. They are the many aspects of the one Godhead. I know this because Maharaj used to see and talk to them.'[35]

## SWAMI TURIYANANDA (HARI)

While Swami Brahmananda was a receptacle of his teacher's spiritual power for the welfare of successive generations, other intimate disciples of Sri Ramakrishna, both householder and monastic, each embodied different spiritual principles which Sri Ramakrishna had instilled in them during their training periods. Swami Turiyananda, for example, more than the others, exemplified the ascetic, since

. . . all his life, even from his boyhood, he treated his body with the same indifference as St. Francis, (who looked upon his body as 'Brother Ass'). Swami Turiyananda . . . demonstrates . . . what austerity really means and what its value is in the life dedicated to God.[36]

### Positive Approach toward Lust

Some incidents in Swami Turiyananda's relationship with Sri Ramakrishna illustrate the direction of his spiritual development. Turiyananda, who sought assiduously to overcome lust, had the habit of remaining aloof from women. As a youth he did not allow even little girls in his company. When questioned by Sri Ramakrishna about his attitude toward women, he replied, " 'Oh, I cannot bear them." His teacher's answer was,

'You talk like a fool!' . . . 'Look down upon women! What for? They are the manifestation of the Divine Mother. Bow down to them as to your mother and hold them in respect. That is the only way to escape their influence. The more you hate them, the more you will fall into the snare.'[37]

[35] *Ibid.,* pp. 87-88.
[36] Swami Ritajananda, *Swami Turiyananda* (Mylapore, Madras: Sri Ramakrishna Math, 1963), pp. 1-2.
[37] *The Apostles of Sri Ramakrishna,* p. 306.

When on another occasion he asked Sri Ramakrishna how he could get beyond the idea of sex, his teacher replied that one need not destroy lust in the attempt to lead a celibate life, but rather give it another direction. Instead of encouraging merely a negative effort at self-control, he advocated the positive approach of directing the emotions toward God.[38]

### Reluctance to Accept Personal God

These and other teachings were aimed at Turiyananda's reluctance to accept devotion to the personal form of God, as he had been inclined toward the ultra-radical school of Advaita Vedanta[39] when he met Sri Ramakrishna, with its emphasis on knowledge rather than love of God and consequent reliance on self-effort as opposed to God's grace. Turiyananda recalled later, in his conversation with a younger Swami,

> 'When I was of your age (in the early twenties), I was an extreme Vedantist. . . . But Sri Ramakrishna scolded me again and again and gave me another ideal. He pointed out that the path of knowledge was not my way. He made me a devotee instead. I can still remember how the Master disciplined me.'[40]

The following incidents show Turiyananda's transformation in this regard:

> Like a true Vedantin, Harinath lived a life of asceticism and continence. The deeper he dived into Vedanta, the more its lofty ideal appealed to him. Plunged in the study of books on this subject, he did not come to Dakshineswar for some days. Sri Ramakrishna noticed his absence and said to him one day, 'Hallo, you do not come here now so frequently. They say you are studying and meditating on Vedanta nowadays. It is good. But what does the Vedanta philosophy teach? Brah-

---

[38] Turiyananda states in this connection, "Mere suppression of passions helps little. There must be a high ideal along with self-restraint. Without a high ideal, the passions will find another outlet. You must give them a new direction, then you will be automatically rid of them. 'Take refuge in Me and control the senses.'" *Spiritual Talks*, p. 118. "The Master asked me to increase my lust infinitely. I was amazed to hear it. He then explained, 'What is lust? It is the desire to get. Then desire to get Him and strengthen this desire greatly.'" *Ibid.*, p. 116.

[39] "It was Shankara who moulded my life. Before I came to the Master, a single verse of Shankara would lift me a step up and give me a flood of light." *Ibid.*, p. 126.

[40] Ritajananda, pp. 15-16.

man alone is real and everything else is unreal,—isn't that its substance or is there anything more? Then why don't you give up the unreal and cling to the real?' These words threw a new light on Vedanta and turned Hari's thoughts in a new direction. A few days later Sri Ramakrishna went to Calcutta and sent for Harinath; when he came he found the Master in a state of semi-consciousness. 'It is not easy to see the world of phenomena as unreal,' the Master began addressing the assembled devotees. 'This knowledge is impossible without the special grace of God. Mere personal effort is powerless to confer this realisation. A man is after all a tiny creature, with very limited powers. What an infinitesimal part of truth can he grasp by himself!' Harinath felt as if these words were directed to him, for he had been straining every nerve to attain illumination. The Master then sang a song eulogising the miraculous power of divine grace. Tears flowed down his cheeks, literally wetting the ground. Harinath was deeply moved. He too burst into tears. After that he learned to surrender himself at the feet of the Lord.[41]

## Subsequent Reliance on Grace

In the course of Turiyananda's subsequent spiritual life he learned more and more to depend on the Divine Will. Especially

---

[41] *Life of Sri Ramakrishna,* pp. 478-479. Later in his life, in a conversation concerning his attitude on the superiority of devotion to knowledge *(bhakti* vs. *jnana),* Turiyananda stated: "Jnana fully evolved becomes Bhakti. Practice of knowledge leads the mind higher and higher, beyond the bounds of duality. But true Bhakti is its own end. . . . Knowledge is necessary in the first stages of spiritual life to master the senses. Afterwards it is one continuous enjoyment of the beatific love of God. And how beautiful are these words of Thomas à Kempis: 'Speak, O Lord, for Thy servant heareth. Silence, all ye teachers! And silence, ye prophets! Speak Thou alone, O Lord, unto my soul!' " *Spiritual Talks,* p. 287. One day, referring to Swami Vivekananda, he said: "It was the opinion of Swamiji that all heart and no brain is preferable to all brain and no heart. He used to say that the heart does everything." *Ibid.,* p. 289. On self-reliance, he commented: "Reliance on one's apparent self leads to ruin. To presume to be all-knowing is extremely harmful. Self-reliance or self-confidence means faith in the Higher Self." *Ibid.,* p. 100. "Merely saying 'I am Brahman' is no use as long as there is the least ignorance left in you. You must worship God." *Ibid.,* p. 294. Cf. *ibid.,* pp. 213-215, and the following elaboration by Turiyananda on Divine Mother: "The philosophy of the *Chandi* has established the unity of Brahman and Shakti. 'She, the Divine Mother is the Absolute and yet the relative in the form of the universe. She pervades everything.' Mahamaya (the Great Illusion) has veiled everyone with delusion that Her play may continue undisturbed. She vouchsafes both worldly enjoyment and spiritual emancipation. . . . How is it that we *know,* and yet cannot *act?* This is due to Her Maya. She must be propitiated. 'She being propitiated grants the boon of Freedom.' Aye, without Her grace, no man can

during his wanderings and pilgrimages after his Master's death, when he led a life of extreme asceticism and self-denial, he felt as if the Divine Mother of the Universe was guiding his every step. Although his mind often dwelled for long periods in the state of *turiya* (fourth plane of consciousness),[42] he would always pray to the Divine Mother for devotion and self-surrender. He fully recognized God's sovereignty in the world as well as in the realm of spiritual experience. In his own words,

'A person who returns to the world after the experience of nirvikalpa samadhi does not do so on his volition. It is by the grace of God that one gets samadhi, and one's re-entry into the world is also by the will of God. Everything happens only by the will of the Lord.'[43]

*Reminiscences of Sri Ramakrishna*

Turiyananda's mind would always turn to the days spent in the company of Sri Ramakrishna with nostalgia and longing, as he reminisced with young novices and disciples in his later years:

Dakshineswar was in those days as divine and blissful as Kailasa (the celebrated abode of Shiva). From morning till one in the afternoon, all were busy preparing for the worship of the Deities and then worshipping them; while Shri Ramakrishna himself was always talking about God, and people sat spellbound listening to him. The atmosphere vibrated with thoughts of God. Even his jokes and funs related to God and culminated in Samadhi. He would rest after the midday meal, but only for a short while. The rest of his day was given to discoursing about God. In the evening he would visit the Kali temple and there fan the Mother, then return to his room reeling under divine intoxication. He would often ask those who practised Sadhana if they felt a kind of intoxication in the morning and evening. . . . At night there was scarcely any sleep for him. No sooner had he lain down that he would get up and rouse all who slept in his room, saying, 'Do not sleep so much. Get up and meditate.' He would then lie down again and get up by early dawn and recite the names

---

get out of this net-work of illusion. Only through worship can the common man realize the supreme beatitude, the state of universal consciousness." *Ibid.,* p. 279. Cf. *ibid.,* pp. 325-326.

[42] Akhilananda, *Hindu Psychology,* p. 207. " 'During that period,' he later recalled, 'my mind always stayed on a high level. There was a constant stream of God-consciousness, unbroken like the flow of oil from one vessel to another.' " Ritajananda, pp. 41-42.

[43] Ritajananda, p. 43.

of God in his inimitable sweet voice. Others also would get up and sit down to Japa and meditation. Now and then he would go to them and correct their postures.[44]

Shri Ramakrishna used to give no other blessing except this, 'Mother, let them have illumination—let them be conscious of their real nature.'[45]

Questioned by a disciple, "You once told us that the joy of one day's company with . . . [Sri Ramakrishna] was enough compensation for the sufferings of a whole life," he answered:

Yes, it is true. An hour of congregational singing in the company of the Master used to fill us with such an exuberant joy that we would feel transported, as it were, into an ethereal region. But now even meditation fails to evoke that celestial bliss, or even a semblance of it. That bliss would abide in us for a week continually. We used to feel intoxicated, though we did not know the why or how of it. Who will believe it? It is difficult to convince anyone. Yet I must speak out.[46]

*Later Life: His Austerity*

Turiyananda's austere temperament, strength of mind and life of God-consciousness led Swami Vivekananda to send him to America as a living example of the Indian ideal of monasticism. He told Turiyananda, " 'Can you lecture like I have done?' " " 'Of course not,' " was the reply, " 'what are you saying?' " " 'Well then,' " Vivekananda retorted, " 'do not trouble yourself about lecturing. You just live the life. Be an example to them. Let them see how Sannyasins live!' "[47] Turiyananda's personal self-discipline was such that he could even withdraw his mind from his body at will, as the following event illustrates, related by Akhilananda:

Sri Ramakrishna had cancer of the throat. When the doctors would go

[44] *Spiritual Talks,* pp. 94-95.

[45] *Ibid.,* pp. 187-188.

[46] *Ibid.,* pp. 282-283.

[47] *With the Swamis in America* by A Western Disciple (2d ed.; Mayavati, Almora: Advaita Ashrama, 1946), pp. 50-51. For a documentation of Swami Turiyananda's experiences in America, see *op. cit.* and Ritajananda, pp. 45-91. Turiyananda hints at the kind of power he manifested as a *guru* in America: see *Spiritual Talks,* pp. 271-273; cf. the following: "Formerly my nerves were very fine, and I had great powers of explaining things. Whenever anyone put me a question, I could see everything from its very origin to its outer expression—I could see from what motive he spoke and why. And there was a flood of light in a single word of mine." *Ibid.,* p. 123.

to treat it, He would say to them: 'Wait a minute.' After a short time He would add: 'Now you can go on.' He had withdrawn His mind completely from the body. Then the doctors could do anything, for He could not feel it. We never saw Sri Ramakrishna; we saw His disciples. Swami Turiyananda, one of the disciples, had to undergo a serious operation. His heart was weak because of age and long suffering. The doctors were hesitant about giving him an anesthetic. They reported this to Swami Brahmananda, our Master, who was then President of the Ramakrishna Mission. Swami Brahmananda went to the bedroom of the sick Swami and said, 'You will just have to endure!' The Swami replied: 'Yes, Maharaj, certainly.' And all the preparations were made for this major operation in his room. He began to talk about *Brahman* to some of the young Swamis who were present while the operation was going on. The surgeon was amazed. After finishing everything he asked: 'Swami, can you sing a song?' And Swami Turiyananda sang a devotional song. His mind was completely withdrawn from the body. There was not the slightest distortion of the facial muscles during the operation.

Sri Ramakrishna used to say that when Jesus was crucified, He withdrew His mind completely from His body; He was in another state altogether, a state of *samadhi* or superconsciousness. The nails pierced through His body but the mind was unaffected.[48]

## SRI RAMAKRISHNA'S VERSATILITY AS GURU

*Swami Vijnananda*

It becomes evident from the foregoing that Sri Ramakrishna's close disciples offer rich testimony of the spiritual experiences[49] by

[48] Akhilananda, *Mental Health,* pp. 126-127. Cf. A. J. Appasamy, *Christianity as Bhakti Marga: A Study in the Mysticism of the Johannine Writings* (London: Macmillan, 1927), "Can God Suffer?," pp. 116-122, esp. p. 117; Akhilananda, *Hindu View of Christ,* chap. vii, "Christ and the Cross," pp. 179-197; Abhedananda, *Christian Science and Vedanta* (Calcutta: Ramakrishna Vedanta Math, 1952); Swami Paramananda, *Spiritual Healing* (rev. ed.; Boston: Vedanta Centre, 1923).

[49] For a fairly comprehensive cataloguing of the spiritual experiences of the disciples of Sri Ramakrishna, see Saradananda, *The Great Master; The Disciples of Ramakrishna; Spiritual Talks;* Isherwood, *Sri Ramakrishna and His Disciples;* Swami Shivananda, *For Seekers of God,* trans. by Swami Vividishananda (Mayavati, Almora: Advaita Ashrama, 1954); Vividishananda, *A Man of God* (Mylapore, Madras: Sri Ramakrishna Math, 1957); *Story of a Dedicated Life;* Ritajananda, *Swami Turiyananda; The Eternal Companion; Sri Sarada Devi, The Holy Mother; Life of Swami Vivekananda; Life of Sri Ramakrishna;* Nivedita, *The Master as I*

which their lives were transformed and blessed as a result of contact with their preceptor. He communicated to them, by one means or another, the experience of God according to their capacities and temperaments; he transmitted to them all the spirit of understanding of other religions. Additional illustrations of his teaching method will demonstrate the unique flexibility of Sri Ramakrishna's approach, and further corroborate its effectiveness. Swami Vijnananda, who met his master in his early teens and lived to become the fourth president of the Order until his death in 1938, describes his first encounter with Sri Ramakrishna in the following manner:

'I felt in Sri Ramakrishna's room a tangible atmosphere of peace. The devotees present seemed to be listening in blissful absorption to the words which poured from the Master's lips. I don't recall what he said, but I still remember the transport of delight I experienced then as if it was yesterday. For a long time I sat there, beside myself with joy, and my whole attention was concentrated on Sri Ramakrishna. He did not say anything to me, nor did I ask him anything. I thought it was time for me to depart, so I prostrated before him. As I stood up to go, he asked, "Can you wrestle? Come, let me see how well you wrestle!" With these words he stood up ready to grapple with me. I was very much surprised at this kind of challenge. I thought to myself, "What kind of holy man is this?" Anyhow, I replied, "Yes, of course I can wrestle."

'Sri Ramakrishna came closer, with a smile on his lips. He caught hold of my arms and began to shove me. But I was a muscular young man, and pushed him back to the wall. He was still smiling and holding me with a strong grip. Gradually I felt a sort of electric current coming out of his hands and entering into me. That touch made me completely helpless; I lost all my physical strength. I went into ecstasy, and the hair of my body stood on end. Then Sri Ramakrishna let me go. He said, smiling, "Well, you are the victor." With these words he sat down on his cot again. I was speechless. Wave after wave of bliss was engulfing my whole being. After a while, Sri Ramakrishna got up from his seat. Patting me gently on the back, he said, "Come here often." Then he offered me some sweets as prasad, and I returned to Calcutta. For days the spell of the intoxicating joy lingered, and I realized that he had transmitted spiritual power to me.'[50]

On his second visit with Sri Ramakrishna, Vijnananda said that

---

*Saw Him* and her *Notes on Some Wanderings;* Ashutosh Ghosh, *Swami Abhedananda, The Patriot-Saint* (Calcutta: Ramakrishna Vedanta Math, 1967).
[50] Isherwood, pp. 236-237.

he was unable to meditate as he wished. Sri Ramakrishna touched his tongue, then told him to meditate in the Panchavati. Vijnananda made his way with difficulty to the Panchavati in a state of spiritual intoxication; he then sat in meditation and lost all outward consciousness. Sri Ramakrishna subsequently assured him that from then on he would always have deep meditation.[51]

*Testimony of Swami Shivananda*

Swami Shivananda, another great soul of high spiritual attainments who succeeded Swami Brahmananda as President of the Order, wrote a letter to a lady from Boston about his life and experiences with Sri Ramakrishna in response to her inquiries. It evidences the intimacy which pervaded Sri Ramakrishna's relationship with his disciples, as well as the universality that always characterized his teachings. Shivananda writes to Mrs. Anna M. Worcester, known as "Annapurna":

> I am very glad to receive your letter of January 5, 1932. . . .
>
> 'Yes, I am writing a short note regarding my personal life, as I promised previously. . . . From my early boyhood I had a deep longing to know God and to realize Him. That longing grew with age. Urged by it, I would go to the Brahmo Samaj and visit holy men, who I thought would be able to help me. . . . In Calcutta I first met Sri Ramakrishna at the house of Ram Chandra Datta. Next I met him at Dakshineswar.
>
> In the dim light of an oil lamp I saw the Master seated cross-legged in his room with three or four others seated on the floor in front of him. The short audience was enough for me: at once I felt a deep attachment for the Master. I felt as if I had known him for a long time. My heart became filled with joy . . . with the confidence, faith and certitude of a child, I surrendered myself to him, placing myself entirely under his care. I became certain that at last I found him for whom I had been searching all these days. Since then I looked upon the Master as my mother. He also treated me the same way. After this momentous visit my life at home and work at the office seemed to be like a heavy load. I would often run to him, visiting him at Dakshineswar or in Calcutta.
>
> During my second or third visit, as I was serving him, the Master, in an ecstatic mood, touched my chest. The magic touch took away my outward consciousness, plunging me into a deep meditative state. I do not know how long I remained in that state. As a result of the touch everything became revealed to me; I realized that I was the Soul, eternal

[51] *Apostles of Sri Ramakrishna,* p. 384.

and free; I realized that the Master was . . . born . . . for the good of mankind, and that I was on earth to serve him. He bestowed upon me the blessing of a similar experience again under the Banyan tree at Panchavati.

Notwithstanding this, he would not allow us to rest on our laurels, but would constantly urge us, with infinite patience, to taste the fruits of his realization by our own efforts. He watched our efforts and directed us to proceed on our own lines. Bigotry and fanaticism had no place in his life and teaching. He would accept all of all denominations with equal love and sympathy. To come in contact with him was to become spiritual forever. To live with him was to live in the presence of God.

I had to marry against my wish, and that was a great trial for me. My determination to renounce the world deepened as I prayed night after night with tears in my eyes, asking God not to bind me down with chains of the world. On the death of my wife I was relieved of all bondages and I ran straight to Dakshineswar. I begged the Master to allow me to stay with him. He kindly accepted me. Since then for the next three years he was with us in the body, I lived almost constantly with him. At Dakshineswar I met Swamiji as well as the Swamis Brahmananda and Premananda. Amongst us Swamiji was loved and trusted most by the Master.

After the Master's passing away I travelled all over India and endeavored much to know God in His different aspects. I liked the Himalayas very much and also spent some time in South India and Ceylon. Benares, the city of Shiva, I loved much. All my efforts have ended in realizing Him everywhere. Sri Ramakrishna is the centre from which all the radii have travelled towards the circumference.[52]

---

[52] As reprinted in Vividishananda, *A Man of God,* pp. 260-263. Mrs. Worcester was closely associated with Swami Akhilananda in his work in America for thirty-five years until his death in 1962 (see Akhilananda, *Modern Problems,* p. 8). She died in 1970, and was well known to this writer. For brevity and emphasis in this chapter, only four of the monastic disciples of Sri Ramakrishna have been highlighted with respect to their discipleship experiences. But even a casual survey of the documented history of Sri Ramakrishna as a spiritual teacher will show that the occurrence of superconscious experience among his disciples was by no means limited to his monastic followers. Householder disciples such as Purna Chandra Ghosh, Nag Mahashay, Balaram Bose, "M," Girish Ghosh, Keshab Chandra Sen, along with many others, as well as his numerous women disciples, attest to the variety of types of personalities which reached God-consciousness under his guidance. See Saradananda, Part III; Isherwood, pp. 127-305; *The Disciples of Ramakrishna,* pp. 295-504; Ghanananda, "Some Holy Women"; *The Saint Durga Charan Nag;* and *The Gospel of Sri Ramakrishna,* Nikhilananda translation. Note especially the event of New Year's Day, 1886, as recorded in the closing pages of Saradananda's biography (pp. 894-898), when Sri Ramakrishna lifted a number of householder devotees simultaneously to a higher plane.

# CHAPTER XII

# Swami Akhilananda: Practical Application of Sri Ramakrishna's Approach

## MINISTRY AMONG CHRISTIANS

"The Swami and I," Paul E. Johnson recalls, "were devoted friends during all the years of his residence in Boston. He was surely a saint who manifested overflowing love from the Infinite Spirit to all who knew him."[1]

The life of the Reverend Swami Akhilananda, "a representative of modern Hinduism,"[2] is an outstanding example of the practical application of Sri Ramakrishna's approach to the dilemma of religious plurality in the context of contemporary American society. This writer had the privilege of knowing him as a spiritual teacher during the period 1953-1962, and can testify to the contributions he made in the course of his ministry, especially to the Christian community. In this connection Walter H. Clark recalls the Swami's appreciation of Christian values in the following manner:

I never knew him to engage in proselytizing, and I never felt anything from him but a keen appreciation for my Christian convictions expressed in such a manner as to heighten my understanding of Jesus and

---

[1] Letter to this writer dated September 22, 1972, from Paul E. Johnson, Professor Emeritus, Boston University School of Theology.

[2] De Smet, review of *Avatar and Incarnation,* p. 173.

162

to strengthen my sensitivities to the mystical and eternal values of Christianity. . . . I never knew him to cast a slur on anyone's faith, and I never knew anyone who disliked him. As to his threat to Christianity, I several times told him that he was 'the best Christian' I knew.[3]

As a direct product of Sri Ramakrishna's succession of discipleship, Swami Akhilananda was fully at home in the Christian faith.[4] Edgar S. Brightman states,

Swami Akhilananda . . . has made many friends in educational circles, especially at Brown, Boston, and Harvard Universities. He is welcome among Jews and Christians alike. He is prized both as a scholar and as a religious leader and counselor. It is a great privilege for me to be counted among the friends of this broad-minded and noble man. He is modest, gentle, and tolerant; yet at the same time firm, well-poised, and saintly. . . . The Swami lives by the principles which he . . . recommends to others. . . . The faith which he represents is an outgrowth of the teaching and religious experience of Sri Ramakrishna, a nineteenth-century saint, whose immediate disciple, the Swami Brahmananda, was the teacher of the Swami Akhilananda. To know [him,] then, is analogous to knowing one of the early Christians who was separated from Jesus by only one generation.[5]

With respect to the nature of his leadership among the young students seeking spiritual guidance in the largely Christian college communities of New England, Robert Ulich writes,

He was a teacher in the truest sense of the term, a guide to youth, and a participant in their troubles and aspirations. . . . he could lead a young seeker more deeply into the essence of Judaism or Christianity than many a minister was able to do. The Swami was not one of those Indian 'Gurus' who pretend to heal our uprooted civilization. To be frank, in some of them I detect a certain vanity. And though it seems to me he was well acquainted with Yoga practices, they were for him not essential.[6]

[3] Walter H. Clark, in *Spiritual Practices,* by Swami Akhilananda, Memorial Edition with Reminiscences (Cape Cod, Mass.: Claude Stark, Inc., 1974), pp. 166-167.

[4] "Sri Ramakrishna . . . experienced God through the Christian way in His spiritual experiences. His disciples, like Swami Vivekananda, Swami Brahmananda, Swami Saradananda, Swami Ramakrishnananda, and others, also had exalted experiences of Jesus and the Christian ideals. . . . He introduced the worship of Jesus as an incarnation [among Hindus]." Akhilananda, *Hindu View of Christ,* p. 13.

[5] Foreword to Akhilananda's *Hindu Psychology,* pp. xii-xiii.

[6] Robert Ulich, in *Spiritual Practices* by Akhilananda, Memorial Edition, p. 200.

Dr. Clark's comment in this connection is significant in that it stresses the same point from a different perspective: Swami Akhilananda, rather than preach Hinduism, sought to deepen the Christian experience. Dr. Clark recalls:

[As] Dean of the Hartford School of Religious Education at the Hartford Seminary Foundation, . . . I brought the Swami to Hartford to give a lecture on the place of religion in psychotherapy. . . . I can remember with much vividness and pleasure the effect of the Swami's warm personality and spiritual acumen on the students there. . . . It gave me a glimpse into the sources of his influence with Christian youth, whose beliefs in the mystical values of Christianity were thereby strengthened.[7]

Akhilananda's effectiveness as a representative of Sri Ramakrishna's approach to the dilemma of religious plurality can be evaluated from the perspective of his acceptability to prominent members of the Christian academic community. The following statement by Harold DeWolf, former Professor of Systematic Theology at Boston University, affords one among many possible examples of the ready exchange of views and of speaking engagements that characterized Akhilananda's work in Christian circles. Dr. DeWolf states,

My personal memories of the Swami include many friendly discussions of philosophy and religion in his headquarters home on Bay State Road. . . ; Akhilananda speaking, at my request, in the chapel of Boston University College of Liberal Arts, and his invitation, which I accepted, to be speaker at the Sunday service in the Center. In the college chapel he spoke on criteria by which one could judge whether a person who claimed to have experienced the presence of God had, in fact, or whether he might be deceiving or self-deceiving. . . . I recall with appreciation his emphasis, like that of Jesus, on the idea that 'by their fruits you shall know them.' The closer a person's acquaintance with God, he said, the more his life would show a sensitive, loving concern for other people.[8]

## FORMATIVE PERIOD

Swami Akhilananda was born in East Bengal on February 25, 1894. His mother died when he was still young. Because of the abundance of family members which is usual under the Indian sys-

[7] Walter H. Clark, *op. cit.,* p. 165.

[8] Harold DeWolf, in "Reminiscences," *Spiritual Practices,* p. 171.

tem of family life, he did not lack love in his formative years. His father was a lawyer. His grandfather regularly practiced spiritual disciplines and devotional exercises, and it was from him that the Swami, at an early age, first learned the habit of meditation.[9]

He came into contact with several of the swamis of the Ramakrishna Order while in his early teens. Inspired by their lives and example, he decided to devote his own life to the monastic ideal. Before long he developed close association with almost all of the monastic disciples of Sri Ramakrishna. He never met Swami Vivekananda, who had passed into *mahasamadhi* in 1902. It has already been described in the previous chapter how Swami Brahmananda became his teacher. One or two illustrations of his devotion to his *guru* and of his zeal for the spiritual life will bring his training as a monk into sharper focus.

One day when Akhilananda and a brother disciple were walking in the forest with Swami Brahmananda, a tiger appeared at a clearing. Akhilananda and the other disciple both jumped in front of their teacher to protect him from the tiger. Brahmananda, who even at an advanced age was physically very strong, brushed them aside and stood before the tiger, only ten paces away. The teacher and the tiger looked at each other for a few moments. Then the tiger turned and loped away quietly. Akhilananda used to allude to this incident in his lectures and sermons to demonstrate the great love which is the very nature of a fully developed spiritual personality, not only for his disciples, but a universal love which does not stop at human beings alone but includes animals as well, even normally destructive animals (cf. St. Francis and the wolf). The implication was that the tiger felt the great swami's love and fearlessness, and thus turned away and did not molest them.

Another incident of those early days is as follows: Young Akhilananda (Nirode Sannyal) would regularly come to the Math after school to sit in the presence of his teacher, often without conversation, as would some of the other disciples. One day "Maharaj" said to him, "Hello! I have not seen you for some time. Where have you been?" The boy replied, a little startled: "But, Maharaj, I just

---

[9] As Gordon Allport writes, "American psychology would improve in richness and wisdom if it accommodated in some way the wise things that [Akhilananda] says about meditation." *Hindu Psychology,* Introduction, p. x.

came the day before yesterday." With a smile and an impatient gesture, Brahmananda said, "Oh, you and your 'day before yesterday!' "[10]

One of his brother disciples, Swami Prabhavananda, offers gracious testimony to Swami Akhilananda's devotion to his spiritual teacher. He writes,

> Swami Akhilananda was a loving soul—having wonderful love for everyone. I was envious of his love for Maharaj, his guru. I remember one occasion when he visited here. We got together with other monastic members and asked him to speak about Maharaj. While he spoke he was sobbing and weeping. His love was so great.[11]

Swami Premananda was the manager, or "mother," as he was called, of the Math. He made no formal disciples, yet showered his love and blessings on all the young monks. He had a particular fondness for Akhilananda, for whom he would often prepare a bed in his own room. One day Swami Premananda instructed Akhilananda without further explanation to "study science." Years later Akhilananda gave full credit to Swami Premananda's foresight: "I cannot help remembering what Swami Premananda, one of the great disciples of Sri Ramakrishna, told me in 1915 about studying science."[12] "He used to insist on our study of scientific methods."[13] "He evidently foresaw the world situation and suggested to me to study the contemporary thought-current."[14] In this connection Walter Clark writes,

> In the broadest possible sense the contribution of Swami Akhilananda was the lessening of cultural gaps between the East and the West. With a grounding in western science and western culture through his studies in India and with an empathy for them and an interest in them, the Swami came to the United States to perform what became his life's mission. Hospitable to all walks of people, he was nevertheless most at home with intellectuals like himself: students, scholars and scientists, particularly

---

[10] From lectures by Akhilananda attended by this writer.

[11] Prabhavananda, in *Spiritual Practices* by Akhilananda, Memorial Edition, p. 194. Swami Prabhavananda is head of the Vedanta Society of Southern California, and was a disciple of Swami Brahmananda.

[12] *Modern Problems,* p. 15.

[13] *Hindu Psychology,* p. xvii.

[14] *Modern Problems, loc. cit.*

those who shared his devotion to the religious quest, even though few had advanced along the path as far as he. Professors Pitirim Sorokin, Gordon W. Allport, Robert Ulich, and O. Hobart Mowrer as well as Clarence Faust and Dean Walter G. Muelder were examples of the type of person he sought out as friends. To them he not only imparted his own wisdom but he also was open to learning from them in what was a truly creative dialogue. It was not in his nature to be authoritarian, narrow, or intolerant either in his teaching or his writing, and it was his humility that brought out the wisdom in others at the same time that it recommended his own.[15]

The happiness and contentment that Akhilananda knew during his days as a *brahmacharin* (novice) was complete. He delighted in cooking for his brother monks and for the great swamis. On looking back and speaking of those days, he would disclose that his only desire was to remain a cook in the presence of his master, preparing a variety of Bengali dishes (cf. Brother Lawrence). His only opportunity to continue this activity in the West was on occasions when banquets were held to celebrate the birthday of Śri Ramakrishna. He would spend most of the night cooking huge pots of delicately curried rice, which would be served to the guests along with the catered dinner, customarily held at the University Club in Boston.

After Akhilananda's completion of academic studies at the University of Calcutta in 1919, he had a variety of assignments, one of which was directing flood and famine relief work in South India. He related that he would swim day after day, forging flooded rivers to bring help, accompanied by snakes and crocodiles. At night the villagers would offer him a small bowl of rice, and on again he would work the next day. He confided to a group of friends in America, "I can never forget the two young boys who swam along with me, oblivious of the danger. None of us felt any fear."

Then he had the more sedate task of managing a boys' dormitory at a school, and later assisted at the Ramakrishna Center at Madras. During another period he taught philosophy and religion at Annamalai University.

## AMERICAN EXPERIENCE

In 1926 he left for America. At this point he was offered some

[15] Clark, "Reminiscences," p. 167.

advice by the then Secretary of the Order, Swami Saradananda. This advice held him in good stead, and he often referred to it to characterize his experience in America. Coming to see him off at the boat along with Swami Akhandananda and others, Swami Saradananda spoke endearingly to him as follows: "I have been to America twice. Learn from my experiences. Some people will praise you to the skies, and glorify you. Others will throw mud on you. Take both equally."

Akhilananda began work immediately. He first founded the center in Providence, Rhode Island, and then in the early forties founded the Boston Center.[16] He kept both up, working full time at both centers until his death in 1962. The scope of his activities in America was considerable. He travelled country-wide constantly to lecture and attend meetings, and assisted a number of the Ramakrishna Vedanta Societies in this country to keep going in difficult times (e.g., New York, St. Louis, Chicago, Seattle). He attempted to start centers in Philadelphia and Washington, D. C., without success. His main influence, however, was not in center building but in the sphere of character building and intellectual culture.[17] He attracted doctors, philosophers, scientists, professors, psychologists, theologians, sociologists, and students in addition to the aver-

[16] See Paul E. Johnson, *Psychology of Religion* (Nashville, Tenn.: Abingdon Press, 1959), pp. 157-159, for Professor Johnson's description of the worship service he attended at Swami Akhilananda's invitation, on the occasion of the dedication of the Boston Vedanta Center.

[17] Jacob Needleman, Chairman of the Department of Philosophy at San Francisco State College, writes of the Vedanta movement in America: "Finally, when considering the Indian influence in America, a special place must be reserved for the Vedanta Societies throughout the country. Historically, Vedanta Society was the first Eastern religious tradition that took root on our soil, having been brought here late in the nineteenth century by Swami Vivekananda, the chief disciple of the great Indian master Sri Ramakrishna. Intellectually, the influence of this form of Vedanta has been enormous. It was because of the American Vedantists—numbering some of the best minds of our time—that the East was first taken seriously here. And though, when compared to more recent movements, it now seems sedate, its activities constitute a very wide and solidly based spiritual discipline." *The New Religions* (Garden City, N. Y.: Doubleday, 1970), p. 213. Cf. Swami Gambhirananda, *History of the Ramakrishna Math and Mission* (Mayavati, Almora: Advaita Ashrama, 1957); Swami Tejasananda, *The Ramakrishna Movement: Its Ideals and Activities* (Howrah: The Ramakrishna Mission Sarodapitha, 1956); Swami Ranganathananda, *The Ramakrishna Mission: Its Ideals and Activities* (Calcutta: The Ramakrishna Mission Institute of Culture, 1966).

age men and women seeking the religious life. He drew them by his sweet nature, loving kindness and sharp intellect. Professor Ulich comments,

Without any pose he moved among us simply, modestly, and naturally. . . . When I met him for the first time I intuitively felt the presence of an unusual personality. He was a lover of life and men.[18]

His bursts of laughter and humorous comments during long, serious conferences are still remembered by those who were present, as the highlight of his company was a wonderful, sparkling sense of humor. This writer attended several such conferences in the early and mid-fifties, such as the Conference on Altruistic Love at the Massachusetts Institute of Technology Auditorium, when Swami Akhilananda was on the platform with Eric Fromm and others, and the Conference on Science, Philosophy, and Religion.[19] We can never forget the quiet, sweet way he sat there, and the good humor he lent the proceedings. Dr. Clark states in this regard,

Several years after I first met him both of us were asked by Professor Pitirim A. Sorokin, the distinguished founder of the Department of Sociology at Harvard, to become founding members of his Research Society for Creative Altruism, along with Igor Sikorsky, F. S. C. Northrop, Senator Ralph Flanders, Henry Margenau, A. H. Maslow, President Daniel Marsh of Boston University and other distinguished men. . . . I

[18] "Reminiscences," *loc. cit.*

[19] According to the *Providence Evening Bulletin* obituary article on September 25, 1962, Akhilananda "was a member of many organizations including the University Club of Boston, the Universal Club of Ministers in Rhode Island, the Rhode Island World Affairs Council, the Rhode Island Philosophical Society, the American Philosophical Association, the American Academy for the Advancement of Science, the American Academy of Political and Social Science, the National Association of Biblical Instructors, the Oriental Society of America, the Foreign Policy Association of America, the Fellowship of Reconciliation of America, the Conference of Science, Philosophy and Religion, the Society of Scientific Study of Religion, the Conference on Religion in a Scientific Age, the Institute of Pastoral Care, the Religious Education Association, the Congress of the Inter-American Psychological Association, the American Psychological Association and the American Metaphysical Association. He was vice president and board member of the World Parliament of Religions and was a founding member of the American Foundation of Religion and Psychiatry in New York. He was a charter member of the American Academy of Religion and Mental Health in New York and also was a founding member of the Society of Altruistic Love in America."

can remember very vividly several of the stormy Council meetings that threatened the demise of the Society even earlier than it actually occurred. Those of us on the Council who were Christian required the calming and tolerant offices of the Hindu Swami to remind us that patience and a focus on our great goals were an essential if the society were to achieve its purpose. This he did with patience and a wit that again and again served to pour oil on troubled waters.[20]

Though a representative of Vedanta to the West, the Swami dressed in traditional Western ministerial garb: clerical collar and black attire. Only on worship days did he put on the ochre robe of the Hindu monk. The following quotation from a televised talk on "We Believe" (WHDH-TV), March 18, 1960, by Dr. Edwin Booth of Boston University gives further indications of Akhilananda's life in America:

There is a sentence in our Christian tradition that God has not left Himself without a witness at any time. . . . I wish to pay my tribute, therefore, this morning, to a witness to the Eternal that comes out of a tradition not my own. . . . For thirty years now, I have personally known the leader of one of the Vedanta Society groups, the one settled here in Boston and working jointly with the one in Providence. . . . And the Society to which I refer now, to which I pay tribute this morning, has arisen out of the following of the teachings of an Indian named Sri Ramakrishna. Sri Ramakrishna was born in 1836 and died in 1886, so it is a very modern movement. There is representing the Sri Ramakrishna Vedanta Society here in Boston a Swami whom many of us have learned to love. . . . Now the Swami who bears witness in our American Christian society for the deep intensities of the spiritual life is named Akhilananda. . . . This means . . . 'Akhil the blessed.'

. . . We have sent our testifiers to India for many, many years. One of my mother's great-uncles was the first missionary of the Church of Scotland to India. . . . And now I sit in Boston and bear tribute to the reverse, to the validity and the value of a missionary from the Hindu tradition, from India, to us in our society here. What a marvelous thing it is for us to build bridges between our faiths! . . .

The Swami Akhilananda was won into the fellowship of Sri Ramakrishna's group when he was a young boy. He never dreamed of being a teacher or a preacher. All he wanted to do was to be a cook in the society of the Brothers of Sri Ramakrishna, that he could know their peace and

[20] "Reminiscences," p. 164.

understand their friendship. Well, the little lad that long ago wanted to be a cook in the Brothers of Sri Ramakrishna has now for thirty years magnificently defended in Providence and Boston, in Brown University and Boston University, in Massachusetts Institute of Technology and Harvard College, the faith he loves. This is a remarkable story. . . .

It is interesting always to know him. He is a marvelous person. He does not live according to the customs of the East, for he speaks peace to us of the West, so he lives according to our customs. He has a good home, he wears our Western clothes, he drives a big good Western automobile. But everywhere he goes, his smiling face, his quiet word, his gentle hand, is a blessing of peace to all of us. I was ill once, quite seriously, a few years ago. He stepped in my hospital room on several occasions, and quietly out of the ancient East I heard his words: 'Peace, peace, peace.' Well it is marvelous to know that the religions communicate to each other through living individuals, warm and gentle, quiet and patient.

Viewed in the light of Dr. Booth's address, Akhilananda was among the pioneers of reverse missionary work, started by Swami Vivekananda in England and America at the turn of the century.[21] Akhilananda was no stranger to Christianity, which has been largely in the custodianship of Western institutions. Early in his spiritual life he developed an intense devotion to Christ while a disciple of Swami Brahmananda. He recalled to some of us the memorable Christmas Eve ceremony at Belur Math when Swami Brahmananda went into *samadhi,* creating an intense spiritual atmosphere. Akhilananda's *Hindu View of Christ* is a landmark in the field, and testifies to his personal devotion and reverence for Jesus. Walter G. Muelder once commented, "There was a man who *really* understood the New Testament."[22]

In Akhilananda's lectures and books he frequently cited St. Francis, who was among his favorite personalities in the Christian tradition. Once, while in Italy, he visited the chapel where St. Francis had his spiritual experiences, and commented on the atmosphere

---

[21] See Akhilananda, *Hindu View of Christ,* chap. xii, "Christian Missions," pp. 245-284, especially the following: "We are firmly convinced that sharing of religious experiences should be the basis of missionary activities of any group" (p. 248). "Insofar as a Hindu takes Jesus as the embodiment of divine love in human form, he worships Jesus as veritable God. Therefore, he understands something of the real spirit of Christianity" (pp. 261-262). Cf. also p. 275 ff.

[22] Statement made to this writer in May, 1970.

there. "Not the big cathedral," he remarked, "but the little one around the corner," was the church where he had felt that spirituality still present. He was also especially fond of St. Anthony, to whom he was compared by an intimate friend because he combined intellect and devotion as did the saint of Padua.[23]

Humility was the keynote of Akhilananda's personality. He was humble to the core. At trains or bus stations he would be the last one out. On other occasions, during the automobile ride from Providence to Boston after an evening lecture Sunday night, he would suddenly awaken abruptly from a nap in the back seat and say, "We must get liver for the cats!" No stores were open Sunday night for liver, so upon arrival at Back Bay, the hour nearly midnight, and the Swami exhausted from the day's platform work, he would proceed carefully to pick the chicken off some cooked chicken bones so that the two cats could enjoy a chicken dinner instead of canned cat food.

## PUBLISHED WORKS

Regarding Akhilananda's published works, Professor Hal Bridges of the University of California comments:

> Swami Akhilananda—author, it will be remembered, of the *Hindu View of Christ*—has published two books expressing mystical thought as psychology. His *Hindu Psychology: Its Meaning for the West* was introduced to American readers in 1946 by Gordon W. Allport of the Harvard psychology department and Edgar Sheffield Brightman of the philosophy department of Boston University. It mingles learned discussion of Western and Hindu psychological theory with unreserved acceptance of the mystical 'superconscious state.' Akhilananda takes issue with Jung for identifying superconscious experiences with the 'deep unconscious state,' describing them as 'vast but dim,' and declaring that they are

[23] Akhilananda states in this connection: "When an individual is spiritually transformed, his influence affects society tremendously. In fact, the whole ideal of a society is changed. Let us refer to the great mystics of the Middle Ages in Europe. We all know what the condition of Christianity was during their lifetime. If personalities like St. Francis, St. Anthony, and some others had not come at that period, Christianity would have been practically lost without their influence. John Wesley, the founder of the Methodist Church, really saved England from a social revolution. His influence with that of a few others changed the thought current of the people in England." *Hindu View of Christ,* pp. 239-240.

172

'scarcely to be recommended anywhere north of the Tropic of Cancer.' Jung's comment is 'unscientific,' he argues. 'Any man who has had these realizations will laugh at such conclusions.' The superconscious state, samadhi, is not dim, but 'vivid and definite.' North of the Tropic of Cancer it has been recommended by 'Judaeo-Christian types' like St. Teresa and Meister Eckhart who, unlike Jung, speak from experience. And far from its being identical with the unconscious state, it is, in its profound awareness, the very opposite. 'To identify the superconscious state with the unconscious state is to mix darkness and light. In one case man is completely oblivious of the existence of God; in the other case man is fully aware of the existence of God, nay, identified with Him.'

Mysticism also permeated Akhilananda's *Mental Health and Hindu Psychology* (1951). In this study he declares that Hindu psychology grew out of spiritual experience, and is closely related to the mental health field, since the Hindus 'fully realize that until and unless the mind is wholly unified and integrated there is no possibility of spiritual realization or mystical experiences.' He goes on to argue that the fears and anxieties, the conflicts and frustrations that make for mental illness can be overcome by yogic meditation and mystical attainment. Meditation strengthens the will, stabilizes the emotions, and calms the mind, and when mystical experience results it is even more conducive to mental health. The man who truly realizes his oneness with God lives free of negative tensions—in peace and love.[24]

The Swami's fourth book, published posthumously, was *Modern Problems and Religion*. It deals with a wide spectrum of personal and communal problems of life, attempting to show how religion best solves these, and that without sincere religious commitment there is no permanent solution. Akhilananda's fifth and final book, published posthumously a decade after his death, was characterized by Dean Muelder as "autobiographical."[25] In his second Introduction to this work, *Spiritual Practices,* Muelder writes,

Swami Akhilananda's death has terminated the valuable practical counsel and guidance in spiritual matters which characterized his leadership

[24] Hal Bridges, *American Mysticism, From William James to Zen* (New York: Harper & Row, 1970), pp. 121-122. Professor Bridges' book was notably the first survey of its kind "devoted entirely to the history of mysticism in America" (from the flap).

[25] As told to this writer during the summer of 1971.

173

in the Vedanta movement. I look back on years of close friendship with him with special gratitude and can only wish that many who will read this book with profit could have felt the spiritual power of his personal solicitude.[26]

When Akhilananda's works were reintroduced in paperback form recently, Paul E. Johnson wrote, "This is a notable service to bring the Swami's definitive books into circulation again with this new publication, and we hope the clarity of his mind and the radiance of his spirit may in this way bless a continuing circle of readers."[27]

His books did not originate from a desire to publish or from motives of personal ambition as may be the case for some scholars, but from the suggestions of others, namely scholarly friends who felt the Swami had something to share. He worked on them during time snatched from interviews, trips, conferences, letter-writing, and lecturing. His motive was the spirit of service. He did not even keep the rights to the books, but left them in the hands of his publishers, Philosophical Library, Harper Brothers, and Bruce Humphries. His works on Hindu psychology represent a major contribution to scholarship in that the insights of Patanjali's *Yoga Aphorisms* are made understandable and dynamic in the light of modern Western developments in psychology. What is most interesting in these works is Akhilananda's thorough grasp of the history and practice of psychology in the West, from Charcot and Janet to his contemporary times. Yet this was as it should be, as he had prepared himself for it, following the advice of Swami Premananda to study science.

His effectiveness was most pronounced on the personal level with men and women who held the reins of contemporary intellectual culture. One day this writer was asked to deliver a small book to a gentleman at Harvard Square—the then greatest living astronomer, Dr. Harlow Shapley. The book was Swami Vivekananda's *Jnana-Yoga.* Subsequently Dr. Shapley reported to the Swami that he carried the book in his pocket everywhere. More than that, Shapley, once an agnostic seeking an answer to the universal dilemma, began touring the country lecturing at universities on science and

[26] *Spiritual Practices*, p. 11.
[27] Letter from Dr. Johnson dated September 22, 1972.

religion. His book, *Of Stars and Men*,[28] shows the effect of this new direction.

## AS A SPIRITUAL TEACHER

Akhilananda's teaching method was in the tradition of his teacher, Swami Brahmananda, and his teacher's teacher, Sri Ramakrishna. He was always encouraging, never negative. His universality knew no bounds. His understanding of the goal of life was to realize God, and "Love thy neighbor as thyself"[29] was both the path and the result. All religions for him were legitimate ways to attain knowledge and love of God, provided a person is sincere. Speaking to a student with a Catholic background he would turn the person's mind to Jesus or the Madonna.[30] Husband and wife would receive individual instruction and training in religious life, varying with the nature and temperament of each.

Philosophically he was an Advaitist, but an Advaitist who included all forms of personalism. In his second Introduction to *Hindu View of Christ*, Walter G. Muelder writes of the Swami, "His deep appreciation for Christ does not compromise his Vedantist faith that loyalty to Christ is consistent at the practical level with non-dualistic ultimate monism."[31] This did not make him a syncretist, for he fully acknowledged the distinctiveness and worth of each religious tradition. He celebrated with worship ceremonies or special lectures the birthdays of the founders of the world's great religions and commemorated the holy days of Islam and Judaism. He instilled in his students a deep veneration for all religions.

Temperamentally he was an extremely balanced person. Dr. James Houston Shrader writes, "We can almost say that he radiated the peaceful composure that dominated his life. His demeanor

[28] (Boston: Beacon Press, 1959). Note Akhilananda, *Modern Problems*, p. 66.

[29] Leviticus 19:18.

[30] This writer personally knew of instances when Swami Akhilananda directed Christians back to their churches. His approach may be compared with Swami Bhavyananda of the Ramakrishna Vedanta Centre in London, who was asked by some priests to give them instruction in the technique of meditation. After he gave the instruction, the priests asked what they should meditate on. The Swami's reply was "Jesus, of course."

[31] Dated November, 1971 (Boston: Branden Press, 1972 [c. 1949]).

175

never changed. He was always the same cheerful, peaceful Swami."[32] Those who knew him saw him angry only on rare occasions, and then in the spirit of reprimand to students who had committed blunders. His anger then was, as one of the disciples of Sri Ramakrishna had said, "like a line drawn in water: when it is finished, it is gone." When he saw evil, he would either turn away or laugh, but never condemn. He had only sympathy for the suffering of his fellow man. This type of even-mindedness, it may be recalled, is constantly reasserted in the *Bhagavad-Gita* as a primary test of a knower of God. Dr. Shrader remarks of the Swami,

> His spirituality was deep-seated. He never spoke about 'believing' this or that. He knew. I once asked him whether he had ever enjoyed the experience of breaking through to contact Reality, known as mysticism. He said that he had. This gave him an assurance that was stimulating to behold. . . . His spiritual certainties transcended my beliefs. I told him that his assistant had said that India had three million gods. He sniffed his dissent and said that there was only one God.[33]

What was most memorable was his constant selfless spirit, an attitude which was effortless. During the last few years of his life he had various painful illnesses. At one time a condition in his left side was especially bothersome. Yet he continued his round of normal activities: lecturing, travelling, officiating at weddings and funerals, holding dinners and conferences—smiling and laughing, yet holding his side all the while. His comment on the life he was leading in service to God and man was, "A slave is a slave; what can I do?"

This writer once composed the following poem in testimony to Swami Akhilananda's dedicated life, and presented it to him. He read it without a word, and smiled faintly.

### Love's Soldier

O wondrous soldier! golden complexioned.
    You fight Mother's battles with sympathy's sword.
The war cries—"Struggle! Struggle!
    Struggle to reach That. For That thou art!
Thou art all, and all is One!"—

[32] "Reminiscences," pp. 198-199.
[33] "Reminiscences," *loc. cit.*

Spring from your heart
To urge onward your erring arrowmen.

Your eyes, Sita-like sweet,
    Smile, saddened
By the suffering they see,
    Pierce through misery's veil
Beholding the Spirit breathing in all.

By your loving service to Him
    You teach us, tired divinities,
How to reach the goal.

When we would ask him, in youthful enthusiasm, "What can we do for you, Swami?"—his reply was always, "Live the life, live the life." And if we "lived the life," we would carry out the ideal to which his own life had long ago been fully dedicated, the ideal of Sri Ramakrishna.

# Conclusion

In the foregoing presentation, Sri Ramakrishna's approach to the dilemma of religious plurality has been documented as an exposition of his experiences of God-consciousness in different religious traditions. It is hoped that this exposition, in and of itself, represents a contribution to interreligious understanding. As Arnold Toynbee points out, "Sri Ramakrishna's message was unique," and "his religious activity and experience were, in fact, comprehensive to a degree that has perhaps never before been attained by any other religious genius, in India or elsewhere."[1] The only surprise is that his life and teachings have not yet been explored in a systematic and thoroughgoing manner by the scholarship community. This presentation is intended as a start in such a direction; and humbly so, for it is recognized that only a few of the many facets of Sri Ramakrishna's life and experiences are dealt with here.

The foregoing chapters portray the many positive aspects of Sri Ramakrishna's life, but in the following, some critical issues will be considered.

---

[1] See p. vii, *supra*.

## LIMITATIONS OF SRI RAMAKRISHNA'S APPROACH

Sri Ramakrishna's background precluded any scholarship activity. He could barely write simple prose. Mathematics gave him a headache. Meticulous study was therefore not possible; nor did he express particular interest in theological speculation. He hungered only for the mystic's vision of ultimate Reality.

While many of his utterances had profound theological and philosophical meaning,[2] they were couched in home-spun village vernacular, often spoken with a slight stammer. His sayings resisted the framework of speculative philosophy and theology. Thus his approach may seem unacceptable to modern scholars of religion. It took Swami Vivekananda, educated in Western ways, to translate Sri Ramakrishna's ideals for the scholar. Were it not for him, they might well have remained unintelligible or inaccessible to the contemporary student of religious life. Thus a disparity exists between the methods of speculative theology of the different world religions and the teachings of Sri Ramakrishna, a disparity which has forestalled the appreciation and utility of his approach in academic circles.

There have been figures in Islamic, Christian, Buddhist, and Hindu religious history who have combined the intellectual power of persuasive scholarship with the depth of mystic realization: al-Ghazali, St. Thomas Aquinas, Nagarjuna, and Shankara respectively. Theirs was a particular mission, as was Sri Ramakrishna's. The comparison is made only to point up Sri Ramakrishna's limitation in this regard, a limitation which he himself, in fact, relished.

Perhaps this limitation stemmed from another: the fact that his approach was predominantly devotional. Granted, he scaled the peak of Advaita Vedanta, but he returned always to his Divine Mother. While his foremost disciple, Vivekananda, preached monism in India, Europe, and America, Sri Ramakrishna himself advocated *bhakti* according to Narada, or wholehearted devotion to God, as the most effective means to the experience of God in this present age. To many who first come into contact with Sri Ramakrishna's and Swami Vivekananda's personalities, this apparent antithesis is most confusing. Westerners in particular find the Hindu

---

[2] See, for example, Satis Chandra Chatterjee, *Classical Indian Philosophies: Their Synthesis in the Philosophy of Sri Ramakrishna.*

devotional exercises difficult to understand or relate to. In this sense, Sri Ramakrishna's emotional participation in ecstasy, his *bhavas,* his identification with Hanuman or Radha, are incomprehensible— not only to the Westerner but to many a Hindu—and represent a limiting factor at present in the utility of his approach to the vast majority of religious seekers of all traditions.

A further limitation in Sri Ramakrishna's approach is the very choice he made in Divine Mother as an aspect of God. This frankly repels many people, especially those of the Judeo-Christian and Islamic traditions, who identify God with the Father. For these traditions, God admits to no "consort," and to worship the divine feminine is no less than idolatry.

To put Sri Ramakrishna's devotion to Kali and the Hindu position itself in fair perspective, it is not necessarily the "consort" of God that is being worshipped in Durga, Kali, Parvati, Sarasvati or Annapurna, but the one God seen from the feminine rather than the masculine perspective. This does not, however, negate the limitation that Sri Ramakrishna's approach suggests to those religions having a Semitically-based origin. Scripture and history reveal the moral abuses of the Canaanites with respect to their goddess, Asherah, and this is often and unfortunately superimposed on Hindu feminine deities as well by Jewish, Christian, and Muslim thinkers. Let it be noted only that there is a vast difference between the moral practices (temple prostitution, etc.) of the Canaanites with respect to their goddess Asherah and the religious life as exemplified by Sri Ramakrishna in his devotion to Kali as Divine Mother.

Possibly the most glaring limitation of Sri Ramakrishna's approach arises from his very dedication to the mystical path: his life and practices remain a puzzle to all those sincere followers of religious life whose primary aim is not to see God, but to lead a good life in faithful fulfillment of what they honestly believe to be the requirements of their orthodoxy. The majority of us are in that category.

Only a handful of men or women in any given nation or century are born with the capacity or inclination to devote themselves fulltime to the occupation of God-realization. To those Sri Ramakrishna speaks most audibly. But to us, whose lives are burdened with a thousand non-mystical preoccupations, while we still adhere to religious values, his message is hushed and most indistinct.

This presents a limitation in that the vast segment of mankind, engaged in the non-mystical pursuits of faith in the Lord, kindness and ministry to his children, and the workaday world of his service, not only does not want to "see God" as Sri Ramakrishna and others did, but protests that this is a side issue in religious life.

No wonder, then, that the apparent casualness with which Sri Ramakrishna regarded the outer forms and customs of the different traditions he tried represents an unmistakable challenge to the existing religiosity of today. His life poses the question, 'What is the goal of religion? Is it observance of forms and ceremonies, or is it the direct and immediate experience of God? Can religious orthodoxy and the mystic's approach be harmonized, or must they remain opposite poles of fullfillment for the faithful?'

This challenge represents a limitation of Sri Ramakrishna's approach in that to the degree it interferes with or contradicts religious orthodoxy in any given religious tradition, to that degree will it be regarded as a threat rather than an aid to personal growth and interreligious understanding.

This leads to the final and most exasperating limitation of Sri Ramakrishna's approach. Mystical experience can be verified, as he himself, his followers, and others have shown, but this verification is not an easy matter. If one wishes to verify a particular experience of God, one must raise one's level of consciousness to the same level as that of the person one is authenticating. It cannot be done by external methods, such as measurement of alpha waves or other mechanical means.

That is, if one were to authenticate the possibility of experiencing Jesus in the same way as St. Paul, St. Francis, or St. Anthony, one would have to have that experience for himself—by actually seeing Jesus. This requires preparation, one-pointed devotion, and the grace of Jesus himself. But it is possible, as Sri Ramakrishna showed.

The limitation exists as a severe one in that most people do not trouble to qualify themselves for that experience.[3] Without preparation, there is little possibility of verifying the authenticity of such an experience, so that one is led quickly and easily to draw the

---

[3] See Matthew 5:8 in this connection.

conclusion that verification cannot occur. Thus Sri Ramakrishna's approach condemns itself at the outset to be accessible only to those who seek the experience of God.

## THE QUESTION OF CONVERSION

A factor in Sri Ramakrishna's make-up from the start of his religious pilgrimage was that philosophical precepts and religious creeds played a minor role in his search for God. This factor can be seen as both a limitation and a strength simultaneously.

Its strength lies in providing the foundation for a peculiar universality which enabled him to identify spontaneously with many divergent sects and religious ideals holding often contradictory views of the universe, God, man, and salvation. Thus he was able to experience God as a separate personal reality as well as experiencing the unitive state. In later life he acknowledged both of these to be true—the personal God and the oneness of existence—based on his experiences. He never denied that which he had known through experience, so that he could deny neither the personal God nor nonduality.

But to many minds these appear a blatant contradiction. If the Creator exists, can the individual soul be one with the Creator? Can the worm be God? Or if there is only oneness and all differentiation in the cosmos is but an appearance, where is there room for "I and Thou, O Lord"?

When the mystic's vision seems to defy logic, many thoughtful persons whose lives are hinged on careful piety turn away: Christians, Muslims, Buddhists, and Hindus alike. Within Hinduism itself there are non-dualists, of course, but there are just as many who interpret the Vedas according to dualism or qualified non-dualism, and these represent as unshakeable an orthodoxy as Christian, Islamic, or Jewish traditions with respect to the personal God.

The adherent of such traditions would question, therefore, the legitimacy of Sri Ramakrishna's conversion. Was he not always basically a non-dualist, possibly even a pantheist, as he "saw God in all"? Had he not experienced the unitive state before practicing Christianity and Islam? How could he then with complete conviction worship Christ, or Allah, retaining at the same time the conviction that there is only oneness, not the duality essential for worship?

On the relative plane, this is a contradiction, and one which sharpens a critic's judgment on Sri Ramakrishna's conversion.

A Muslim or a Christian may also correctly challenge Sri Ramakrishna's conversion as being not only of limited duration, but all too short. Was he not a Christian for four days only, a Muslim for three days? Did he not take but one day to reach *nirvikalpa samadhi,* a Buddhist might object, when it requires many lives for an *arahant* or *bodhisattva* to attain *Nirvana?*

Sri Ramakrishna was indeed a fast mystic. But is time the unique consideration? The intensity of his purpose and of his longing for communion with God in each instance accelerated the transformations that occurred.

The period of conversion varies considerably among individuals. In some cases it can be an overnight matter, while in other instances conversion takes a complete lifetime. Sir Richard Burton, translator of the *Arabian Nights,* spent fifteen years in fully absorbing Islamic culture for his conversion.

A three-day conversion, such as the one Sri Ramakrishna underwent, with the fullness of mystic vision as the result, is one kind of conversion. It is an experience in itself, with its own quality. It does not strive for the assimilation of a total religious heritage, because that is not its goal. The pursuit from which this conversion results is authentic enough. That pursuit is God.

It should be stressed that Sri Ramakrishna's type of intense three-day conversion is not the only method, nor even the ultimate way. His effort was to establish that spiritual contact alone, in the world of the mystic's empyreum, which many mortals seldom if ever glimpse. His inner need was to create a spiritual link, a bridge over which he himself walked from one tradition to another. Thus he stepped across the cleavages and chasms which divided him from his fellow man in religious life, and which prevented him from tasting other forms of God. His was a warmth, an intimacy of relation with the divine being which permitted a corresponding closeness and love with human beings, and an undoing of alienation.

If in this, it is charged, he remained always a Hindu who never really "converted" to any religion outside the Hindu fold, thereby leaving the dilemma of religious plurality still a dilemma, he was undeniably a special type of Hindu, one who was graced by both Jesus and Allah with their vision.

## THE RESPONSE OF ORTHODOXY

This presentation has delineated Sri Ramakrishna's approach as being the method of a mystic engaged in religious experimentation. In order correctly to portray his activities from this perspective, it has given minimum weight to many of the claims of orthodoxy of classical Islam, Christianity, Buddhism, and even of Hinduism itself (that portion of Hinduism which does not deal directly with direct apprehension of God). No disrespect is intended, however, to the orthodox followers of any religious creed or tradition by this omission. The originality of Sri Ramakrishna's approach requires its presentation in a manner which does not dilute its power in religious history. Nevertheless, the objections from classical orthodoxy that can and have been raised in response to Sri Ramakrishna's approach are summarized as follows:

It is recognized that many Christians would seriously question the authenticity of Sri Ramakrishna's Christian faith,[4] while others may acknowledge his "power of faith"[5] through his vision of Jesus.[6] Thus, while his approach emphasized the universalism of Christianity with its positive offer of the gospel for all, it overlooked the necessity for the gospel's negative check-point, that is, the uniqueness in history of Christ's incarnation.

While classical Buddhists, Theravadins, or those of the many Mahayana schools, would not contest the legitimacy of Sri Ramakrishna's *nirvikalpa samadhi* experience as *Nirvana,* many would contend that his theism both previous and subsequent to this experience was of a non-Buddhistic nature. Theravadins especially might object to the qualified use of the word 'God' in Chapter IV, as God has come to denote the personal Creator which is not posited, though not rejected, in Buddha's recorded discourses.

Many orthodox Muslims, while admiring Sri Ramakrishna's veneration for Allah and Muhammad, might raise the objection that he never really entered into the community of Islamic brotherhood. He failed to share, some Muslims might say, the full spiritual value of *Hadith* and *Shari'a.* Although he participated in the mysticism which has infused orthodox Islam for the past thousand

---

[4] See John 14:6.

[5] Romans 1:16.

[6] See John 14:9.

years since its introduction into orthodoxy by al-Ghazali, Sri Ramakrishna could not temperamentally advocate the universal salvation message which was the prime motive power in Islam's rapid spread. Neither could he relish Islamic folklore based on early conquests, nor participate fully in the non-mystical everyday life style of devout Muslims, nor read the Qur'an in Arabic.

It is also recognized that Sri Ramakrishna's approach did not conform in many respects to the expectations of Hindu orthodoxy. Many Hindu sects have their own exclusivism, as for example the Vaishnavites and Shaivites, among others. Sri Ramakrishna also plainly disregarded the injunctions of caste restriction in a variety of ways. During his spiritual practices it has been noted that he cleaned the house of an untouchable, discarded the sacred thread of the Brahmin, accepted food from lower-caste individuals, and freely associated with non-Hindu devotees. As a spiritual teacher he accepted Christians, Muslims, Jews, and foreigners as disciples.

The mystic's role in religious history contains its own intrinsic freedom and privileges. He sees what we can not see. We cannot bind him, even with our golden chains. Orthodoxy is often based on the mystic's discoveries, but the very freedom that he enjoys presents us with a problem. His freedom becomes a limitation in our eyes when our present orthodoxy cannot contain it.

## CONTRIBUTION TO ROLE OF WOMANHOOD

While Sri Ramakrishna's apprehension of the Motherhood of God is not the main thrust of this presentation, there is a freshness and originality in his approach to God as Mother which cannot escape comment. In his worship of Kali as Divine Mother he accepted the redemptive aspects of suffering in a similar manner as Christians[7] accept the Cross in *imitatio Dei*. Simultaneously, he understood the beneficent, protective, and forgiving aspect of God in this form, "piercing through misery's veil," as do Christians in devotion to Christ, who forgave us all while we crucified him.

---

[7] This is not to obscure the difference between Roman Catholicism and Classical Protestantism on this point: i.e., the Protestant view of the total sufficiency of Christ's suffering; see John Murray, *Epistle to the Romans* (Grand Rapids, Mich.: William B. Eerdmans, 1959), p. 299 (commentary on Romans 8:17).

Sri Ramakrishna's attitude toward women, exemplified by his worshipful respect for his own wife, has significance today. This exalted place of womanhood as a reflection of Divine Motherhood can be viewed as one workable solution to the grave problems besetting contemporary cultures regarding the institutions of marriage and monasticism. The role of sexual gratification, compared with other innate human urges, especially the desire to know and love God, would thereby be modified and given a subordinate role instead of a primary one as prevails today. Woman's place in society would be ennobled, as her self-understanding and her appreciation by men would flow from the religious realization that the Godhead contains both the divine masculine and the divine feminine. Society potentially can therefore be enriched from Sri Ramakrishna's reawakening of Divine Mother as a viable spiritual ideal.

## SYNTHESIS

An attempt has been made in this study to introduce to the Christian scholarship community a life wholly dedicated to God-consciousness in a tradition other than our own.

Sri Ramakrishna's life and teachings form an approach to the dilemma of religious plurality, an approach based on the experience of God, which is worthy of closer examination by sincere adherents of all religious traditions. One may conclude, by the details of his life, that this approach is a significant one.

The fact that Sri Ramakrishna experienced God in different religions is a matter of historical record. The fact also that God or ultimate Reality has been realized directly and immediately by many persons of diverse religious backgrounds cannot be ignored. Whole civilizations have been based on the strength of their testimony.

Sri Ramakrishna taught that any person who wishes to verify the authenticity of the experience of God may do so by raising his or her level of consciousness to a higher plane through prayer and spiritual practices. Then he or she can affirm with Sri Ramakrishna, "I actually *see* God, more clearly than I see you," or declare with Swami Vivekananda, "I *have* touched the feet of God."

# *Afterwords*

## *Sri Ramakrishna's Approach to Religious Plurality*

by JANE I. SMITH

Two basic themes or questions seem to be woven into the fabric of Indian religious thought, recurring throughout the writings of scripture and in the personal experiences of its greatest saints. The first concerns the relationship of one's self to the Being of God (or the nature of Reality); i.e. is God personal and distinct from man, or nonpersonal and identical with man's essence? The second question, closely related to the first, deals with the means of man's salvation. Does he find release from the burdens of existence through his own efforts, or through devotion to a saving being (and if through devotion, can man begin by approaching God himself, or can salvation come only through God's initiatory act of grace)? Tell me, O Krishna, which way is better, pleads Arjuna in the *Bhagavad-Gita.* As Krishna advocates first one approach and then another, with the implication that all have legitimacy in the total picture of man's religious response, so Indian religion as a whole has seemed to revolve around the attempt to come to terms with the questions stated above. It is evident throughout this timely work on Ramakrishna that in his total experience can be found one of the clearest examples of the reconciliation of all of these themes, from pure *nirvikalpa samadhi* to the extremes of devotional response to God as Mother.

If Ramakrishna's involvement shows that no one approach within the Hindu context need necessarily be exclusive of others, it also indicates with great clarity the possibility of having a genuine experience of God within a variety of traditions. Hinduism has often been called a "sponge" religion, soaking up divergent tendencies and absorbing various religious traditions into its vast, amorphous body. Its flexible spirit has been well articulated by Sarvepalli Radhakrishnan: "Toleration is the homage which the finite mind pays to the inexhaustibility of the Infinite."

Actually, however, toleration is but one approach to the dilemma of plurality; or, more specifically, the dilemma of how to deal with an existing situation of religious plurality. The search for a unity of all religions is another. The message of Ramakrishna seems to be that the individual religious *experience* is not bound to either of these. Through his own understanding he could deny neither the personal God nor non-duality; in the same way he could not deny the possibility of having the experience of God in its deepest sense through a variety of religious traditions. There is a tendency in some contemporary Indian thinkers to assume that what is "valid" in all religions, the ultimate unifying factor, is that which is closest to Advaita Vedanta. In Ramakrishna one sees that not only was the experience of a personal God, in his case as Mother Kali, of utmost importance, but that the question of the unity of religions gave way to a clear and overriding concern for the unity of God and of the approaches to God, for an understanding of the oneness of Being, both personal and absolute, and the oneness of the ways in which God has chosen to reveal him/her-self. The emphasis on the unity of God over the unity of religions seems especially important to consider in this age of ecumenicity.

The question of Ramakrishna's involvement in other religious traditions is certainly not without its attendant problems and considerations. Can one in fact use the term "conversion" to refer to his experiences with Christianity and Islam? One way to understand it seems to be as conversion not to another tradition, even for a brief period of time, but rather conversion to a different set of circumstances in which to attain to the presence of God. Some of the statements made in this volume illustrate the difficulties inherent in translating religious experience across traditional lines, such as the indication that Ramakrishna was "immersed in the Muslim attitude" and that he practiced Islamic mysticism. To begin to do justice to the Islamic perspective one must come to terms with the fact that by his own admission Ramakrishna could never affirm the Muslim creed which says that there is no God but Allah. His failure to attest to this would mean that from the Muslim point of view he had never really participated in the Islamic experience, that he was not a Muslim and could not be one without witnessing to that most basic of credal formulations. In the Christian case one can raise questions concerning Ramakrishna's understanding, among other things, of the suffering of Christ.

Similar problems arise in the attempt to equate terminology from one tradition with that of another. Is the Muslim *dhawq,* for example, really equivalent to the Hindu *samadhi?* Finally, obviously, the real question is this: Is the content of one man's religious experience ever in any sense identical with that of another's? If this is carried to the extreme, all terminology as applying to anything more than similarity is ultimately invalid, and communal and traditional definitions become meaningless in the face of pure individual experience. Perhaps this is precisely what Ramakrishna was trying to illustrate with his "conversions" to Islam and Christianity. One of the virtues of this work is that while raising good questions and stimulating the intellect to ponder their answers, as a record of the experience of Ramakrishna it leaves no doubt that real understanding lies outside the realm of speculation. Reconciliation of differences, whether between religious traditions or in one's understanding of God's nature, is beyond the realm of logical definition.

The entire record of Ramakrishna, then, is one of savoring the essence of his communion with God in the form of the theistic Kali and others, both before and after experiencing the non-duality of the Absolute Unmanifest. The important thing for him was that he could do this in the context of Islam or Christianity as well as his native Hinduism, and the specifics of actually being a Muslim or a Christian seem to have interested him little. In Advaitic *sadhana* Ramakrishna had to give up Mother. (The reference to Meister Eckhart's renouncing God for God's sake is reminiscent of the famous Zen statement that the Buddha reveals himself when no more asserted, that for Buddha's sake Buddha is to be given up.) And yet Ramakrishna continued to the end of his life to worship Mother Kali in the most intensely devotional of ways, even to the point of being willing to give back, as it were, the full experience of *nirvikalpa samadhi.* "O Mother, do not plunge me in the knowledge of Brahman and take away my consciousness!" he pleaded at a moment of intense illness not long before his death. "I am but Thy child. I have fears and anxieties! I do want my Mother! A thousand salutations to Brahman-*jnana.* Give it to him who wants it, O Mother." Paradoxes of logic can certainly be the truths of mysticism, seldom more clearly illustrated than in Ramakrishna's ability to maintain devotion in the face of the knowledge of non-duality, to cut across traditional and orthodox lines in the fulfillment of his attempts to participate in the Being of God.

CENTER FOR THE STUDY OF WORLD RELIGIONS
HARVARD UNIVERSITY

# *Sri Ramakrishna, the Son of Woman*

## by MUHAMMAD DAUD RAHBAR

Jesus is remembered as the Son of Man. In the recorded history of religion, Sri Ramakrishna shines as a devotee of the Divine Mother. He should, therefore, be remembered as the Son of Woman.

Four miles north of Calcutta, in the Garden of Temples at Dakshineswar, he began his devotions to Mother Kali and went into rapture when yet only a child. His life from then on is an open book filled with a moving story of worship and adoration. His revelation of the benign Mother of the Universe is a consummation of the spiritual aspirations of matriarchical India.

Like a magnet, Sri Ramakrishna attracted ardent disciples. More than thirty of them maintained intimate association with him. Hundreds of them derived solace and blessing by beholding him and talking to him.

I have read some delightful portions of the one-thousand-page *Gospel of Sri Ramakrishna.* This marvellous volume has extraordinary revelations. Immediately one recognizes a cherishable friend in Sri Ramakrishna. His open, passionate, and transparent devotion humbles and chastens us. He is no common mortal. He is a man of phenomenal gifts. His presence is a haven. His conversations, recorded abundantly in the *Gospel of Sri Ramakrishna* by his disciple M., are charming, inspired. Their literary merit is due to the inspired goodness of Sri Ramakrishna. Somehow they reminded me of the eloquence of Joan of Arc and Abraham Lincoln, a type of eloquence that comes from the phenomenal strength of character.

If we call him a mystic, some of our readers will quickly conclude that here is a spiritual quietist and tranquilist. Whoever reads the *Gospel of Sri Ramakrishna* will think otherwise. You will discover there a man of unusual zest and vivacity. It is quite an example of spiritual or mystical activism. Sri Ramakrishna is a busy man whose incessant acts of devotion are powerfully charismatic and educative.

He is an exemplar with a life reminding us of some precious things modern society is forgetting. The list of his virtues is magnificent: wisdom (as distinct from journalistic encyclopaedism), inspired intellect, devotion, renunciation, concerned detachment, sublimation, genuine gregariousness, brilliant conversationalism, friendliness, gracious wit, variety and vastness of life experience.

The devotional discipline of Sri Ramakrishna is sustained by consistent and natural urges. In it there is childlike eagerness. His love of the lotus feet of the Lord or the lotus feet of the Divine Mother is more than filial piety; it is filial fondness, filial longing. He wants his forehead forever to rest on those feet. From his large repertoire of devotional poetry, he hums, recites, and sings readily some piece appropriate to the mood. He does not wear a wearied expression. He does not sing hymns with mechanical musical precision rehearsed with the aid of relentless staff-notation. His hymns are folk music sung with the flexibility of folk tunes. He can interrupt them for a sigh, a comment, or even a quip. When he sings, he is either in a trance, or has profuse mirth, or weeps and sobs. His yearning is boundless. Its outreach is cosmic in dimensions. He wants to unite with all. He craves to embrace all. Worship rouses him to want to prepare offerings. He performs all rituals with an eagerness that cannot be contained. Hence they turn out to be performances with masterly flares of improvisation. Fragrance, fresh flowers, colorful trinkets, incense, sprightly medley of song and narrative, the mingling tinkle of small and large bells, the rhythmic jingle of the dancers' anklets, the laughter of children, the moaning of ailing sufferers, the festive din of fairs, make him feel at home.

His devotion is not one of sullen moralism and forced austerity. It is a constant pursuit of refreshment of soul and renewal of zeal. It is definitely dynamic. Pilgrimage pleases him more than lavish touristic luxuries. He makes his life a feast of devotional *bhavas* (attitudes), savoring them with the relish of a lover of vintage. This is ensured by his austere control of appetites of flesh, his abstinence, and minimal vegetarian diet.

The temple familiar to Sri Ramakrishna was certainly unlike the churches of America today. It was a resort generally for the poor. Its interior was colorful, but simple and austere. It had nothing of the wooden front-facing fixed pews. Bare-footed devotees came there for unrehearsed supplication.

Although recognized as a mentor by many, Sri Ramakrishha remained a natural son, a disciple, and a learner all his life. His pursuits are exercises aiming at purging him of non-knowledge, that is, perverse consciousness. He did not assimilate factual information alone but worked out faith-building modes of thought. His knowledge is made of direct observation of nature and people. His loyal disposition has the gift of vivid reminiscence and lively reverie. His hunger of novel experience makes him a man of hope. He is enlightened in the sense that life makes good sense to him.

We turn now to another genuine quality of Sri Ramakrishna: renunciation. It is perhaps the virtue most vigorously rejected by the politicized civilization of the emerging world. It is condemned by political activists as if it were an adoption of the way of unconcern. The political activists have to go through self-searching to realize that much of the fever and scramble of politics is a symptom of sick spirit. The implementation of the great movement of democratic thought in the world is not simply a matter of equal opportunity to cultivate ambition. Democratic freedom must learn to respect the freedom to renounce. Perhaps it is true to say that in America today, austere forms of creative renunciation are virtually proclaimed illegal. A mendicant spiritual would be looked upon as a vagrant and a parasite. This is tragic. The excessively politicized intelligentsia in the modern world will hastily detect in Sri Ramakrishna an "escapist quietism." An observation on those lines will be rejected by anyone who reads a substantial part of the *Gospel of Sri Ramakrishna*. In him we find a bustling renunciation full of excitement, but not escapism or quietism. His life is not one of escape for the soul, rather it is a life busy with fortification of the spirit. His ascetic exercises lead to his faith-building charisma. His experiments with psychology of religion are of both spiritual and scientific value for us. He is not running away from responsibilities in the world, he is handling them with eminent creativity. He exercises the privilege of inspired selection of occupation. He investigates the secrets of spirit and soul by turning to experienced men and women. He meditates and is an alert onlooker. He is not bookish but is assiduous in enquiries as a student of folk religion through listening to recital of sacred mythology, direct observation, rigorous introspection, conversation and, most of all, through devotion.

He does all that and does not ask anybody for a salary or a stipend as a reward. Nobody has a reasonable right to object to this arrangement.

Any society that bans renunciation and detachment of this kind is heading for impaired mental health and low level of faith. For it deprives itself of a needed source of holy contagion and vibrations of serenity. Every society needs a mixture of infection of animation and equanimity. Every society needs contagion of selflessness and meditative inspiration.

Peace is not simply cessation or absence of wars. Peace is also equanimity. While so many active statesmen, historians, and journalists make their objective and detached observations on the day-to-day events, detached, sage men of renunciation like Sri Ramakrishna enjoy and offer another kind of detachment and insight. They are aware of a more ultimate perspective that provides cognizance of human mortality, the infinity of time and space as the full context of all historical events. They view everyday life as a mysterious flux with its origin and end related to eternity, the eternal, the ultimate Intelligence and Disposition sustaining existence. The men of the world are often oblivious of these ultimate relations. They are forgetful of their own mortality and continue headlong in pursuit of material goals as if they are going to live on earth forever. The man of renunciation is available to men of the world, with his detachment, his infection of equanimity, and his peaceful enlightenment, to comfort and restore some sanity in a fast and frantic society. He is not an escapist. He is busy sharing salvation with fellow-beings. He is a deliverer by vocation.

Akin to Sri Ramakrishna's renunciation is his sublimation. Like renunciation, this related attitude has become subject to strong criticism. Sexual revolution has been intertwined with the transition to democracy. It has helped expose the realities of undemocratic double standards and diverted our attention fruitfully to many modes of deviousness and dishonesty of people in the matters of status, power, and wealth. The movement of sexual boom is, however, still in the phase of a revolt rather than a stable state. Therefore the crusaders of sexual freedom have forgotten that voluntary sexual continence also has a place in a democratically free society. Those who want to choose the way of sexual abstinence should be given the privilege to enjoy their freedom and be properly respected for it.

Most of the non-Hindu readers of this book will find Sri Ramakrishna's style of married life unfamiliar. This phenomenon is no less understandable than the life of Christian monks and nuns. The only difference is that continence in the Christian case is outside of wedlock while in this case it is within marriage. The latter arrangement of devotional abstinence and sublimation has its own validity if the participants in it are fully free and subject to no coercion. The covenant that existed between Sri Ramakrishna and his wife was a phenomenon of religious culture to which both of them belonged.

Sri Ramakrishna in his childhood identified femininity with divinity. As a devotee he saw only worshipability in womanhood. Through a sexually abstinent marriage he augmented his closeness to the Divine Mother. Within the tradition of Hindu mysticism, the arrangement looks quite natural.

Sublimation is an unpopular word in contemporary Western society. The newly emerging communes of various kinds in the West, with their extemporized untraditional mysticism, depart from traditional mysticism in one important respect: the new communes, by and large, admit both sexes in the same dwellings, with sexual communism as a common enough arrangement. In this respect, modern mysticism is profoundly different from the mysticism of pre-modern periods. Traditional mysticism regarded sublimation as an integral part of ascetic discipline.

Feminist reformers will profit from a serious look at the culture out of which the Son of Woman came. Worship of the Divine Mother is natural in the matriarchical setting of India, with passivity, pacifism, vegetarianism, Vedantic acceptance of the parity of male and female principles, effeminacy of the male, the siesta-inducing climate, all providing a homogeneity of an effeminate mellow civilization. Pacifism, a concomitant of effeminacy of a society, was reinforced in India by climate and the frequency of formidable military invasions from abroad. The matriarchical foundations of society were consolidated. Ramachandra became unthinkable without his Sita, Krishna without his doting mother and his milkmaid lover Radha, Brahma without his Saraswati, Vishnu without his Lakshmi and Shiva without his Parvati. Such a sustained position of womanhood in the tradition of many centuries facilitated the election of Indira Gandhi as the Prime Minister. The same feature facilitated Sri Ramakrishna's mature revelation of the Divine Mother.

The soldierly masculine civilization of the West will have to go through long historical preparation to provide a natural place for the worship of Divine Mother among believers. Nevertheless the assertion of the feminine element has begun. The Western male is not yet effeminate, although perhaps the Western female has become somewhat masculine.

Now we turn to the subject of Sri Ramakrishna's search for harmony with people of other religious traditions. Evidently he did not preach with any pretentious slogan of world peace. It is evident, though, that he strove to be at peace with himself and his neighbors. As a devotee with the complex religious heritage of Hinduism, he lived in an environment of much religious diversity. He was aware of the organized otherness of Buddhist, Muslim, and Christian communities. There is interesting evidence in his life of an effort to achieve harmony with the people and thought of those communities. He took interest in these experiences without assuming altruistic airs. He turned to experiment out of a pressing curiosity and not out of a desire for pietistic exercise, and least for ostentation. He went about his experiments innocently like a child. They have his typical mark of unsophistication. By all evidence they are sincere. It is more considerate to view them not in terms of their influence on intercommunal relations but in terms of how they helped him find greater peace of mind. There is so much unkind criticism from us of how so-and-so failed to be a greater influence on society. Such criticism bespeaks our frustration rather than doing justice to the well-wishing servants of society we criticize. If extraordinary people are instruments of Providence at all, then it is to be granted that Providence itself determines the extent of their influence.

The Emperor Akbar experienced an intimate touch with Hindu revelation by marrying a charming and gifted Hindu princess who fascinated him. He exercised an exception to Muslim law by allowing her to stay Hindu and not converting her to Islam as his wife. In this case his partaking of Hindu experience was aided and conditioned by intermarriage and imperial expediency. His great-grandson, Dara Shikoh, went about appreciating Hindu thought and feelings by pantheistic preoccupation. Al-Beruni enjoyed tasting the flavour of Hindu life by scholarly enquiry among Hindu priests and scholars, without ever stating that he felt the urge to dilute or replace his Islam with Hinduism. Guru Nanak experienced a blend of Islamic and Hindu revelations, refreshed and modified by his own inspiration, that made him see the puzzle of religion's role in power politics and some anomalies of formal ritual, temple, mosque, priesthood, etc. He chose to stay closer to folk-life and appreciate the faith of average people. Sir Richard Burton, Professor Edward G. Browne, Theodore Nöldeke, Louis Massignon, E. W. Lane and their peers experienced intimacy with Islam and the Muslims through scholarship and social contact, without professing any degree of conversion to Islam (though the experience must mean some sort of Muslimising). Richard Burton, in fact, wrote a kind of credo in his amazing *Kasidah* reflecting the spirit of heterodox Arabic and Persian poets.

Many businessmen, diplomats, tourists, artists, and even laborers working with, near, or for people of another religious community inevitably partake of the religious experience of members of that community. Even beholding the faces of men and women and children of another religious community is participation in their religious experience. Even looking at photographs and listening to recorded music provides some of the religious experience of the people.

Thus there are so many ways in which concoction and grafting of religious experience continues all over the world all the time. There is no such thing as pure Islam, pure Hinduism, pure Buddhism, or pure Christianity of any person. Coexistence of communities is a concomitant of mixtures of religious experience. The Jews of Brookline, Massachusetts, warm their eyes on very Muslim motifs on the carpets in their drawing rooms.

I pay tribute to Sri Ramakrishna's device to attain intimacy with Buddhist, Muslim, and Christian life. He demonstrated his own kind of desires and overtures, as against other possible ways of going about the enrichment and broadening of experience. He went about it in a certain mystical way. It is valid, interesting, and meaningful because its motivation was pure.

His origin in a predominantly matriarchical culture equipped Sri Ramakrishna with a natural willingness to find his first mentor in a woman (Bhairavi Brahmani). His delight and trust in the merry nature of the Mother of the Universe helped him identify the divine in his own wife and set a pattern for his continent married life. Jesus experienced the Lord as Father. Muhammad experienced the Lord as the male Monarch. This had profound influence respectively on the Christian and Muslim psychology of religion.

The basic disposition of Jesus was an optimistic sadness. Gautama Buddha observed Vedantic reticence on the Ultimate Mystery. Muhammad lived a life presenting violent challenges to his peace-loving statesmanship. Sri Ramakrishna sought passionate closeness to all three of these.

The mentors he chose to aid him in his experiences of the Buddha, Jesus, and Muhammad had their own equipment. Their experience mediated Sri Ramakrishna's experience. These contacts represented mystical shortcuts. However, alternative modes of devotional quest exist that could have been employed to yield different and yet meaningful experience. For example, one way of quest is to seek experience of the faith directly from a contemporary Buddhist, a contemporary Muslim, and a contemporary Christian, with all the weaknesses and strengths of each.

Concentration aiming at the vision of Muhammad has much merit. Yet a Muslim's heart will be far more warmed if a saint of Hindu background in Bengal recites a Muslim religious poem from the Bengali folklore. Sri Ramakrishna did his best to demonstrate his interest in, for example, the Muslims. But the fact remains that few Muslims know him or remember him. To say that these Muslims are ungrateful to him or deplorably ignorant of him is as unkind as finding fault with Sri Ramakrishna's motivation. Let us put it this way: overtures of cultural identity are far more winning than demonstrations of spiritual earnestness. Paying homage to Muhammad is not enough. The Muslims would have responded with much warmth had Sri Ramakrishna memorized a few hundred verses from the *Masnavi* of Rumi and the *Divan* of Hafiz. They would have welcomed him with shrieks of gladness if he had taken interest in styles of Muslim calligraphy, architecture, love of gardens, and Sufi music. A Muslim individual is not satisfied with simply someone's homage to Muhammad. Each of us wants his or her personality to be enjoyed with all its qualities and heritage. Muslims would have responded to Sri Ramakrishna if he had invited many Muslims to little feasts of curried lamb cooked with his own hands.

Praise of Allah, Muhammad, and the Qur'an by a Hindu is not enough to win the Muslims. It takes much more. It takes perseverance in direct personal relations through sharing of culture and each other's assets.

Christians and Muslims have to accept one major change of historical circumstance emerging in the wake of democracy: authoritarian religion will no longer appeal to people nor work any more. Monotheism, a principal weapon of empire-builders, itself could not have thrived without the authoritarian alliance of emperors. With the subsiding of monarchy as an institution in the statecraft of nations, monotheism is left without zealous champions. Traditional critique of "the polytheism of the Hindus" and "the non-theism of the Buddhists" by the Jews, the Christians, and the Muslims, therefore, has lost its power of bite. Hindu apologetics, hence, have assumed a new kind of cogency in the new age. Christians and Muslims, for many centuries, dismissed Hindu religious ideas as primitive and underprivileged. During the centuries of subjugation, Hindu religious thought was looked down upon by the Muslims and the Christians. With the political liberation of the Hindus from the Muslims and then the Christians, the scene has changed and the profundity of Hindu religious experience and the keenness of Hindu religious articulation have gained dignity. In fact much in Hindu attitude and formulations has gained relevance to the religions of all mankind. Here are some of the points of relevance: conscious and deliberate syncretism; religious existentialism; absence of doctrinal abrogation; fusion of opposites; accommodation to polytheism and monotheism in the same tradition; intellectual detachment; religious introspection; recognition of the importance of the psychological needs of man along with that of his moral needs; vegetarianism; celebration of the feminine attributes of divinity; the postulate of inseparability of good and evil on earth; cyclical view of time; recognition of sport as a fundamental element in divine motivation.

These ideas and attitudes deserve contemplation today. Muslims and Christians generally do not take them seriously. But Muslims and Christians are going to sound more and more outdated if they continue to preserve the jargon of authoritarian monarchical monotheism, with a dogmatic authoritarian tone. All religious communities now have to pay attention to the call to democratize the spirit of religion. Hymns that speak of God as the king have no appeal now that kings are no longer popular. The age of monarchy is gone. God will now be adored for his attributes as Friend.

There is a great deal of power politics connected with religion. The scientists and secularists have no doubt contributed much to the removal of dishonesty in religious leadership. But now some of the presumption which used to be the trait of some priests is manifest among many secularist men of science. The autonomy of science and intellect has been overdone. The time has arrived when forces of spirit have to be released. Insight and wisdom are lacking in the intellectual world of today. The faces of secularist scientists seldom have a radiance and magnanimity.

Was not the unsophisticated Sri Ramakrishna a gifted scientist in his own right? In his blissful life we find a happy union of religion and science.

My dear friend, Dr. Claude Alan Stark, is a disciple of Swami Akhilananda, who in turn was a disciple of a disciple of Sri Ramakrishna. I am grateful to Dr. Stark for bringing into my life an enthusiasm for the shining life of Sri Ramakrishna. I confess that contact with the pure life of this saint brought waves of repentance to me and gave me renewed strength. May this book of tribute through scholarship be blessed. By writing these lines I have offered a lit candle in memory of a very superior man.

Dr. Stark has produced an authentic piece of scholarship. Yet he has kept scholasticism from judgmental airs. He has managed to write both as a scholar and a disciple. This aspect of his success deserves special congratulations.

SCHOOL OF THEOLOGY
BOSTON UNIVERSITY

# *Sri Ramakrishna from a Christian Perspective*
## by PER HASSING

It should be made clear that it is important that Western students of religion engage in the study of the many men and movements of the East in order to understand at least to some extent the great variety and devotion found in the Eastern religions. It is also important to stress that the raising of critical questions from a Christian perspective goes hand in hand with respect for Sri Ramakrishna's life, devotion, and search for religious truth. Religious dialogue can only be profitable if a participant speaks from the center of his or her being to that of the other. With this understanding a few observations and questions will be recorded.

In the foregoing pages the claim is made that Ramakrishna experienced God as a Hindu, a Muslim, and a Christian, that he was truly a Muslim and a Christian, and that in each stage his personality went through a complete transformation. The question which at once comes to mind is if he in fact went through a Christian experience?

In the foregoing pages there is an underlying assumption that religion can be defined in individualistic, private, subjective terms. To define religion, historically speaking, has proved to be a very hazardous enterprise, but from a Christian point of view religion can never be adequately understood in only individualistic, personal terms. At the beginning of the Christian life there is baptism into a community, the church; there is the sacramental life centering in the eucharistic, communion meal; there is public instruction and the testing of one's experience against the teaching and experience of the community itself; in addition, there is the command to love one's neighbor which leads to a strong sense of social justice aimed at a transformation of the whole society. For the Christian the experience of the life "hidden with Christ in God" is no doubt intensely personal, but is never entirely subjectivistic, because in Jesus Christ God is personal, the Other, and the primary element is not the personal feeling or the intensity of the personal devotion, but what God objectively has done in Christ Jesus. Central for the Christian is the Christ event, the total life, death, and resurrection of Jesus Christ. The object of the devotion is so important that Christian mystics refrain from the complete identification or union of the self with God; there is always the 'I' and the 'Thou.'

In Christian history there are numerous recordings of conversion, but some of the more famous are St. Paul's in the first, Martin Luther's in the sixteenth, and John Wesley's in the eighteenth century. Common to all three was a strong sense of personal sin. Paul wrestled with this problem and in his Letter to the Romans interpreted salvation in Christ Jesus as freedom from sin and death (8:2). Central to Martin Luther was the question: how could he, a sinner, find a merciful God? He found release and a new life in the freely-given grace of God by faith alone, faith in what God had done for him in Christ Jesus. When John Wesley had his memorable experience in Aldersgate Street, London, he described it as a heartwarming experience based on the insight that in Jesus Christ his personal sin and failure had been forgiven. In all three cases these experiences became turning-points not only in their own personal lives, but in the historical life of the ongoing Christian community. They were life-transforming, determinative experiences, the effects of which lasted as long as they lived.

Compared to these central elements of classical, personal Christian experience and the common life of the community of Christians, one is bound to ask to what extent Ramakrishna's experiences, covering a period of three days, can in any real sense be called a Christian experience of God?

It has been suggested that as Ramakrishna moved from Hinduism to Islam and Christianity he in each case underwent a complete transformation of his personality. The history of Christian missions shows that the idea of *tabula rasa,* i.e. that converts from other religions to Christianity erased all their pre-Christian experiences from their personality, soon proved to be false. It was found that the converts indeed made a decisive break with the past and entered into a new life, moved in a new direction, but they also brought with them into their new existence a deep and broad legacy from the past, so that the old and the new in various degrees existed and grew together in the same persons. In light of this long history, and in the light of modern psychological insight, is it really possible to claim that Ramakrishna in a very short period underwent three complete personality changes?

Finally, Ramakrishna was a Hindu, brought up in a completely Hindu environment, a devotee of various Hindu deities and imbued with the basic Hindu philosophy. Hindu philosophy is monistic; distinctions are blurred, interpreted as not real, but as appearances, even illusions. One of the goals of Hindu thinking is to realize that all is one, that fundamentally there is unity in all existence, not duality. In contrast, Christian as well as Muslim thinking is basically dualistic. The question then arises as to what happened in Ramakrishna's life when he moved from one religion to another? Did he shed his monistic philosophy in order to enter fully into the Muslim and Christian dualistic philosophical outlook? If not, was it not a simple matter for him to regard the differences between the Christian and Muslim outlook, on the one hand, and the Hindu view, on the other, as well as the differences between Christian and Muslim thinking, as only varieties of the one monistic view, and therefore really as non-existent differences? In other words, did Ramakrishna really become a Muslim and a Christian, or did he, through it all, remain a Hindu?

Other questions could also be raised, but they may never be conclusively answered, because Ramakrishna himself is no longer among us, and there is little possibility that new evidence will be found in the ample historical material available. But honesty in scholarship demands that the hard questions in religious history be taken with the utmost seriousness.

SCHOOL OF THEOLOGY
BOSTON UNIVERSITY

# *The Interfaith Dimension*
## by AMIYA CHAKRAVARTY

If ecumenism, why not interfaith? The inclusiveness of human conscience cannot leave out any significant expression of man's divinity. This was the spiritual logic of saint Ramakrishna: Dr. Stark raises it in the context of modern movements in Christianity and in other world religions. Mystics and certain types of transcendentalists have often, both in West and East, offered a similar challenge. But today an insistent awareness of unities, in spite of uniqueness, calls for a new perspective of faith. Closer proximity and knowledge of man's basic history, in addition to the sharing of integral experience, have made religion more relational than divisive. This applies to the dynamism of spiritual culture, not to orthodox creeds which are less concerned with revival than with mere revivalism.

With erudition and a remarkable understanding of the Indian civilization as a whole—I refer to the mainstream, not to the cults and coteries—the author has given us the witness of the Ramakrishna-Vivekananda tradition which itself was rooted in India's perennial philosophy. Truth is One; men call it by different names: this was the Vedic view and it was carried on through the Upanishads, the Gita, and the medieval Indian sages to the nineteenth century saint Ramakrishna. Nearly illiterate but supremely knowledgeable, he not only absorbed the great Indian inheritance but accepted the revelations of other religions, mainly Christianity and Islam. This book unfolds the exciting story of a Hindu Brahmin who discarded sectarianism, used imagism in a highly symbolical and personal way, who dramatically moved from dualistic worship to monism and then to a balance of both, and finally and effortlessly emerged as a world teacher. The entire picture is here. Details of his periodic identification with other religions even in matters of dress and deportment may puzzle some readers, the apparent mixture of visionary experience with ecstatic imagination (as in the case of several Western saints and Sufi mystics) may leave us wondering, but the divine truth of his realization remains. Without seeking to "explain," Dr. Stark has sought to interpret; his own Christian tradition, and the use of "reason" in its fullest modern sense, have led him to a new encounter. We are grateful to a devoted and careful scholar for avoiding the extremes of scepticism and credulity; dogmatism in either direction would obscure truth. The deepest insights of religion, also some of the external and perplexing factors, demand a new approach. More satisfying insights may come through an "interfaith ecumenicity."

From here we can go to "miracles"—and as every student of religion knows, there are "miracles" enough, inexplicable, baffling, often unacceptable, though filled with elements of higher probability. Aspects of reality unknown to us shine through the words and actions of sages and saints. They illumine the miracle of that which is, the "supernatural" being the further revelation of the "natural." Dr. Stark has given us extraordinary instances from saint Ramakrishna's life, as stated by the master or by his devotees, without direct evaluation. To many of us, more important than any incident is the miracle of Ramakrishna himself, the miracle that he could be what he was and give us—for all time—his life's truth.

The above position is taken by many Biblical scholars who cannot be charged either with evasion or literal acceptance: demythologization of the mythical and legendary element in Christianity (myths and legends too have their meaning) is not a proof of unfaith. Indeed, the courage of faith may lie in researching beyond the literal and in rejecting the literal meaning.

Certain references to sex, love, asceticism, and theories of sublimation are open to controversy. Here, too, the author has recorded statements but refrained from hurried conclusions. "What is purity?"—this question, evidently, can be asked only by those who have understood the meaning of love. Saints have not given us a unified answer. Not all have separated spiritual life from marriage; highly moral and lofty lives, whether canonized or not, have defined purity in the simplest and fullest human sense. The sages of Vedic India and of other great civilizations bear a socially valid witness to the human divine: dogmatic assertions about methods and states of purity may sometimes be a sin against the creator rather than sinlessness. Again, no single answer suffices. We have to accept the spirit of divine love which was implicit in Sri Ramakrishna's relationship with others: over-simplification or specification could misrepresent his view of life.

A further point: Dr. Stark has done well to correct the notion that Indian spiritual traditions have stressed the experiential and inspirational factors but suppressed the actional motive. The Ramakrishna-Vivekananda movement has proved again that the finest social service, concerned action and commitment spring from pure goodness, from the realization of beatitude and the divinity of life. If service does not proceed from a sense of devotion, service itself can be a tyranny; again, devotion without any sense of service is not seen in supremely dedicated men of faith. Here too, we enter interstices of truth without which the full truth cannot be recovered; it must be recognized that a saintly person while not seeming to do anything utilitarian for society is actually fulfilling the highest social responsibility by igniting a moral conscience. Through precept and example he is changing individuals and therefore society. Every act of truth is also an act of service. Sri Ramakrishna transformed the hearts of men; he gave them an exalted view of life, the fruits of which can be seen in the work done by the Ramakrishna Mission and by those who helped the movement. The tireless work done by the devotees in hospitals, labor centers, in stricken rural areas, and city slums is well-known; they have been pioneers in spreading education and an international outlook in India and served in other countries. Not only in disaster situations but in daily crises involving drug addiction, broken homes, racism, and economic injustice they have followed the ancient Indian pattern in making compassionate and effective *Karma* (work) a part of the highest *dharma* (religious truth). Thus we trace a continuous history from the Upanishads to Sri Ramakrishna, from Buddha to Gandhi and Tagore. This is not to deny the aberrations and social failures but to confirm the structural norms of Indian religion which have gained from modern science and from the inspired teachings of great Western religious leaders. Dr. Stark's book deals mainly with saint Ramakrishna and his eminent followers, but it is also a critical and affectionate commentary on India, which, along with Africa, has won his American—and, shall I add?—his Bostonian allegiance.

STATE UNIVERSITY COLLEGE
NEW PALTZ, NEW YORK

# Minds of One Accord
## by LAL MANI JOSHI

The wide popularity in modern India of the belief in the unity of religions may be due to the influence of the teaching of Ramakrishna through the efforts of Vivekananda and Gandhi. Swami Vivekananda, Mahatma Gandhi, Dr. Bhagawan Das and Acharya Vinoba Bhave, the leading teachers of the Hindu tradition in its modern form, have devoted their lives to the task of building harmony among the votaries of different religious faiths.

While a large number of moral principles are common to all major religions of the world, there are also fundamental and radical doctrinal differences among them. The Hindus, with whom the notion of the equality of all religions is so popular, do not seem to realize the formidable difficulties rooted in doctrinal differences and diametrically opposed theological presuppositions of different religious traditions.

Dr. Claude Alan Stark has rightly invited our attention to some of the limitations of Sri Ramakrishna's approach to the problem of the plurality of religions. On the other hand, historians of religion and theology can hardly ignore the value of Dr. Stark's pioneer contribution to the preparation for the cooperation of religions[1] based on an exposition of Sri Ramakrishna's spiritual experiments.

The profound declarations of religious truth are based on religious authority. The source of this authority is the spiritual experience of enlightened sages or seers *(rsis)* of ultimate Reality. Thus Sakyamuni's experience of enlightenment is the source of religious authority for his followers. The word of the Buddha is authentic because the Buddha has known and seen the reality as reality and falsity as falsity. Ramakrishna was a seer *(rsi)* of the Divine. His experiences are the foundations of the philosophy of religion expounded by Swami Vivekananda. What is remarkable and, per-

---

[1] *Cf. Friedrich Heiler, "The History of Religions as a Preparation for the Cooperation of Religions" in The History of Religions: Essays in Methodology,* ed. by Mircea Eliade and Joseph M. Kitagawa, The University of Chicago Press, 1959, pp. 132-160; *World Religions and World Peace,* ed. by Homer A. Jack, Boston, Beacon Press, 1968.

haps, unique, is that Ramakrishna is reported to have seen the same ultimate Reality through different windows. Thus he is said to have made experiments not only with Bhagavata and Sakta methods but also with Christian and Islamic paths to salvation. He was a mystic of the first order in the sense of being a direct witness of the Divine. A mystic is a holy person who makes direct assault on the citadel of Truth and in a flash of undifferentiated ecstasy *(nirvikalpa samadhi)* becomes one with the Absolute.

The neo-Brahmanical or Hindu doctrine of the validity of different religious paths is based not only on the authority of the experiments and experiences of Ramakrishna but also on Brahmanical scriptures. Ramakrishna resolved the contradictory doctrines and unified the diverse paths taught by different religious systems. For him religious plurality disappeared and religious exclusivism became a meaningless superstition of the fanatics. How can we challenge Ramakrishna's opinion that the Vedantic, Vaisnava, Saiva, Sakta, Christian and Islamic religious disciplines when rightly practised lead to one and the same supreme goal? His opinion is based on his practical experiences. He does not seek to support his opinion by any scriptural authority, logical argument, or any other indirect means of proof. Those of us who are not convinced of his views will have to make experiments with Truth in our own spiritual laboratory. Direct experience is the supreme authority. Questions of religious truth are to be decided and defined in an operational or practical manner. As Romain Rolland has remarked, "The first qualification for knowing, judging, and if desirable condemning a religion or religions, is to have made experiments for oneself in the fact of religious consciousness."[2] The approach of Ramakrishna is thus a great challenge to all those who are wedded to a narrow and exclusive theology of religious perfection.

The relevance of Ramakrishna studies for inter-religious understanding and intercultural hermeneutics can hardly be gainsaid. The days of religious isolation are gone. The encounter of religions has taken a friendly and constructive turn and the dialogue of religions is making a steady progress. The Ramakrishna approach to

[2] Romain Rolland, *The Life of Ramakrishna,* Advaita Ashrama, Mayavati, vol. I. 1931, p. 5.

the religious pluralism of mankind may play an important part in bringing about peace in the world and cooperation among religions.

It is significant to note that Ramakrishna was not an intellectual or scholar like Ram Mohun Roy or Dayananda Saraswati, founders of the Brahmo Samaj and the Arya Samaj respectively. But his personality had a deeper appeal and his simple message influenced vast multitudes of educated as well as illiterate village folks of India. His simple and unassuming portraits have a natural appeal to all those who are aware of Indian concepts of piety. He is perhaps the greatest figure in the religious history of modern India. Nor was Ramakrishna a philosopher. Philosophy is not a road to spiritual perfection. He was a devotee *(bhakta),* a worshipper of the Divinity. We may call him a Sakta, a worshipper of Sakti or the Goddess Mother, although he was above sectarian labels and his teachings present a wonderful synthesis of the entire religious heritage of India. The fact that he was equally at home with *vedanta* and *bhakti, yoga* and *tantra,* may be taken as a measure of his greatness as a spiritual giant. No other person is known to have adopted so many means of spiritual perfection *(sadhanas)* as Ramakrishna did. His success *(siddhi)* in all these *sadhanas* made him a *siddha* of the first order.

It has been remarked that Ramakrishna "was the embodiment of all the past religious thought of India." The catholic attitude towards different sects and the synthetic approach towards the plurality of deities were characteristic of Ramakrishna's religious experience. His religious genius quickly discovered and he emphasized the underlying unity behind the apparent multiplicity of gods worshipped by the Indians. But this unity had perhaps been foreseen by the Vedic seers. As early as the later Vedic age we find the development of the monotheistic idea. The Vedic scriptures firmly declared that the one God can be worshipped in many forms, and that he who is formless is also capable of assuming numerous forms. The seers saw the truth that the one becomes many and is known under a variety of forms and names. Such a conclusion has been derived from the following verse of the *Rgveda:* "They call him Indra, Mitra, Varuna, Agni, and he is heavenly nobly-winged Garutman. To what is one, sages give many a title; they call it Agni, Yama,

Matarisvan."[3] Those who advocate the gospel of the unity of religions may find their justification in this scriptural authority, and may proceed further to say that the one Reality is known as Brahman, Nirvana, Siva, Visnu, Rama, Krsna, Kali or Sakti. It is interesting to note that this verse occurs in a hymn to Visvedevas, the "All Gods."

Divine Reality is neither male nor female; or, one can say that it is both. Ramakrishna often referred to the divine as Goddess Mother even as the Judeo-Christian scriptures refer to the divinity as God the Father. In fact, ultimate Reality is beyond the formulation of patriarchal and matriarchal theologies. It will be recalled that the early Indo-Aryans had a patriarchal society and the Vedic pantheon was dominated by male deities. The autochthonous religious ideas of non-Aryan origin seem to have entered the Vedic Aryan theology towards the close of the Vedic epoch. Consequently, the earlier *upanisads* display a manifest influence not only of the spiritual and moral ideas of non-Vedic ascetic sages called *munis* and *sramanas*, but also of the conception of deities of non-Aryan races of India who had a matriarchal set-up. It is now generally maintained by the historians of Indian culture that the worship of Rudra-Siva, and especially of Mother Goddess, is of non-Vedic or non-Aryan origin. In other words, the ultimate origins of Saivism, Saktism, *yoga* and *tantra* can be traced to pre-Aryan and non-Vedic streams of culture. In their historical manifestations, however, these systems had been enriched and transformed by Brahmanical rituals and puranic theologies.

It is significant that the upanisadic term for ultimate Reality, *Brahman,* is neuter. Reality is beyond all genders. Sri Ramakrishna worshipped Mother Kali as one personification of the unconditioned Absolute. The idea of a chosen deity *(ista-devata)* or the freedom of worshipping the Divine under any one name and form is a characteristic feature of the Brahmanical Hinduism. In historic times Indians evolved the notion of a composite deity, so to speak, of *ardhanarisvara,* 'half female-half male.' In Tantrika theology Siva (male) and Sakti (female) are not two polarities; they are only

---

[3] *Rgveda* I. 164. 46, translated by Ralph T. H. Griffith, Varanasi, Chaukhamba Sanskrit Series (reprint), 1963.

two apparent aspects of one non-dual Truth *(tattva)*. He who worships Siva worships Sakti, and *vice versa,* he who worships Sakti worships Siva. This concept of the Two-in-One *(yuganaddha)* is essentially monistic *(advaita)*. This concept also resolves the dichotomy of male and female. In a late Vedic scripture we read the following with respect to Brahman: "Thou art woman, thou art man, thou boy, or also girl; thou when aged, totterest with a staff; thou when born, becomest facing all ways."[4]

The idea of the unity of Siva and Sakti, Isvara and Maya, Avalokitesvara and Tara, Purusa and Prakrti, Vajra and Padma, Upaya and Prajña became the central theme of Tantrika philosophy and esoteric *yoga.* The unified principle is known as *yuganaddha, prajñopaya, sahaja,* and *samarasa.* In Tibetan this principle is called *yabyum.* The ultimate aim of religious culture is to attain this state of union *(yoga)*.

In medieval Indian poetry of Vaisnavism, Sufism, Kabirpanth and Sikhism, we often come across the erotic imagery in which the Lord is symbolically conceived as husband and the devotee as wife. Intense love *(prema)* of and devotion *(bhakti)* to the Lord are the pathway to union *(yoga)*. The joy of union of the two was conceived as Great Delight *(mahasukha)*. The Buddhist *siddhas* were the first to use the word *mahasukha* for Nirvana. Since this Great Delight is inherent in every being, it is called the Innate *(sahaja),* another word for Nirvana.

This great ultimate and unifying principle is also called Mahamudra in Buddhist *tantras.* Sarahapada (A. D. 800), the first of the eighty-four Buddhist *siddhas* or 'Adepts' in Tantrika Buddhism, had given the following description of the indescribable Mahamudra:

Having no shape or colour, being all-encompassing,
Unchanging, and stretching across the whole of time.
Like celestial space without end or beginning,
With no real meaning as when a rope is seen to be a snake,
Being the indivisibility of Dharmakaya, Sambhogakaya and Nirmanakay?
Its actuality transcends the regions of the intellect.

---

[4] *Atharvaveda,* X.8. 27, translated by W.D. Whitney, vol. 2, Delhi, Motilal Banarsidass (reprint), 1963, p. 599.

Mahamudra which is instantaneous experience of Buddhahood
Manifests itself in Sambhogakaya and Nirmanakaya for the benefit
of sentient beings.[5]

*Tantra* and *hathayoga* seem to have flourished in medieval India
as much as Vedic ritualism and devotional Vaisnavism. Tantrika
*yoga* was a modified form of classical *yoga* associated with Patañ-
jali's text. The *Guhyasamajatantra* gives only the outlines of esoteric Buddhist *yoga* which again was quite different from the classical system of Buddhist meditations expounded in the *Satipatt-
hanasutta.* Like the *upanisads,* the *tantras* became the sacred as well
as secret scriptures representing an esoteric path. The technology of
Tantrika practice *(sadhana)* is, broadly speaking, the same in Saiva,
Vaisnava, Sakta and Buddhist texts. These texts sought to harmonize the philosophical ideologies of Brahmanical and Buddhist origins. A non-dual philosophy and a profound technique of devotional mysticism were the two basic elements of all *tantras,* Buddhist as
well as Brahmanical. These texts denounced the caste-system and
untouchability; they asserted individual freedom in social and religious life. Women had the same opportunity as men in matters of
*sadhana.* Several women reached the status of a *siddha.* Indulgence
in scholasticism and hairsplitting epistemological theories did not
find favour with these *siddhas.* Simple life, strict discipline, and direct experience of the taste of *dharma* were the hallmarks of Tantrika culture in its pristine stage. In the life and teachings of Ramakrishna we find the culmination of that tradition of harmonious
socio-religious culture which the great *siddhas,* the perfected ones,
had taught and practised during the early medieval period (A.D.
800-1200).

Respect for the faith of other men is an essential feature of that
enlightened attitude which seeks to perceive harmony among the
traditions of mankind. By harmony we do not mean monotonous
uniformity or monolithic unity among religious traditions. Harmony lies in the freedom from narrow-mindedness, in the capacity
to appreciate different perspectives, and in the feeling of fellowship
in a common higher quest. Harmony among different traditions

---

[5] *Kayakosamrtavajragiti* after Herbert V. Guenther, *The Life and Teachings of
Naropa,* Oxford University Press, 1963, p. 223.

and faiths can possibly be achieved by respecting and participating in different manifestations of religious quest, by understanding and admiring the diversities and distinctive visions of each tradition, and not by mystifying or ignoring the differences which are essential. The differences exist essentially, not only because men differ in their equipment and efforts but also because all the approaches are human and phenomenal, whereas the ultimate goal is transcendental. Unity is the nature not of the phenomenal but of the Absolute.

Ramakrishna's respect for all faiths singles him out in the galaxy of sages and mystics of the world. His successful practice of more than one path was at the basis of his conviction of the validity of several pathways. Like the Jaina mystics he recognized that reality does not exclude contradictory features, which means that it is indeterminate *(anekanta)*. The Jaina doctrine of the indeterminate nature of reality does not mean that it is of indefinite nature; the doctrine teaches that it cannot be determined, cannot be defined adequately or absolutely. We must admit that no single statement of reality can exhaust the possibility of other statements about it, and that no single manifestation of the Holy is adequate, for the Holy is more than all its descriptions and manifestations.

A pagan philosopher, Quintus Aurelius Symmachus, is reported to have told the church father Ambrosius that "the heart of so great a mystery can never be reached by following only one way."[6] Those who admit, with Symmachus, that mystery can be reached by following many ways, will feel called upon, with Ramakrishna, to accord equal reverence to all the valid ways. The richness and variety of religious ideas and practices, prevalent among the civilized races of man, should be viewed as a tribute to the deeply religious nature of mankind.

Schleiermacher's appeal for the fellowship of faiths, though resting on a different ground, deserves quotation here: "If you want to compare religion with religion as the eternally progressing work of the world spirit, you must give up the vain and futile wish that there ought to be only one; your antipathy against the variety of religions must be laid aside, and with as much impartiality as possible you must join all those which have developed from the eternally abun-

---

[6] After Arnold J. Toynbee, *An Historian's Approach to Religion,* Oxford University Press, 1956, p. 297.

dant bosom of the Universe through the changing forms and progressive traditions of man."[7]

A constructive and practical suggestion towards building harmony among religious traditions had been made as early as the third century B. C. by Emperor Asoka. In his vast empire lived not only the votaries of Buddhism, Brahmanism, Jainism and Ajivikism, but also the followers of Zoroastrian and Hellenistic religions. Though himself a devout Buddhist by faith and practice, he showed a remarkable degree of reverence for all the other faiths. He sincerely believed that all religious sects aimed at holy life and that there should be a growth of the essence of religiousness. He was aware of sectarian controversies and *odium theologicum* among his subjects. He studied the doctrines of all sects and attended to all religious communities. "I have honored," he tells us, "all religious sects with several forms of honor. But I consider a personal respectful approach towards people as the principal duty."[8] A most remarkable document of religious tolerance and respect for the faiths of men together with an appeal for concord among the followers of diverse faiths is to be found in his Rock Edict No. XII:

> King Priyadarsi, the Beloved of the gods, reveres persons of all religious sects, monks as well as householders, with liberality and with various kinds of reverence. However, the Beloved of the gods does not consider so highly the offering of liberality or reverence for the people as the following, namely, that there ought to be a growth of the essentials of religion *(Dharma)* among the men of all sects. The growth of the essentials of *Dharma* can be promoted in many ways. But its first foundation is restraint of speech, which means that there should not be praise of one's own religious faith or disparagement of another's religious faith on inappropriate occasions, and that it should be moderate indeed even on appropriate occasions. As a matter of fact, the religious faith of other men should be respected in every manner and on all occasions. When a person behaves in this way, he not only promotes his own religious faith but also benefits that of others. But if a person behaves otherwise, he harms not only his own religious faith but also that of others. Indeed, if a person praises his own religious sect and disparages other religious sects

[7] After Friedrich Heiler, *op. cit.* p. 155.

[8] Asoka's Pillar Edict No. VI. Author's free translation. The original text of the edicts of Asoka can be seen, among others, in Radhagovinda Basak, *Asokan Inscriptions,* Calcutta, Progressive Publishers, 1959.

only with a view to glorifying his own religious sect and just out of attachment to it, he harms his own religious sect greatly by doing so. Concord, therefore, is commendable, and the people should know and respect the essentials of one another's religious faith.

For the realization of this end are engaged many of my officers, such as the ministers in charge of religious affairs, ministers who are heads of the matters relating to the ladies, the officers in charge of the settlements of herdsmen, and other groups of officers. And the result of this arrangement is the promotion of every one's religious sect as well as the illumination of *Dharma*.[9]

Asoka taught concord or harmony *(samavaya)* among the religions of the world. It will be noticed that Asoka, one of the noblest followers of Buddhism, does not argue for a synthesis or syncretism of all religious sects. This was also the position adopted by Ramakrishna, who, as has been pointed out by Dr. Stark, did not found a new religion based on the tenets of several religions. Asoka teaches that one must respect the faith of other men and endeavor to understand the teachings of all religious systems. By doing so, he points out, one will be promoting not only one's own religious sect but also contributing to the growth of religiousness among the people in general.

According to Ludwig Feuerbach the essential act of religion is prayer.[10] Prayer, as we understand it, is the holy wish or pure intention expressed out of a sense of ultimacy and total commitment. Prayer is an aspect of worship, one of the manifestations of religious consciousness. Religious consciousness cannot be separated from the consciousness of the unity of all forms of existence. The highest form of religiousness expresses itself fully in an individual freed from the self-system. This reminds us of the Bodhisattva or the Christ, who aims at the liberation of all beings. The best type of prayer is, therefore, the one that is offered by a Bodhisattva:

As long as the space exists and as long as the world exists, so long may I exist for destroying the world's sufferings. Whatever the sufferings of the world, may all those (sufferings) ripen in me; and may the world be blessed by all the religious merits of the Bodhisattva.[11]

[9] Asoka's Rock Edict No. XII. Author's free translation.

[10] *The Essence of Christianity,* translated by George Eliot, Harper, New York, 1957, p. 193.

[11] *Bodhicaryavatara* K. 55-56. Author's translation. The translation of Marion L.

214

Ramakrishna was like a Bodhisattva, who, having realized the unity of all sentient beings, wished every blessing for everybody. The greatest need of the hour is to perceive the underlying unity of all forms of life. He who will discover this profound unity will realize the equivalence of the self and the neighbour *(paratma-samata)* and transcend all barriers whether religious or racial. As we have said above, the diverse religious systems and paths are phenomenal; only the highest goal is transcendental. This single point, namely, that the ultimate quest of all forms of holy culture is concerned with the transcendental, is perhaps a ground upon which thinking minds can build the hope of unity and harmony in the world.

PUNJABI UNIVERSITY
PATIALA, INDIA

# *Prayer of Religious Harmony*

May He Who is the Father in Heaven of the Christians, Holy One of the Jews, Allah of the Mohammedans, Buddha of the Buddhists, Tao of the Chinese, Ahura Mazda of the Zoroastrians and Brahman of the Hindus lead us from the unreal to the Real, from darkness to light, from disease and death to immortality. May the All-Loving Being manifest Himself unto us, and grant us abiding understanding and all-consuming divine love. Peace. Peace. Peace be unto all.

—Used by SWAMI AKHILANANDA

---

Matics, *Entering the Path of Enlightenment,* New York, Macmillan Company, 1970, is far from being precise.

# Bibliography

Abhedananda, Swami. *Christian Science and Vedanta*. Calcutta: Ramakrishna Vedanta Math, 1952.

———. *Great Saviors of the World*. 3d ed. Calcutta: Ramakrishna Vedanta Math, 1966.

———. *Human Affection and Divine Love*. Calcutta: Ramakrishna Vedanta Math, 1952.

———. *Memoirs of Ramakrishna*. 3d ed. Calcutta: Ramakrishna Vedanta Math, 1967.

———. *Sri Ramakrishna*. Calcutta: Ramakrishna Vedanta Math, 1940.

———. *The Thoughts on Sankhya Buddhism and Vedanta*. Calcutta: Ramakrishna Vedanta Math, 1967.

———. *True Psychology*. 3d rev. ed. Calcutta: Ramakrishna Vedanta Math, 1965.

———. *Yoga, Its Theory and Practice*. Calcutta: Ramakrishna Vedanta Math, 1967.

———. *The Yoga Psychology*. Calcutta: Ramakrishna Vedanta Math, 1967.

à Kempis, Thomas. *The Following of Christ*. New York: D. & J. Sadlier, 1885.

Akhilananda, Swami. "Extra-Sensory and Superconscious Experiences." *The Cultural Heritage of India*. Vol. I: *The Philosophies*. Edited by Haridas Bhattacharyya. 2d ed. Calcutta: The Ramakrishna Mission Institute of Culture, 1953.

216

———. *Hindu Psychology: Its Meaning for the West.* Introduction by Gordon W. Allport and Foreword by Edgar Sheffield Brightman. Boston: Branden Press, 1946.

———. *Hindu View of Christ.* Introduction by Walter G. Muelder. Boston: Branden Press, 1949.

———. *Mental Health and Hindu Psychology.* Boston: Branden Press, 1951.

———. *Modern Problems and Religion.* Boston: Branden Press, 1964.

———. *Spiritual Practices.* Introduction by Walter G. Muelder. Boston: Branden Press, 1972.

———. *Spiritual Practices.* Memorial Edition with Reminiscences. Cape Cod, Mass.: Claude Stark, Inc., 1974.

———. *Sri Ramakrishna and Modern Psychology.* Providence: The Vedanta Society, 1937.

Allport, Gordon W. "Introduction." *Hindu Psychology: Its Meaning for the West,* by Swami Akhilananda. Boston: Branden Press, 1946.

Ananda. *Spiritual Practice.* Mayavati, Almora, Himalayas: Advaita Ashrama, 1930.

Appasamy, A. J. *Christianity as Bhakti Marga: A Study in the Mysticism of the Johannine Writings.* London: Macmillan, 1927.

*The Apostles of Shri Ramakrishna.* Edited by Swami Gambhirananda. Calcutta: Advaita Ashrama, 1967.

Appleton, George. *On the Eightfold Path: Christian Presence amid Buddhism.* Edited by M. A. C. Warren. Christian Presence Series. New York: Oxford University Press, 1961.

Arberry, A. J. *Discourses of Rumi.* London: John Murray, 1961.

———. *Sufism: An Account of the Mystics of Islam.* London: Allen & Unwin, 1950.

Ashokananda, Swami. *Memories of Swami Shivananda.* San Francisco: Vedanta Society of Northern California, 1969.

———. *My Philosophy and My Religion.* San Francisco: Vedanta Society of Northern California, 1970.

———. *Spiritualizing Everyday Life.* San Francisco: Vedanta Society of Northern California, 1969.

———. *Swami Brahmananda.* San Francisco: Vedanta Society of Northern California, 1970.

———. *Swami Vivekananda in San Francisco.* San Francisco: Vedanta Society of Northern California, 1969.

*Ashtavakra Samhita.* Translated by Swami Nityaswarupananda. Calcutta: Advaita Ashrama, 1969.

*At Holy Mother's Feet (Teachings of Shri Sarada Devi).* By Her Direct Disciples. Mayavati, Almora, Himalayas: Advaita Ashrama, 1963.

Atmananda, Swami. *The Four Yogas.* Bombay: Bharatiya Vidya Bhavan, 1966.

Atmaprana, Pravrajika. *Sister Nivedita of Ramakrishna-Vivekananda.* 2d ed. Calcutta: Sister Nivedita Girls' School, 1967.

Attar, Farid al-Din. *Muslim Saints and Mystics.* Translated by A. J. Arberry. Chicago: University of Chicago Press, 1966.

Aurobindo, Sri. *The Life Divine.* New York: The Greystone Press, 1949.

Avalon, Arthur. [Sir John Woodroffe]. *Hymns to Kali.* Madras: Ganesh, 1965.

————. *Hymns to the Goddess.* Madras: Ganesh, 1964.

————. *Kama-Kala-Vilasa.* Madras: Ganesh, 1961.

Axelson, Sigbert. *Culture Confrontation in the Lower Congo.* Falköping, Sweden: Gummessons, 1970.

Bagchi, P. C. "Evolution of the Tantras." *The Cultural Heritage of India.* Vol. IV: *The Religions.* Edited by Haridas Bhattacharyya. 2d ed. Calcutta: The Ramakrishna Mission Institute of Culture, 1956.

Balandier, Georges. *Daily Life in the Kingdom of the Kongo: From the Sixteenth to the Eighteenth Century.* New York: World Publishing Co., 1968.

Barban, P. Bernardino. *Saint Anthony of Padua.* Translated by Alexander Piasentin. New York: Society of St. Paul, 1933.

Batsikama ba Mampuya ma Ndwala, R. *Ndona Beatrice: Serait-Elle Témoin du Christ et de la Foi du Vieux Congo?* Kinshasa: Éditions du Mwanza, 1969.

*The Bhagavad-Gita with the Commentary of Sri Sankaracharya.* Translated by A. Mahadeva Sastri. Madras: V. Ramaswamy Sastrulu & Sons, 1961.

Bhaktivedanta Swami, A. C. *Teachings of Lord Chaitanya.* New York: International Society for Krishna Consciousness, 1968.

Blofeld, John. *The Tantric Mysticism of Tibet.* Dutton Paperbacks. New York: E. P. Dutton, 1970.

Bridges, Hal. *American Mysticism: From William James to Zen.* New York: Harper & Row, 1970.

Brightman, Edgar S. *A Philosophy of Religion.* New York: Prentice-Hall, 1940.

————. "Foreword." *Hindu Psychology: Its Meaning for the West,* by Swami Akhilananda. Boston: Branden Press, 1946.

————. *The Problem of God.* New York: Abingdon Press, 1930.

Brown, Peter. *Augustine of Hippo.* Berkeley: University of California Press, 1969.

Bucke, Richard Maurice. *Cosmic Consciousness.* New York: E. P. Dutton, 1967.

*Buddhist Wisdom Books.* Containing the Diamond Sutra and the Heart Sutra. Translated by Edward Conze. London: Allen & Unwin, 1958.

Bultmann, Rudolf. *Jesus Christ and Mythology.* New York: Charles Scribner's Sons, 1958.

Burke, Marie Louise. *Swami Vivekananda in America: New Discoveries.* Calcutta: Advaita Ashrama, 1958.

Chakravarti, Chintaran. "Sakti Worship and the Sakta Saints." *The Cultural Heritage of India,* Vol. IV: *The Religions.* Edited by Haridas Bhattacharyya. 2d ed. Calcutta: The Ramakrishna Mission Institute of Culture, 1956.

Chatterjee, Satis Chandra. *Classical Indian Philosophies: Their Synthesis in the Philosophy of Sri Ramakrishna.* Calcutta: University of Calcutta: 1963.

Chesterton, G. K. *St. Francis of Assisi.* Image Books. Garden City, N. Y.: Doubleday, 1957.

Clark, Walter H., in *Spiritual Practices,* by Swami Akhilananda. Memorial Edition with Reminiscences. Cape Cod, Mass.: Claude Stark, Inc., 1974.

Clasen, Sophronius. *St. Anthony.* Translated by Ignatius Brady. Chicago: Franciscan Herald Press, 1961.

*The Confessions of St. Augustine.* Translated by John K. Ryan. Image Books. Garden City, N. Y.: Doubleday, 1960.

Conze, Edward. *Buddhism: Its Essence and Development.* Harper Torchbooks. New York: Harper & Row, 1959.

———. *Buddhist Meditation.* Ethical and Religious Classics of East and West, No. 13. London: Allen & Unwin, 1956.

———. *Buddhist Thought in India.* Ann Arbor Paperbacks. Ann Arbor: University of Michigan Press, 1968.

———. *Thirty Years of Buddhist Studies.* London: Bruno Cassirer, 1967.

———; Horner, I. B.; Snellgrove, David and Waley, Arthur, eds. *Buddhist Texts Through the Ages.* Harper Torchbooks. New York: Harper & Row, 1964.

Cowell, E. B.; Müller, F. Max; and Takakusu, J., eds. *Buddhist Mahayana Texts.* New York: Dover Publications, 1969.

*The Cultural Heritage of India.* 2d ed. Vols. I-IV.

Dayal, Har. *The Bodhisattva Doctrine in Buddhist Sanscrit Literature.* Delhi: Motilal Banarsidass, 1970.

de Smet, Richard V. Review of *Avatar and Incarnation,* by G. Parrinder. *The Journal of Religious Studies,* III (Spring, 1971), 171-173.

Deutsch, Eliot. *Advaita Vedanta: A Philosophical Reconstruction.* Honolulu: East-West Center Press, 1969.

Devi, Kalpalata. "The Life Divine (A Tribute to Sri Sarada Devi)." *Prabuddha Bharata,* LIX (March, 1954), 120-125.

*The Devi-Mahatmyam or Sri Durga Sapsati.* Translated by Swami Jagad-isvarananda. Mylapore, Madras: Sri Ramakrishna Math, 1955.

DeWolf, Harold, in *Spiritual Practices,* by Swami Akhilananda. Memorial Edition with Reminiscences. Cape Cod, Mass.: Claude Stark, Inc., 1974.

*The Dhammapada.* Translated by Irving Babbitt. New York: New Directions, 1965.

*The Dhammapada.* With Pali text, translation and notes by S. Radhakrishnan. London: Oxford University Press, 1966.

*Dignaga, On Perception: Pramanasamuccaya.* Translated by Masaaki Hattori. Cambridge: Harvard University Press, 1968.

*The Disciples of Ramakrishna.* Mayavati, Almora, Himalayas: Advaita Ashrama, 1955.

Diwakar, R. R. *Bhagawan Buddha.* Bhavan's Book University. Chaupatty, Bombay: Bharatiya Vidya Bhavan, 1967.

Dix, Dom Gregory. *The Shape of the Liturgy.* London: Dacre Press, A. & C. Black, 1945.

*The Documents of Vatican II.* Edited by Walter M. Abbott. London: Geoffrey Chapman, 1967.

Durrwell, F. X. *The Resurrection: A Biblical Study.* Translated by Rosemary Sheed. New York: Sheed and Ward, 1960.

Eddington, A. S. *Philosophy of Physical Science.* New York: Macmillan, 1929.

Eliade, Mircea. *The Myth of the Eternal Return.* Translated by Willard Trask. Bollingen Series XLVI. Pantheon Books. New York: Random House, 1954.

———. *Patterns in Comparative Religion.* Translated by Rosemary Sheed. Meridian Books. Cleveland: World Publishing Co., 1968.

———. *The Quest: History and Meaning in Religion.* Chicago: University of Chicago Press, 1969.

———. *Rites and Symbols of Initiation: The Mysteries of Birth and Rebirth.* Translated by Willard R. Trask. Harper Torchbooks. New York: Harper & Row, 1958.

Erickson, Joan Mowat. *Saint Francis and His Four Ladies.* New York: W. W. Norton, 1970.

*The Eternal Companion: Brahmananda.* Records of His Teaching, with a biography by Swami Prabhavananda. Hollywood, Calif.: Vedanta Press, 1947.

*The Eternal Companion: Brahmananda.* Teachings and Reminiscences with a Biography by Swami Prabhavananda. 3d ed., revised and enlarged. Hollywood, Calif.: Vedanta Press, 1970.

Evans-Wentz, W. Y., ed. *Tibetan Yoga and Secret Doctrines.* 2d ed. London: Oxford University Press, 1958.

Ferrando, Guido. "St. Francis and Sri Ramakrishna." *Vedanta for the*

*Western World.* Edited by Christopher Isherwood. New York: Viking Press, 1969.

Gambhirananda, Swami. *History of the Ramakrishna Math and Mission.* Calcutta: Advaita Ashrama, 1957.

———. *Holy Mother, Shri Sarada Devi.* Madras: Sri Ramakrishna Math, 1955.

Ghanananda, Swami. "The Beatitudes." *Vedanta for East and West,* No. 122 (November-December, 1971), pp. 15-26.

———. "Some Holy Women Figuring in the Life of Sri Ramakrishna." *Women Saints of East and West.* London: Ramakrishna Vedanta Centre, 1955.

———. *Sri Ramakrishna and His Unique Message.* 3d ed. London: Ramakrishna Vedanta Centre, 1970.

al-Ghazali. *Ihya' 'Ulum Al-Din (The Revival of the Religious Sciences).* Translated by L. Zolondek. Leiden: E. J. Brill, 1963.

Ghose, Shishir Kumar. *Lord Gauranga.* Bhavan's Book University, No. 92. Bombay: Bharatiya Vidya Bhavan, 1961.

Ghosh, Ashutosh. *Swami Abhedananda, The Patriot-Saint.* Calcutta: Ramakrishna Vedanta Math, 1967.

Ghosh, Atal Behari. "The Spirit and Culture of the Tantras." *The Cultural Heritage of India.* Vol. IV: *The Religions.* Edited by Haridas Bhattacharyya. 2d ed. Calcutta: The Ramakrishna Mission Institute of Culture, 1956.

Gilson, Étienne. *The Christian Philosophy of St. Augustine. Translated by L. E. M. Lynch. New York: Random House, 1967.*

Gnaneswarananda, Swami. *Ramakrishna: The Man and the Power.* Chicago: Vedanta Society, 1936.

Gonda, J. *Change and Continuity in Indian Religion.* The Hague: Mouton & Co., 1965.

*The Gospel of Ramakrishna.* Revised by Swami Abhedananda from M's original English text. New York: Vedanta Society, 1947.

*The Gospel of Sri Ramakrishna.* Translated with an Introduction by Swami Nikhilananda. New York: Ramakrishna-Vivekananda Center, 1942.

Govinda Nath, Radha. "A Survey of the Caitanya Movement." *The Cultural Heritage of India.* Vol. IV: *The Religions.* Edited by Haridas Bhattacharyya. 2d ed. Calcutta: The Ramakrishna Mission Institute of Culture, 1956.

*Great Women of India.* The Holy Mother Birth Centenary Memorial. Edited by Swami Madhavananda and Ramesh Chandra Majumdar. Mayavati, Almora, Himalayas: Advaita Ashrama, 1953.

Gustafson, James M. *Christ and the Moral Life.* New York: Harper & Row, 1968.

Harman, Willis. "The New Copernican Revolution." *The Journal of Transpersonal Psychology,* I (Fall, 1969), 21-29.

*The Harmony of Religions: A Teaching of Ramakrishna.* London: Ramakrishna Vedanta Centre, 1965.

Heard, Gerald. "Vedanta as the Scientific Approach to Religion." *Vedanta for the Western World.* Edited by Christopher Isherwood. Compass Books. New York: Viking Press, 1960.

Hocking, William Ernest. *The Meaning of God in Human Experience.* New Haven: Yale University Press, 1912.

Hügel, Baron Friedrich von. *The Mystical Element of Religion as Studied in Saint Catherine of Genoa and Her Friends.* 2 vols. London: J. M. Dent & Sons and James Clarke & Co., 1961.

*India's Contribution to World Thought and Culture.* Edited by Lokesh Chandra, Devendra Swarup, Swarajya Prakash Gupta and Sitaram Goel. Madras: Vivekananda Rock Memorial Committee, 1970.

Isherwood, Christopher. *Ramakrishna and His Disciples.* London: Methuen, 1965.

*Jaina Sutras.* Translated by Hermann Jacobi. 2 vols. New York: Dover Publications, 1968.

James, William. *Essays in Pragmatism.* New York: Hafner, 1952.

——. *The Meaning of Truth.* Ann Arbor: University of Michigan Press, 1970.

——. *The Varieties of Religious Experience.* The Modern Library. New York: Random House, 1902.

Jayatilleke, K. N. *Ethics in Buddhist Perspective.* Kandy, Ceylon: Buddhist Publication Society, 1972.

Jeremias, Joachim. *The Eucharistic Words of Jesus.* New York: Charles Scribner's Sons, 1966.

Johnson, Paul E. Letter to Claude Alan Stark, September 22, 1972.

——. *Psychology of Religion.* Nashville: Abingdon Press, 1959.

Jones, Howard Mumford. *Education and World Tragedy.* Cambridge: Harvard University Press, 1946.

Jones, Rufus M. *Studies in Mystical Religion.* London: Macmillan, 1925.

Jorgensen, Johannes. *St. Francis of Assisi.* Translated by T. O'Conor Sloane. Image Books. Garden City, N. Y.: Doubleday, 1955.

Joshi, Lal Mani. *Brahmanism, Buddhism and Hinduism.* Kandy, Ceylon: Buddhist Publication Society, 1970.

——. "Gaudapada's Rapprochement between Buddhism and Vedanta." *Journal of Akhila Bharatiya Sanskrit Parishad,* I (July, 1969), 11-12.

——. *Studies in the Buddhistic Culture of India.* Delhi: Motilal Banarsidass, 1967.

——. "Truth: A Buddhist Perspective." *Journal of Religious Studies,* IV (Spring, 1972), 65-76.

Judd, James M. "The Universality of Mother God." *Vedanta for East and West,* No. 122 (November-December, 1971), pp. 9-15.

Jung, Carl G. *Integrity of the Personality.* Translated by Stanley Dell. London: Kegan Paul, 1939.

Kirtidananda, Swami. *The Glory of the Divine Mother.* Calcutta: The Ramakrishna Mission Institute of Culture, 1969.

Kraemer, Hendrik. *Religion and the Christian Faith.* Philadelphia; Westminster Press, 1956.

———. "The Role and Responsibility of the Christian Mission." *Philosophy, Religion and the Coming World Civilization: Essays in Honor of William Ernest Hocking.* Edited by Leroy S. Rouner. The Hague: Martinus Nijhoff, 1966.

Kumarappa, Bharatan. *The Hindu Conception of the Deity.* London: Luzac, 1934.

Lacombe, Oliver. "Swami Vivekananda and Practical Vedanta." *Swami Vivekananda Memorial Volume.* Calcutta: Swami Vivekananda Centenary Committee, 1963.

Lawrence, Brother. *The Practice of the Presence of God.* London: A. R. Mowbray, 1965.

Leclerq, Jean. *The Love of Learning and the Desire for God: A Study of Monastic Culture.* Translated by Catharine Misrahi. Mentor Omega Books. New York: New American Library, 1962.

Leeuw, G. van der. *Religion in Essence and Manifestation.* Translated by J. E. Turner. 2 vols. Gloucester, Mass.: Peter Smith, 1967.

LeShan, Lawrence. "Physicists and Mystics: Similarities in World View." *The Journal of Transpersonal Psychology,* I (Fall, 1969), 1-20.

Lewis, Leta Jane. "Eastern Philosophy and Western Problems." *Vedanta for East and West,* No. 124 (March-April, 1972), pp. 3-15.

*The Life of St. Teresa of Jesus.* Translated by David Lewis. London: Thomas Baker, 1924.

*The Life of Sri Ramakrishna.* 6th ed. Mayavati, Almora, Himalayas: Advaita Ashrama, 1948.

*The Life of Swami Vivekananda.* By His Eastern and Western Disciples. 4th ed. Mayavati, Almora, Himalayas: Advaita Ashrama, 1949.

Linssen, Robert. "The Idea of Love-Energy of Teilhard de Chardin and the Bhakti-Yoga of Swami Vivekananda." *Vedanta for East and West,* No. 118 (March-April, 1971), pp. 25-32.

McVeigh, Malcolm J. "The Interaction of the Conceptions of God of African Traditional Religion and Christianity in the Thought of Edwin W. Smith." Unpublished Ph.D. dissertation, Boston University, 1971. To be published as *God in Africa.* Cape Cod, Mass.: Claude Stark, Inc., 1974.

Madan, Mrs. Lajwanti. "Mira Bai." *Women Saints of East and West.* London: Ramakrishna Vedanta Centre, 1955.

Marozzi, E. R. "The Making of Swami Vivekananda." *Swami Vivekananda in East and West.* Edited by Swami Ghanananda and Geoffrey Parrinder. London: Ramakrishna Vedanta Centre, 1968.

Matsunaga, Alicia. *The Buddhist Philosophy of Assimilation.* Tokyo: Sophia University, 1969.

Maxwell, William D. *An Outline of Christian Worship: Its Development and Forms.* London: Oxford University Press, 1936.

Mazoomdar, Protap Chandra. *Ramakrishna Paramahamsa.* Calcutta: Udbodhan Office, 1928.

*Meditation.* By Monks of the Ramakrishna Order. London: Ramakrishna Vedanta Centre, 1972.

Mendenhall, George E. *Law and Covenant in Israel and the Ancient Near East.* Pittsburgh: Pa.: Presbyterian Board of Colportage, 1955.

*The Message of Our Master.* By the First Disciples of Shri Ramakrishna. Calcutta: Advaita Ashrama, 1955.

Moffitt, John. Review of *The Unknown Christ of Hinduism,* by Raymond Panikkar. *The Journal of Religious Studies,* IV (Spring, 1972), 163-168.

Mohom Nath, Raj. "Sankara Deva and the Vaishnava Movement in Assam." *The Cultural Heritage of India.* Vol. IV: *The Religions.* Edited by Haridas Bhattacharyya. 2d ed. Calcutta: The Ramakrishna Mission Institute of Culture, 1956.

Morgan, Kenneth W., ed. *The Path of the Buddha.* New York: Ronald Press, 1956.

Muelder, Walter G. "Introduction." *Hindu View of Christ,* by Swami Akhilananda. Boston: Branden Press, 1949.

————. "Introduction." *Spiritual Practices,* by Swami Akhilananda. Memorial Edition with Reminiscences. Cape Cod, Mass.: Claude Stark, Inc., 1974.

Mujeeb, M. *The Indian Muslims.* London: Allen & Unwin, 1967.

Mukerji, Dhan Gopal. *The Face of Silence.* New York: E. P. Dutton, 1926.

Müller, Max. *Ramakrishna: His Life and Sayings.* 2d ed. London: Longmans, Green & Co., 1923.

Munck, Johannes. *Paul and the Salvation of Mankind.* Translated by Frank Clarke. Richmond, Va.: John Knox Press, 1959.

Munshi, K. M. *Bhagawan Parashurama.* Bhavan's Book University. 2 vols. Bombay: Bharatiya Vidya Bhavan, 1965.

Murti, T. *The Central Philosophy of Buddhism.* London: Allen & Unwin, 1955.

*The Mystic Vision: Papers from the Eranos Yearbooks.* Edited by Joseph

Campbell. Bollingen Series XXX, Vol. 6. Princeton, N. J.: Princeton University Press, 1968.

*Narada Bhakti Sutras.* Translated by Swami Tyagisananda. Mylapore, Madras: Sri Ramakrishna Math, 1955.

*Narada Sutra.* Translated with commentary by E. T. Sturdy. 2d ed. London: John M. Watkins, 1904.

*Narada's Way of Divine Love: The Bhakti Sutras.* Translated with commentary by Swami Prabhavananda. Hollywood, Calif.: Vedanta Press, 1971.

Needleman, Jacob. *The New Religions.* Garden City, N. Y.: Doubleday, 1970.

Neill, Stephen. *The Story of the Christian Church in India and Pakistan.* Grand Rapids, Mich.: Wm. B. Eerdmans, 1970.

Nelson, J. Robert. "Signs of Mankind's Solidarity." *No Man is Alien: Essays on the Unity of Mankind.* Edited by J. Robert Nelson. Leiden: E. J. Brill, 1971.

Nicholson, Reynold A. *The Mystics of Islam.* London: Kegan Paul, 1966.

———. *Studies in Islamic Mysticism.* Cambridge, England: The University Press, 1921.

Nikhilananda, Swami. *Vivekananda: A Biography.* Mayavati, Almora, Himalayas: Advaita Ashrama, 1953.

Nirvedananda, Swami. *Sri Ramakrishna and Spiritual Renaissance.* Calcutta: The Ramakrishna Mission Institute of Culture, 1940.

Nivedita, Sister. *Kali the Mother.* Mayavati, Almora, Himalayas: Advaita Ashrama, 1950.

———. *The Master as I Saw Him.* 10th ed. Calcutta: Udbodhan Office, 1966.

———. *Notes of Some Wanderings with the Swami Vivekananda.* 5th ed. Calcutta: Udbodhan Office, 1967.

Otto, Rudolf. *The Idea of the Holy.* 2d ed. London: Oxford University Press, 1950.

———. *Mysticism East and West.* Translated by Bertha L. Bracey and Richenda C. Payne. New York: Macmillan, 1960.

Pande, Govind Chandra. *Studies in the Origin of Buddhism.* Ancient History Research Series, No. 1. Allahabad: University of Allahabad, Department of Ancient History, Culture and Archaeology, 1957.

Pandit, M. P. *Gems from the Tantras.* Madras: Ganesh, 1969.

———. *Lights on the Tantra.* Madras: Ganesh, 1968.

Panikkar, Raymond. *The Unknown Christ of Hinduism.* London: Darton, Longman & Todd, 1968.

Paramananda, Swami. *Spiritual Healing.* Rev. ed. Boston: Vedanta Centre, 1923.

Parrinder, Geoffrey. *Avatar and Incarnation.* London: Faber & Faber, 1970.

*The Path of Purification (Visuddhimagga) of Bhadantacariya Buddhaghosa.* Translated by Bhikku Nyanamoli. 2d ed. Colombo, Ceylon: A. Semage, 1964.

Pavitrananda, Swami. *Modern Man in Search of Religion.* Mayavati, Almora, Himalayas: Advaita Ashrama, 1947.

*Plotinus: The Enneads.* Translated by Stephen MacKenna. Revised by B. S. Page. 3d ed. London: Faber & Faber, 1962.

Portalie, Eugene. *A Guide to the Thought of Saint Augustine.* Translated by Ralph J. Bastian. Chicago: Henry Regnery, 1960.

Prabhavananda, Swami. *The Sermon on the Mount according to Vedanta.* Mentor Books. New York: New American Library, 1963.

———. *Swami Premananda, Teachings and Reminiscences.* Hollywood, Calif.: Vedanta Press, 1968.

*Prabuddha Bharata. The Holy Mother Birth Centenary Number,* LIX (March, 1954).

Pratyagatmananda, Swami. "Philosophy of the Tantras." *The Cultural Heritage of India.* Vol. III: *The Philosophies.* Edited by Haridas Bhattacharyya. 2d ed. Calcutta: The Ramakrishna Mission Institute of Culture, 1953.

———. "Tantra as a Way of Realization." *The Cultural Heritage of India.* Vol. IV: *The Religions.* Edited by Haridas Bhattacharyya. 2d ed. Calcutta: The Ramakrishna Mission Institute of Culture, 1956.

Pritchard, James B. *Ancient Near Eastern Texts.* Princeton: N. J.: Princeton University Press, 1950.

*Providence Evening Bulletin.* Obituary on Swami Akhilananda, September 25, 1962.

Radhakrishnan, Sarvepalli and Moore, Charles A., eds. *A Source Book in Indian Philosophy.* Princeton, N. J.: Princeton University Press, 1950.

Raghavendrachar, H. N. "Madhva's Brahma-Mimamsa." *The Cultural Heritage of India.* Vol. III: *The Philosophies.* Edited by Haridas Bhattacharyya. 2d ed. Calcutta: The Ramakrishna Mission Institute of Culture, 1953.

Rahbar, Daud. "Muhammad and All Men." *No Man Is Alien: Essays on the Unity of Mankind.* Edited by J. Robert Nelson. Leiden: E. J. Brill, 1971.

Rajagopalachari, C. *Ramayana.* Bhavan's Book University, No. 44. Bombay: Bharatiya Vidya Bhavan, 1965.

———. *Sri Ramakrishna Upanishad.* 4th ed. Mylapore, Madras: Sri Ramakrishna Math, 1964.

Ramakrishnananda, Swami. *God and Divine Incarnations.* Madras: Sri

Ramakrishna Math, 1947.

———. *Sri Krishna: Pastoral and Kingmaker.* Madras: Sri Ramakrishna Math, 1960.

Ranganathananda, Swami. *The Ramakrishna Mission: Its Ideals and Activities.* Institute Booklets: 12. Calcutta: The Ramakrishna Mission Institute of Culture, 1966.

———. *Swami Vivekananda: His Life and Mission.* Calcutta: The Ramakrishna Mission Institute of Culture, 1963.

———. *Swami Vivekananda's Synthesis of Science and Religion.* Calcutta: The Ramakrishna Mission Institute of Culture, 1967.

———. *Vedanta and Science.* Calcutta: The Ramakrishna Mission Institute of Culture, 1966.

Reck, Andrew J. "Hocking's Place in American Metaphysics." *Philosophy, Religion, and the Coming World Civilization: Essays in Honor of William Ernest Hocking.* Edited by Leroy S. Rouner. The Hague: Martinus Nijhoff, 1966.

Richardson, Alan. *A Dictionary of Christian Theology.* Philadelphia: Westminster Press, 1969.

Rist, J. M. *Plotinus: The Road to Reality.* Cambridge, England: The University Press, 1967.

Ritajananda, Swami. *Swami Turiyananda.* Mylapore, Madras: Sri Ramakrishna Math, 1963.

Robinson, Richard H. *The Buddhist Religion: A Historical Introduction.* The Religious Life of Man Series. Belmont, Calif.: Dickenson, 1970.

Rolland, Romain. *The Life of Ramakrishna.* Translated by E. F. Malcolm-Smith. 7th ed. Calcutta: Advaita Ashrama, 1965.

———. *The Life of Vivekananda and the Universal Gospel.* Calcutta: Advaita Ashrama, 1965.

Rouner, Leroy S., ed. *Philosophy, Religion, and the Coming World Civilization: Essays in Honor of William Ernest Hocking.* The Hague: Martinus Nijhoff, 1966.

*Rumi, Poet and Mystic.* Selections from his writings. Translated with Introduction and Notes by Reynold A. Nicholson. London: Allen & Unwin, 1950.

*Saddharma-Pundarika or The Lotus of the True Law.* Translated by H. Kern. The Sacred Books of the East, Vol. XXI. New York: Dover Publications, 1963.

*The Saint Durgacharan Nag (The Life of an Ideal Householder).* Madras: Sri Ramakrishna Math, 1951.

Saradananda, Swami. *Sri Ramakrishna, The Great Master.* Translated by Swami Jagadananda. 2d ed. Madras: Sri Ramakrishna Math, 1952.

Sarma, D. S. *The Master and the Disciple.* Mylapore, Madras: Sri Ramakrishna Math, 1967.

————. *The Prince of Ayodhya*. Madras: Sri Ramakrishna Math, 1946.

Sastri, K. S. Ramaswami. *Sri Ramakrishna Paramahamsa*. Mylapore, Madras: Sri Ramakrishna Math, 1928.

Satprakashananda, Swami. *Methods of Knowledge according to Advaita Vedanta*. London: Allen & Unwin, 1965.

————, ed. *The Use of Symbols in Religion*. St. Louis: Vedanta Society, 1970.

*Sayings of Sri Ramakrishna*. 7th rev. ed. Madras: Sri Ramakrishna Math, 1949.

Schrödinger, Erwin. *Science and Humanism*. London: Cambridge University Press, 1952.

————. *What is Life?* New York: Macmillan, 1947.

Schul, Bill D. "Science & Psi: Transcultural Trends." Report of a symposium at the American Psychiatric Association Convention. *Psychic Magazine,* September, 1972, pp. 40-44.

Schweitzer, Albert. *The Quest of the Historical Jesus*. New York: Macmillan, 1968.

*Selections from the Sacred Writings of the Sikhs*. Translated by Trilochan Singh, Bhai Jodh Singh, Kapur Singh, Bawa Harkishen Singh and Khushwant Singh. Revised by George S. Fraser. Introduction by S. Radhakrishnan. Foreword by Arnold Toynbee. UNESCO Collection of Representative Works: Indian Series. London: Allen & Unwin, 1960.

[Sgam.po.pa.] *The Jewel Ornament of Liberation*. Translated and annotated by Herbert V. Guenther. The Clear Light Series. Berkeley, Calif.: Shambala Publications, 1971.

Shah, Idries. *The Sufis*. Introduction by Robert Graves. Anchor Books. Garden City, N. Y.: Doubleday, 1971.

Shankaracharya, Sri. *Atmabodha (Self-Knowledge)*. Translated by Swami Nikhilananda. Mylapore, Madras: Sri Ramakrishna Math, 1967.

————. *Aparokshanubhuti or Self-Realization*. Translated by Swami Vimuktananda. Calcutta: Advaita Ashrama, 1938.

————. *Brahma-Sutra-Bhasya*. Translated by Swami Gambhirananda. Calcutta: Advaita Ashrama, 1965.

————. *The Quintessence of Vedanta (The Sarva-Vedanta-Siddhanta-Sarasangraha of Acharya Shankara)*. Translated by Swami Tattwananda. Introduction by Swami Agamananda. Kalady, Kerala: Sri Ramakrishna Advaita Ashrama, 1960.

————. *Upadeshasahasri (A Thousand Teachings)*. Translated with notes by Swami Jagadananda. Mylapore, Madras: Sri Ramakrishna Math, 1961.

————. *Vakyavritti and Atmajnanopadeshavidhi*. Translated by Swami Jagadananda. Mylapore, Madras: Sri Ramakrishna Math, 1967.

——. *Shankara's Crest-Jewel of Discrimination (Viveka-Chudamani).* Translated by Swami Prabhavananda and Christopher Isherwood. Hollywood, Calif: Vedanta Press, 1947.

——. *Vivekachudamani of Shri Shankaracharya.* Translated by Swami Madhavananda. 7th ed. Calcutta: Advaita Ashrama, 1966.

Shapley, Harlow. *Of Stars and Men.* Boston: Beacon Press, 1959.

Sharma, I. C. *Ethical Philosophies of India.* Edited and revised by Stanley M. Daugert. Harper Torchbooks. New York: Harper & Row, 1965.

Shastri, S. B. "Buddhist Ethics and Social Ideas in Buddhism." *Buddhism.* Guru Nanak Quincentenary Celebration Series. Patiala: Punjabi University, 1969.

Shikuh, Prince Muhammad Dara. *Majma'-Ul-Bahrain or The Mingling of the Two Oceans.* Edited with translation and notes by M. Mahfuz-ul-Haq. Bibliotheca India No. 146. Calcutta: Asiatic Society of Bengal, 1929.

Shivananda, Swami. *For Seekers of God.* Translated by Swami Vividishananda. Mayavati, Almora, Himalayas: Advaita Ashrama, 1954.

Shrader, James Houston, in *Spiritual Practices,* by Swami Akhilananda. Memorial Edition with Reminiscences. Cape Cod, Mass.: Claude Stark, Inc., 1974.

Siddheswarananda, Swami. *Meditation according to Yoga-Vedanta.* Translated by V. A. Thyagarajan. Foreword by S. Radhakrishnan. 2d ed. Puranattukara, Trichur: Sri Ramakrishna Ashrama, 1969.

Singer, Milton and Ingalls, Daniel H. H., eds. *Krishna: Myths, Rites and Attitudes.* Honolulu: East-West Center Press, 1966.

Sinha, Jadunath. "Bhagavata Religion: The Cult of Bhakti." *The Cultural Heritage of India.* Vol. IV: *The Religions.* Edited by Haridas Bhattacharyya. 2d ed. Calcutta: The Ramakrishna Mission Institute of Culture, 1956.

Smith, Wilfred Cantwell. *The Faith of Other Men.* Mentor Books. New York: New American Library, 1963.

——. *The Meaning and End of Religion: A New Approach to the Religious Traditions of Mankind.* New York: Macmillan, 1963.

Sorokin, Pitirim. *The Crisis of Our Age.* New York: E. P. Dutton, 1941.

——. *A Long Journey.* New Haven, Conn.: College and University Press, 1963.

——. *The Reconstruction of Humanity.* Bhavan's Book University, No. 54. 3d ed. Bombay: Bharatiya Vidya Bhavan, 1962.

—— and Lunden, Walter A. *Power and Morality: Who Shall Guard the Guardians?* Extending Horizons Books. Boston: Porter Sargent, 1959.

——. *The Ways of Power and Love.* Chicago: Henry Regnery, 1967.

Spencer, Sidney. "Vivekananda and the Unity of Churches and Religions."

*Swami Vivekananda in East and West.* London: Ramakrishna Vedanta Centre, 1968.

*The Spiritual Exercises of St. Ignatius.* Translated by Anthony Mottola. Image Books. Garden City, N. Y.: Doubleday, 1964.

*Spiritual Life.* Madras: Sri Ramakrishna Math, n.d.

*Spiritual Talks.* By the First Disciples of Sri Ramakrishna. Mayavati, Almora, Himalayas: Advaita Ashrama, 1955.

*The Spiritual Teachings of Swami Brahmananda.* 2d ed. Mylapore, Madras: Sri Ramakrishna Math, 1933.

*Sri Sarada Devi, The Holy Mother.* Madras: Sri Ramakrishna Math, 1949.

*Srimad-Bhagavad-Gita.* Translated by Swami Swarupananda. 8th ed. Mayavati, Almora, Himalayas: Advaita Ashrama, 1948.

Stark, Claude Alan. "Swami Vivekananda as a Devotee." *The Journal of Religious Studies,* IV (Spring, 1972), 89-106.

*The Story of a Dedicated Life* (The Biography of Swami Ramakrishnananda). Madras: Sri Ramakrishna Math, 1948.

Streng, Frederick J. *Emptiness: A Study in Religious Meaning.* Nashville: Abingdon Press, 1971.

Stromberg, Gustaf. *The Soul of the Universe.* Philadelphia: David McKay, 1940.

Strunk, Orlo, Jr., ed. *The Psychology of Religion: Historical and Interpretive Readings.* Nashville: Abingdon Press, 1971.

Sundkler, Bengt. *The Christian Ministry in Africa.* London: S.C.M. Press, 1960.

*The Sutra of the Sixth Patriarch on the Pristine Orthodox Dharma.* Translated by Paul F. Fung and George D. Fung. San Francisco: Buddha's Universal Church, 1964.

Suzuki, Daisetz Teitaro. *Mysticism: Christian and Buddhist.* New York: Macmillan, 1969.

―――. *On Indian Mahayana Buddhism.* Edited by Edward Conze. Harper Torchbooks. New York: Harper & Row, 1968.

*Swami Vivekananda Centenary Memorial Volume.* Edited by R. C. Majumdar. Calcutta: Swami Vivekananda Centenary, 1963.

*Swami Vivekananda in East and West.* London: Ramakrishna Vedanta Centre, 1968.

Tawney, R. H. *Religion and the Rise of Capitalism.* Mentor Books. New York: New American Library, 1954.

Tejasananda, Swami. *The Ramakrishna Movement: Its Ideals and Activities.* 2d ed. Belur Math, Howrah: Ramakrishna Mission Saradapitha, 1956.

Teresa, Saint. *Way of Perfection.* London: Thomas Baker, 1935.

Thakur, S. C. *Christian and Hindu Ethics.* London: Allen & Unwin, 1969.

Thera, Piyadassi. *The Buddha's Ancient Path.* London: Rider, 1964.

Thomas, Edward J. *The History of Buddhist Thought.* London: Routledge & Kegan Paul, 1951.

*Thus Spake the Holy Mother.* Compiled by Swami Suddhasatwananda. Mylapore, Madras: Sri Ramakrishna Math, 1953.

Tillich, Paul. *Systematic Theology.* 3 vols. in one. New York: Harper & Row, 1967.

Toynbee, Arnold. *Christianity among the Religions of the World.* New York: Charles Scribner's Sons, 1957.

————. "Foreword." *Sri Ramakrishna and His Unique Message,* by Swami Ghanananda. London: Ramakrishna Vedanta Centre, 1970.

*Uddhava Gita or The Last Message of Shri Krishna.* Text with English translation and notes by Swami Madhavananda. 3d ed. Calcutta: Advaita Ashrama, 1971.

Ulich, Robert, in *Spiritual Practices* by Swami Akhilananda. Memorial Edition with Reminiscences. Cape Cod, Mass.: Claude Stark, Inc., 1974.

Underhill, Evelyn. *Mysticism.* 4th ed. London: J. M. Dent, 1912.

————. *Practical Mysticism.* London: J. M. Dent, 1964.

Upanishads:

    *The Brhadaranyaka Upanishad.* With the Commentary of Sri Sankaracarya. Translated by Swami Madhavananda. 4th ed. Calcutta: Advaita Ashrama, 1965.

    *Eight Upanisads.* With the Commentary of Sankaracarya. Translated by Swami Gambhirananda. 2 vols. 2d ed. Calcutta: Advaita Ashrama, 1965-66.

    *The Principal Upanisads.* Edited with Introduction, Text, Translation and Notes by S. Radhakrishnan. The Muirhead Library of Philosophy. London: Allen & Unwin, 1953.

    *The Upanishads.* A one-volume abridgement translated and edited by Swami Nikhilananda. Harper Torchbooks. New York: Harper & Row, 1963.

    *The Upanishads: Breath of the Eternal.* Translated by Swami Prabhavananda and Frederick Manchester. Hollywood, Calif.: Vedanta Press, 1947.

*Vedantasara of Sadananda Yogindra Saraswati.* Translated by Swami Nikhilananda. Calcutta: Advaita Ashrama, 1968.

*Vedartha-Sangraha of Sri Ramanujacharya.* Translated by S. S. Raghavachar. Mysore: Sri Ramakrishna Ashrama, 1968.

Venkataraman, R. K. "Sakti Cult in South India." *The Cultural Heritage of India.* Vol. IV: *The Religions.* 2d ed. Calcutta: The Ramakrishna Mission Institute of Culture, 1956.

Vittengl, Morgan, "Many Paths Ascend Mt. Fuji." *Maryknoll Magazine,* January, 1972, pp. 17-20.

Vivekananda, Swami. *The Complete Works of Swami Vivekananda.* Mayavati Memorial Edition. 8 vols. and Index. Calcutta: Advaita Ashrama, 1948-53.

———. *The East and the West.* Calcutta: Advaita Ashrama, 1963.

———. *In Search of God and Other Poems.* 2d ed. Calcutta: Advaita Ashrama, 1968.

———. *Inspired Talks, My Master and Other Writings.* Rev. ed. New York: Ramakrishna-Vivekananda Center, 1958.

———. *Jnana-Yoga.* Rev. ed. New York: Ramakrishna-Vivekananda Center, 1955.

———. *Karma-Yoga and Bhakti-Yoga.* Rev. ed. New York: Ramakrishna-Vivekananda Center, 1970.

———. *Lectures from Colombo to Almora.* Calcutta: Advaita Ashrama, 1963.

———. *Letters of Swami Vivekananda.* Mayavati, Almora, Himalayas: Advaita Ashrama, 1964.

———. *Memoirs of European Travel.* Calcutta: Advaita Ashrama, 1963.

———. *Our Women.* Calcutta: Advaita Ashrama, 1965.

———. *Practical Vedanta.* 5th ed. Mayavati, Almora, Himalayas: Advaita Ashrama, 1946.

———. *Raja-Yoga or Conquering the Internal Nature.* 8th ed. Mayavati, Almora, Himalayas: Advaita Ashrama, 1947.

———. *Raja-Yoga.* Rev. ed. New York: Ramakrishna-Vivekananda Center, 1955.

———. *Thoughts on the Gita.* Mayavati, Almora, Himalayas: Advaita Ashrama, 1967.

Vividishananda, Swami. *A Man of God.* Mylapore, Madras: Sri Ramakrishna Math, 1957.

Warnick, Kenneth. "Mysticism and Schizophrenia." *The Journal of Transpersonal Psychology,* I (Fall, 1969), 49-66.

Warfield, Benjamin B. *The Inspiration and Authority of the Bible.* Grand Rapids, Mich: Baker, 1948.

Watt, W. Montgomery. *Muslim Intellectual: A Study of Al-Ghazali.* Edinburgh: Edinburgh University Press, 1963.

*The Way of a Pilgrim.* Translated by R. M. French. New York: Seabury Press, 1965.

Webster, Geoffrey. "Some Reflections on Mahayana Buddhism." *Vedanta for East and West,* No. 128 (November-December, 1972), pp. 25-30.

Weil, Andrew. *The Natural Mind: A New Way of Looking at the Higher Consciousness.* Boston: Houghton Mifflin, 1972. As excerpted in *Psychology Today,* October, 1972, pp. 51-96.

Weiman, H. N. "Empiricism." *Philosophy, Religion, and the Coming World Civilization: Essays in Honor of William Ernest Hocking.* Edited by Leroy S. Rouner. The Hague: Martinus Nijhoff, 1966.

Welbon, Guy Richard. *The Buddhist Nirvana and Its Western Interpreters.* Chicago: University of Chicago Press, 1968.

Winternitz, M. *A History of Indian Literature.* Vol. III, Part I: *Classical Sanskrit Literature.* Translated by Subhadra Jha. Delhi: Motilal Banarsidass, 1963.

*The Wisdom of God (Srimad Bhagavatam).* Translated by Swami Prabhavananda. Hollywood, Calif.: Vedanta Press, 1943.

*With the Swamis in America.* By a Western Disciple. 2d ed. Mayavati, Almora, Himalayas: Advaita Ashrama, 1946.

*Women Saints of East and West.* Foreword by Vijaya Lakshmi Pandit. Introduction by Kenneth Walker. London: Ramakrishna Vedanta Centre, 1955.

Woodroffe, Sir John. *The Garland of Letters.* Madras: Ganesh, 1969.

——— . *Introduction to Tantra Sastra.* Madras: Ganesh, 1969.

——— . *Sakti and Sakta.* Madras: Ganesh, 1965.

——— . *The Serpent Power.* Madras: Ganesh, 1964.

——— . *The World as Power.* Madras: Ganesh, 1966.

*Words of the Master.* Compiled by Swami Brahmananda. 10th ed. Calcutta, Udbodhan Office, 1945.

*The Works of St. John of the Cross.* Translated by David Lewis. London: Thomas Baker, 1919.

Wright, G. Ernest. *God Who Acts.* London: S.C.M. Press, 1966.

——— . *The Old Testament and Theology.* New York: Harper & Row, 1969.

*The Writings of St. Francis of Assisi.* Translated by Benen Fahy. Chicago: Franciscan Herald Press, 1963.

Yamunacharya, M. *Ramanuja's Teachings in His Own Words.* Bhavan's Book University, No. 111. Chaupatty, Bombay: Bharatiya Vidya Bhavan, 1963.

Zimmer, Heinrich. *Philosophies of India.* Princeton, N. J.: Princeton University Press, 1967.

# Index

235